# Urban Teacher Education and Teaching

*Innovative Practices*
*for Diversity and Social Justice*

# Urban Teacher Education and Teaching

## *Innovative Practices for Diversity and Social Justice*

*Edited by*

### R. Patrick Solomon
*York University*

### Dia N. R. Sekayi
*Walden University*

**LAWRENCE ERLBAUM ASSOCIATES, PUBLISHERS**

2007  **Mahwah, New Jersey**                    **London**

Lawrence Erlbaum Associates, Inc., Publishers
10 Industrial Avenue
Mahwah, NJ 07430

Cover design by Tomai Maridou

**Library of Congress Cataloging-in-Publication Data**

Urban teacher education and teaching : innovative practices for diversity and social justice / edited by R. Patrick Solomon and Dia N. R. Sekayi.
      p. cm.
Includes bibliographical references and index.
ISBN 978-0-8058-5501-2 — 0-8058-5501-7 (cloth)
ISBN 978-0-8058-5502-9 — 0-8058-5502-5 (pbk.)
ISBN 978-1-4106-1435-3 — 1-4106-1435-2 (e book)
    1. Education, Urban—United States. 2. Teachers—Training of—United States. 3. Urban schools—United States. 4. Minorities—Education—United States. 5. Training—Social aspects—United States. I. Solomon, Rovell Patrick. II. Sekayi, Dia N. R.

LC5119.8.U73 2006
370.71'1091732—dc22                    2006010477

Books published by Lawrence Erlbaum Associates are printed on acid-free paper, and their bindings are chosen for strength and durability.

Printed in the United States of America
10  9  8  7  6  5  4  3  2  1

# Contents

## PART II:  PRE-SERVICE TEACHER PREPARATION FOR URBAN TRANSFORMATION

## PART III: CULTURALLY RELEVANT PEDAGOGY AND ADVOCACY IN URBAN SETTINGS

# Foreword

Peter C. Murrell, Jr.
*Northeastern University*

The editors and contributors of this volume ask and address perhaps the most critical question in urban education: Have urban schools failed us, or have we failed urban schools? The question is profound on a number of levels, in light of three troubling developments in the field of urban education in the last two decades. First is a greater entrenchment of a "deficit mentality" in regard to urban schools and schooling. There are perspectives and approaches in the contemporary educational literature that too closely mimic the popular image of urban schooling as one of increasing degradation, despair, and dysfunction. Just as in the public discourse and print media, the scholarly and professional literature in urban education increasingly views *urban school* as a synonym for a troubled school that conjures imagery of dilapidated buildings filled with African American, Hispanic American, émigrés, and children of color from third-world countries. In this deficit imagery, typical urban-school students are further constructed as those from materially, linguistically, and scholastically impoverished homes, whose diminished social resources [are tacitly assumed to] account for the so-called achievement gap—their underperformance on aggregated scores on standardized tests of achievement when compared with their European American counterparts. Certainly there are differences in experiences, interests, and scholastic readiness among diverse populations of urban public school students. But, are the difficulties of urban students a matter of *their* failing school, or the schools failing *them*? This volume offers a fresh critical perspective on framing transformational approaches to problems of urban education.

ix

A second disturbing development in urban education is that it has become big business, set against the interests of children, youth, and their families in urban settings. The woes of urban schools and urban schooling have become the engine of a new education industry. The proliferation of prepackaged curricula and prefabricated school reform models dedicated to alleviating the real, imagined, and manufactured ills of urban schooling now constitutes a huge multimillion-dollar market. They produce an array of consumables bought by city school districts, out of desperation and by mandate, ostensibly for the benefit of urban children and youth. But do they benefit urban children, youth, and families who depend on public education? Whether they do or not is an important question. This volume offers a critical analysis of value systems currently driving urban education, using the lens of a critical democracy.

The third, and perhaps most troubling development over the past two decades, has been the diminishing integrity of theory, policy, and practice regarding urban education. Despite the urgency of addressing critical problems of chronic underachievement, increasing dropout rates, oversubscription of minority students in special education, and poorly equipped teachers, the public and scholarly discourse lacks focus and clarity. Without greater clarity as to how we go about serving the interests of urban school students, we are unlikely to expose the reasons for the persistence of the critical problems. This volume offers the critical and theoretical lens that exposes, for example, how the deficit mindset and the urban education industry (engineered to profit from products that ostensibly ameliorate "urban deficits") combine to maintain the status quo of poor educational outcomes for urban schools and communities.

We need a new and more global critical consciousness regarding the issues, problems, and dilemmas of urban education. This volume offers both public and scholarly discourses on urban education and they are offered with critical sensibility, especially as regards school practices across lines drawn by cultural, ethnic, racial, and economic differences. It is time to ask, as this volume does, what integrated vision of urban schooling will move us beyond the interminable discourse on the failures of urban schools, to frames of thought and action that will inspire a pedagogy of possibility.

The collective voice of the scholars in this volume directs our awareness, skills, and sensibilities of critical analysis so that we might unravel the structural impediments of urban inner-city communities, urban school practices and policy, and disrupt the reproductive cycle of failure and degraded schooling. It is a critical theoretic perspective on urban education that calls to the fore critical consciousness in the tradition of John Dewey, Paulo Freire, and Henry Giroux, contextualizing it in a new discourse of possibility and critical democratic values. Urban education is badly in need of this integrated perspective—a lens that keeps in view at all times the macro–structural issues, the mesolevel dilemmas, and the microlevel problems of successful practice in diverse urban contexts. The corpus of work in this volume puts us on the road to that needed integrated perspective. It asks and then addresses precisely the right question: Have urban schools failed, or has the reform movement failed urban schools?

# Preface

This volume is guided by a social reconstructionist tradition in teacher education. One of its best known advocates, George Counts, argues in his 1932 book, *Dare the School Build a New Social Order?*, for institutions that lead rather than reflect sociopolitical ideas and values. From such a tradition, contributors have built their work on the principles and practices of equity, diversity, and social justice education.

Contributors to this volume come from a wide range of geographical backgrounds in Canada, the Caribbean, and the United States. Their ethno–racial heritages and identities are Aboriginal and/or First Nations, African, Asian, and European, which together brings rich and divergent knowledge, perspectives, and cultural experience to their work. The combination of international perspectives and a wide range of diversity allow the work to effectively illuminate the most pressing challenges faced by urban schools, teachers, teacher candidates, and teacher-training programs. As scholars, researchers, teacher educators, teacher practitioners, cultural workers, and activists, their work presented here makes a significant contribution to our understanding of the persisting dilemmas of urban education.

The volume is presented in three parts: the conceptual framing of key issues in urban schooling, pre-service teacher preparation for urban transformation, and culturally relevant pedagogy and advocacy in urban settings. As such, it covers a range of issues, from broadly theoretical to urgently practical.

In their chapters, contributors present a range of insights and possibilities for urban teacher education and teaching. They engage in what Noguera (2003) terms *pragmatic optimism*; that is, determining the realistic possibilities of urban schools given their internal and external constraints, and planning strategically for transformational work. Accordingly, the intention of the authors in this volume is not simply to describe challenges but to explore ways they can be most effectively resisted and overcome. Recognizing that much traditional teacher education often fails to account for the unique challenges that urban teaching presents, they outline concrete approaches to reforming, renewing, and reinvigorating teacher education for urban schools. Acknowledging policy analysts' concerns about the structural problems that restrict urban schooling and the lack of political will to effect real change, these authors convey a deep commitment to the transformational possibilities of schooling. As Cochran-Smith (1995) argues, "To alter a system that is deeply dysfunctional, the system needs teachers who regard teaching as a political activity and embrace social change as part of the job" (p. 494). These authors are convinced that teaching can address these systemic and pervasive problems, strive toward a more just and equitable society, and refuse submission to schooling's reproductive and transmissive propensities. Thus what emerges is an emphatic message of hope for those committed to the ongoing project of improving urban teacher education and working in urban settings.

## ACKNOWLEDGMENTS

We thank the contributors to this volume for sharing their experiences and insights as researchers, educators, and cultural workers in urban settings. They have crossed a number of national, geographical, and institutional borders to provide insights into the transformational challenges of urban schools and communities. We thank Lawrence Erlbaum Associates Senior Editor, Naomi Silverman, Associate Editor, Erica Kica, and their reviewer, Sandra Hollingsworth, for their input and support for moving this project from its inception to completion. We acknowledge the research assistance of Marc Carver, Randa Khattar Manoukian, and Laura Lindo and the input of colleagues John Portelli, Beverly-Jean Daniel, Lara Doan, and Harry Smaller. At the technical level, we are grateful for the proofreading and editing expertise of Trevor Norris and Joan Ffrench. We thank Elma Thomas for "managing" the various iterations of the manuscript and for compiling the final document for publication. Finally, we are indebted to our families and friends for their continued support and understanding as we preoccupied ourselves with the task of completing this project.

—R. Patrick Solomon
—Dia N. R. Sekayi

## REFERENCES

Cochran-Smith, M. (1995). Colorblindness and basketmaking are not the answers: Confronting the dilemmas of race, culture and language diversity in teacher education. *American Educational Research Journal, 312*(3), 493–522.

Counts, G. S. (1992). *Dare the school build a new social order?* New York: The John Day Camp.

Noguera, P. (2003). *City schools and the American dream: Reclaiming the promise of public education.* New York: Teachers College Press.

# Chapter 1

# Introduction

R. Patrick Solomon
*York University*

Dia N. R. Sekayi
*Walden University*

## OLD AND NEW CHALLENGES OF URBAN SCHOOLS

Have urban schools failed or has the reform movement failed urban schools? This Miron and St. John (2003) question has reinvigorated the debates on urban schooling. Whether scholarly reports in professional journals or casual discussions by stakeholders in the schooling enterprise, urban education dominates the discourse. In this volume, we move beyond the animated debates on the failures of urban schools, thus avoiding the potential for despair or complacency. Instead, we reframe perceived and real failures as transformational challenges to be overcome. From our critical democratic perspective on education, we intend to engage the issues of urban schools through teacher education, teaching for diversity, and social justice. From such a perspective, we direct the following questions of structure, politics, ideology, economics, and pedagogy to those of us who are stakeholders (teacher educators, teachers, school administrators, policymakers, parents, students, community workers, cultural workers, etc.) in urban schools and communities:

• How do we provide adequate learning experiences so as to give voice to the most vulnerable in urban, inner-city environments, those who are socially different by virtue of race and ethnicity, social class and poverty location, immigrant status, and language status?

1

- What awareness, skills, and sensibilities do we need in order to critically analyze the link between the structural impediments of urban inner-city communities and those of the schools located within them, to challenge the ideological positioning that both gives rise to and sustains reproductive pedagogical practices in urban schools?
- How do we begin to utilize the historically subjugated community knowledge and other resources as authentic curriculum content?
- How do we establish authentic democratic educational partnerships with the communities served by the school (e.g., parents, families, social, and cultural organizations) in order to develop their social and cultural capital?
- How do we attract and retain teachers with high-level skills for success in urban settings, respond to the struggle for teacher professionalism, and provide an environment for practitioners to grow on the job?
- How do we rise above the rigid hierarchical structures and bureaucracies that paralyze innovative professional ideas and activities in urban settings, so as to develop the political skills and courage to fight resistance to change, and engage in transformational work in urban communities?

Related to these historically based structural, political, ideological, and pedagogical questions are more contemporary, reform-related, policy-driven issues. Some of the most strident top–down policy movements that occupy the imagination of educators and critics of schooling are the accountability movement, standards-based curriculum, business intervention into schooling, and teacher testing. Indeed, all of these movements are poised to have a tremendous impact on urban and inner-city schools and the communities they serve.[1] Central to the educational reform movement is the policy of standardization, which along with evaluation has become the mantra for students as a matter of state/provincial policies. Such standardized outcomes-based learning invariably makes essential the dominant-group, middle-class forms of knowledge, those that are universally accepted across the global marketplace. Such a policy rededicates the functionalist tradition, instituting the kind of curriculum and pedagogy that sorts and selects future workers for the socioeconomic machinery. Excluded from such a market-driven knowledge base is the urban, inner-city community subjugated knowledge, a kind of contextualized knowledge on which communities develop their social and cultural capital.

This volume is intended for teacher educators, teachers, and cultural workers who are in partnership with these teacher educators and teachers. Although some of the educational ideas, pedagogies, and movements taken up in this volume are not entirely new, its contributors offer new and innovative approaches to implementing them in urban schools and communities. Such a rethinking and new application is what educators refer to as a *paradigm shift*. On an ongoing basis, pedagogies reinvent themselves at different times and in different contexts. In a globalized world, there is an unprecedented movement of Caribbean education workers across borders; immigrant teachers have sojourned into Canada and recruited and contracted migrant teachers in the United States. Caribbean teachers educated in Canada and the United States have returned to teach in Caribbean educational institutions. With this movement of educators, there is an urgent need for educators in each region to broaden their perspectives and knowledge base about other regions.

In addition, progressive approaches to schooling in general must be adapted to be effective in urban context. Our organizational strategy in this volume is to identify and develop urban education themes that cut across geopolitical borders without centering on any country in particular. Whether in Chicago, U.S.A., Toronto, Canada, or Kingston, Jamaica, there are common characteristics of "urbanness" (listed so insightfully by Principal Crosby later in this Introduction) that will require similar transformative responses from schooling. And in a rapidly emerging globalized world, educators need to expand their knowledge base from the local to the global; they need to know what works in contexts other than their own.

In the next sections, we focus on two issues: teacher education institutions and the challenges they encounter in preparing teachers for urban settings, and the challenges of practitioners in providing relevant curriculum and pedagogy in urban schools and communities.

## THE CHALLENGES OF TEACHER EDUCATION INSTITUTIONS

At the center of urban schools debates are its teachers, who over the years have been regrettably/unfortunately/incorrectly/mistakenly implicated in the underachievement of students in these institutions. The following questions therefore arise: To what extent should teachers be held accountable? Are they adequately prepared to work competently and productively in urban, inner-city schools? School reform movements sweeping across Western societies, and policymakers operating within them, have been critical of teacher education institutions and their ineffectiveness in preparing teachers for urban school improvement. The critiques are anchored in three crucial areas: (a) teacher candidate[2] selection for teacher education, (b) the preparation process, and (c) the evaluation and certification process.

With regard to selection, institutions are critiqued for continuing to insist on high academic requirements. Their use of such "quantifiable indices" as grade point average (GPA) as the first and sometimes only screening factor reflects their preoccupation with an excessively one-dimensional concern with proven academic achievement. Yet research on teacher selection has revealed a number of other essential elements of teacher knowledge and characteristics that may more accurately predict competency and effectiveness in urban schools and communities (Erskine-Cullen & Sinclair, 1996; Haberman & Post, 1998). Haberman and Post, for example, argued for a selection process that incorporates such essential elements as self-knowledge, self-acceptance, relationship skills, community knowledge, empathy, cultural human development, the ability to understand culturally relevant curriculum, the motivation to generate sustained effort, the ability to cope with violence and function in a chaotic environment. Erskine-Cullen and Sinclair (1996) focused on such personal characteristics essential to the successful urban teacher: empathy, respect for students, flexibility, self-care, patience, sense of humor, collegiality, and a high energy level. They alert us to the evolving role of the urban teacher as social worker, nurturer, appeaser, and counselor, not reflected in the GPA. Haberman and Post (1998) conclude a "[H]igh GPA has nothing to do with teaching children in poverty effectively, or predicting who will remain in teaching" (p. 101). In fact, the reference to the troublesome issue of teacher retention in urban schools is significant here, as research indicates that graduate teachers with a high GPA have a comparatively low retention rate in urban schools (Hunter Quartz & The TEP Research Group, 2003). Additionally, screening for high GPA potentially eliminates minority teachers (who for various reasons are chronic underachievers in dominant group institutions), whose rate of retention in urban schools is much higher than others (Clewell & Villegas, 2001; Haberman & Post, 1998). Given these realities, teacher education institutions must be critical of generic conceptions of teacher quality and rethink access criteria for urban teacher preparation.

Teacher preparation for urban schools and communities has been equally problematic. Historically, teacher education programs have been the key to transmitting dominant cultural capital (Anderson, 1988; Watkins, 2001). For example, consider the Hampton case: In the mid-19th century in the United States, a decision was made that teachers selected to educate recently liberated Blacks must be of a particular attitude, specifically, one that would allow Whites (particularly southern planters) to continue to control freed postslavery Blacks. The ideal teacher candidate was one who valued proficiency at physical labor over intellectual development. Photographs documenting early teacher education programs at Hampton showed students working the fields from morning until night in order to cover their tuition (Anderson, 1988). Even then there were rebels who saw through the motivation behind this policy. As Apple (1990) and Shujaa (1994) note, hegemony is not static; there are constant challenges to domination. At present, there are students and families who rebel against the dominant culture's ideology as it is manifested in the school setting. Furthermore, architects of and participants in teacher education programs today in the United States, Canada, and the Caribbean are posing sufficient levels of challenge to urban teacher education programs in order to resist hegemonic forces.

Although today's institution-based preparation may not place candidates in the fields described in the Hampton case, the ideal candidate is still often thought to be one who is able to coax his or her students into conformity. From such a dominant ideological perspective, good teachers control their classrooms, enforce external discipline, and their students demonstrate proficiency through standardized tests—not necessarily through intellectual development and divergent thinking. Compulsory schooling in the United States, Canada, and the Caribbean provides a captive audience for this kind of indoctrination. One of the keys to interrupting this process is to reform teacher education so that it values equity, diversity, and social justice. Thus emerges the essential role of teacher education from our social reconstructionist perspective, a creative adjustment to contemporary conditions, one that is emphasized and developed fully in this volume.

In contemporary schooling, formal and informal curriculum, pedagogical approaches, and institution-based learning continue to be restrictive. Regarding the curriculum, America's gradual recognition and acknowledgment of its growing cultural diversity and its diminishing tendency to embrace the "melting-pot ideology" have given rise to multicultural education within some schools and the teacher education curriculum. But multicultural education is often presented in "stand-alone" courses, and not integrated across the curriculum. The dilemmas facing cross-curriculum integration of multicultural education are (a) a limited number of faculty with the expertise and knowledge to integrate, and (b) convincing "discipline purists," especially those in the pure and applied sciences, that multicultural education has legitimacy in every subject area. Another critique of multiculturalism as practiced in urban schools is that it does not go far enough in interrogating other issues of social difference. While such courses focus on ethnocultural heritages (often in superficial ways), other issues of social difference such as race, social class, poverty, gender, and sexuality are given a less critical treatment, or contested out of the formal curriculum entirely.[3] In such contexts, pedagogical approaches such as antiracism, antihomophobia, feminism, and anticlassism are perceived by some stakeholders in the schooling process as too contentious, too radical, and potentially disruptive to individuals' sensibilities and institutional harmony.

The informal curriculum of pre-service teachers is a learning environment characterized by competitive individualism. Those learning to teach do so in university and practicum school environments where the culture is highly competitive, and players are socialized into competing against each other for knowledge, grades, recognition, and so forth. Players in this game succeed at the expense of others. To prepare urban teachers for community building, teacher educators must engage their candidates in a culture of collaboration and mutual interdependent learning.

Finally, traditional teacher preparation has resided almost entirely in two institutional domains: the school of education (usually located in universities and colleges), and the field-based practicum school. In these artificial environments, candidates learn their craft without full exposure to the real world from which their students come. Their pedagogy is therefore ungrounded, culturally irrelevant, and unresponsive to the immediate and long-term needs of students and their communities. Teachers without such exposure are unaware of the rich cultural knowledge and resources of urban communities, which in turn does not become legitimate mainstream curriculum knowledge.

Teacher preparation for urban settings must therefore embrace a more synergistic model that incorporates the community as a site of professional learning. Howard (1998) describes such a model in which learning in the community is integrated and reciprocally related to the pedagogical processes, so that each experience in the university setting, the practicum classroom, and the community served by these institutions inform and transform each other. Here we operate on the belief that urban communities do have cultural capital, and teachers must engage with communities in developing not only themselves but also this invaluable resource.

An even more contentious dimension of teacher education is the testing and certification process following initial training. In the policymakers' quest for accountability, excellence, efficiency, standards, and teacher quality, many state and provincial jurisdictions across the United States and Canada have instituted new teacher testing programs. In the case of Ontario, Canada, this program was designed to "assure parents that new teachers know the curriculum and teaching strategies before they enter the classroom" (Ontario Ministry of Education [OME], 2001). The provincial governing body went on to argue "a certification test may be viewed as a safeguard for the public—a mechanism that helps ensure that only individuals who possess important knowledge and skills enter into the classroom" (OME, 2002). The 2001 Elementary and Secondary Education Act in the United States highlighted the concept of *highly qualified teachers* as a path to improved student achievement for all students, thus "leaving no child behind." The racial, ethnic, and socioeconomic disparities in academic performance were addressed in this act. "Although teacher quality has been accepted and internalized as a mantra for school reform, the imperative for diversity is often marginalized rather than accepted as central to the quality equation in teaching" (National Collaborative on Diversity in the Teaching Force, 2004, p. 3). However, the fact remains that the student population in U.S. public schools is steadily diversifying while the population of teachers remains relatively unchanged. The jury is still out on the correlation between the lack of diversity and the difficulty many teachers of color have passing Praxis II.[4] Fewer than 50% of African American teachers nationwide pass teacher tests, with more passing the content areas of Praxis II than the basic skills test that comprises Praxis I (National Collaborative, 2004). In the state of Georgia, for example, there is a clear difference between the pass rates at Historically Black Colleges and Universities (HBCUs) and predominantly White institutions in the favor of the latter. One might surmise that underprepared students from urban settings (largely children of color and socioeconomically disadvantaged children) become underprepared teacher education candidates, and are filtered out of the pipeline early, thus restricting their entry into the teaching force.

In parts of the English-speaking Caribbean (eg., Jamaica, Belize, and the Bahamas) a government instituted body (The Joint Board of Teacher Education [JBTE]) is responsible for quality assurance of pre-service teacher education and manages the evaluation and certification process. Through the process of collaboration with teacher educators that deliver curriculum, a level of standardization of "pencil and paper tests" is achieved. New teachers are certified based on their performance on these criterion-referenced examinations.[5]

A study of teacher candidates' perspectives on the Ontario Teacher Qualifying Test (OTQT; Portelli, Solomon, & Mujawamariya, 2003) raised serious questions about the test's evidential validity (how well the test represents the construct being assessed). According to participants in the study, "The test neither achieves accountability nor does it secure excellence in teaching. TCs' responses challenge the popular, yet at times, empty notion of accountability. Their responses should warn educators about false or 'pseudo notions' of accountability" (p. 7).

Despite the research that questions test validity, state and provincial officials continue to threaten teacher education institutions with decertification and withdrawal of funding from those facilities with poor and unacceptable passing rates. (For the state of Massachusetts, see Cochran-Smith & Dudley-Marling, 2001; Flippo & Richards, 2000. For the State of New York, see Kincheloe, 2004.)[6]

Even more damning for urban schools was the test's "consequential validity," which has value implications and social consequences. Those candidates identified as potentially vulnerable to failing are groups that are educationally exceptional and "different" from the mainstream in their social identities, linguistic and cultural background, and perspectives on the teaching–learning process (Portelli et al., 2003). These include immigrants, English as a second language speakers, racial and ethnic minorities, and the working class. Indeed, the initial teacher certification testing in Massachusetts realized the worst fears of the Ontario research. Flippo and Richards (2000) revealed disproportionate failures in the ranks of Africn Americans and Hispanics, the social groups identified by teacher educators to have the appropriate knowledge base and characteristics to function well in culturally diverse environments and to stay in urban schools (Clewell & Villegas, 2001; Haberman & Post, 1998; Hunter Quartz & The TEP Research Group, 2003).

Many critics perceive this standardizing, essentializing, and testing of mainstream knowledge (and the corresponding marginalization of "other" teacher knowledges, competencies, and skills) as technicizing teachers and the teaching profession. As Kincheloe (2004) analyses it:

> Study of the aims of democratic education are replaced by reductionist proficiencies and competencies articulated in the language of behavior objectives or outcomes.... The organizations [colleges, schools/departments of education] find themselves becoming more and more technicized, dehumanized, and standardized and less and less scholarly, learning-oriented, and student-centered. (pp. 10–11)

We agree with Kincheloe and others who argue that in the era of globalization, market forces are dictating the content and process of schooling. Urban schools become particularly vulnerable to such forces that ensure they reproduce the social, economic, and political stratification in society.

## THE CHALLENGES OF TRANSFORMING URBAN SCHOOLS AND COMMUNITIES

Over the years, educational researchers, scholar-activists, and practitioners such as Jean Anyon, Emeral Crosby, Jonathan Kozol, Peter Murrell, Pedro Noguera (2003), Malawi Shujaa, Lois Weiner, and others have provided vivid portrayals of what ails urban schools and the challenges of improving such spaces for urban youth. Emeral Crosby, a Detriot urban high school principal, identifies the most pressing structural and organizational challenges in his 1999 article, "*Urban Schools: Forced to Fail*":

- the self-generating, self-regulating, self-perpetuating bureaucracy and management hierarchy that slows decision making and blocks innovation and change;
- physical infrastructure (buildings and equipment) that are old and outmoded provide an unwholesome and oppressive learning environment for students;
- overload of responsibilities that stretch school personnel beyond the call of academic duty to many other areas of social service;

- continuous urban demographic shifts as new immigrant and refugee groups settle in urban spaces and the old, more established White, middle-class population moves to suburbia;
- the increasing cost of security and the gradual shifting of resources and personnel away from teaching kids to securing buildings;
- the inadequacy of the professional staff for the demanding urban school environment; the high turnover rate of competent teachers, the lack of mentoring and professional development for new teachers, teacher disengagement from urban communities; and
- the lack of political courage to transform urban schools by those who have invested in, and benefit from the way things are. (pp. 298–303)

Crosby concludes, "the current pseudo-revolution that is benefiting no one is called 'restructuring the urban school.' The social engineers want to rebuild urban education on a shaky foundation; they want to build pyramids on an eroding base of sand" (p. 303).

In her book, *Ghetto Schooling: A Political Economy of Urban Educational Reform,* Anyon (1997; see also 2005a, 2005b) argues that school reform in inner-city neighborhoods will continue to be ineffective until there is social and economic reform in the urban space in which schools are located. She also identified several issues of urban schooling, from which we have deduced three urgent preconditions for urban transformation:

- a reduction of the social–cultural differences among school reformers, parents, and school personnel;
- a reduction of differences between the sociocultural content of reform (e.g., curriculum and learning materials), and the school population; and
- the development of positive social relations between teachers and students.

Given the different values, perspectives, and ideological positioning of stakeholders in urban schools and communities, achieving these socioeducational objectives will indeed be a challenge. For example, sociocultural differences among school reformers and school staff on one hand and urban, inner-city dwellers on the other hand, are marked by their social locations in the system and in the broader society. School reformers and policymakers function as agents in the system's bureaucracy and tend to "operate from a distance." School staff becomes the machinery of school reformers, uncritically participating in the importation of a kind of curriculum and pedagogy that does not fit the inner-city context.

The kind of social relations that characterize teachers and their students from such diametrical social locations are ones of alienation, rigidity, antagonism, and distance. As revealed in Evans and Tucker's chapter (chap. 9, this volume) in the Jamaican setting, these relations are further character-ized by authoritarian rule and may well be a legacy of a colonial past and a socially stratified educational system. The experiences of social distancing in inner-city American and Canadian schools also operate on a kind of colo-nial mentality, with those in position of power and authority unilaterally im-posing a kind of schooling on the "powerless" rather than collaborating democratically in the schooling process. The achievement gap between ur-ban, inner-city learners, between the rich and those living in poverty, be-tween Whites and people of color will not close if reform initiatives do not include context-specific and culturally relevant pedagogy.

Building on critical insights about developing the social and economic capital of the community, we draw on Reed's (2004) notions of social capital and teachers' role in its development. He attaches significant value to "so-cial relationships" and "interpersonal connectedness," which he considers "a resource, a form of capital, which provides a foundation for the neigh-borhood's health and prosperity" (p. 74). He concludes, the "amount of so-cial capital in a community can be a significant influence on its economic prosperity, productivity, safety and health" (p. 74).

The discourse on urban schools and social capital (Putman, 2000; Reed, 2004; Runyan, Hunter, Socolar, et al., 1998) presents an important paradigm shift from essentializing urban communities as "spaces of pathology" to sites of social capital development. It is to this task that teacher educators, teacher practitioners, and cultural workers must prepare new urban teachers.

The organizational strategy in this volume is not to offer a comparative study of the three geographical areas represented in the works of the contri-butors. More importantly, we present unique insights into their urban con-texts and provide ideas as to how their work may inform the practices of others. However, contributors have deliberately resisted provided non-contextual pedagogical prescriptions, especially across the geographical boundaries of this volume's potential readership.

## ENDNOTES

[1]Although not all urban spaces are inner city, in this volume we use the terms *urban* and *inner city* interchangeably and focus on those environments characterized by socioeconomic disenfranchisement and marginalization: (a) those with high-density populations living below the poverty line; and (b) those with an entrenched "underclass" and unstable, transient communities of immigrants and refugees with limited or no economic and educational re-sources, living in government-assisted housing, with limited social and health services. In some jurisdictions, neighborhoods with inner-city characteristics can also be located in what McLaren (1980) refers to as the new suburban

ghettos in the Canadian context. These are "inner suburbs" or pockets of socioeconomically depressed communities existing side by side with affluent communities.

[2]In this text, contributors have used such terms as *teacher candidates, student teachers, pre-service teachers*, and *novice teachers* to describe those who are engaged in initial teacher education. These terms are sometimes used interchangeably by the same author.

[3]Examples of contested pedagogies are antiracism, perceived by many as inflammatory and antithetical to the more harmonious multiculturalism; and antihomophobia, perceived by conservatives and the "religious right" as unbefitting for the public school curriculum. Such a response is well documented in the teaching video, "It's Elementary: Talking About Gay Issues in School" (long version; Chasnoff & Cohen, 1997).

[4]The United States has several formal tests of teacher quality at various stages. The most widely used is the Praxis series, developed by the Educational Testing Service (ETS). Praxis I is a test for pre-service teachers in the early stages of a teacher preparation program. It is similar in content to the Scholastic Achievement Test (SAT) used for college admissions. Praxis II, formally known as the National Teacher Exam (NTE) is an assessment of general and specific content and pedagogical knowledge and is used to certify teachers. Some states have adopted Praxis III, which is an assessment of the classroom performance of beginning teachers. Cultural competence is certainly given lip service on the gatekeeper assessment, Praxis II, and in some states, Praxis III. The National Council for the Accreditation of Teacher Education (NCATE), an independent professional accrediting body for schools, departments, and colleges of education, recognized by the U.S. Department of Education, acknowledges the importance of diversity through its fourth standard. Standard four addresses the diversity of college and university faculty, and of teacher candidates.

[5]The Joint Board of Teacher Education (JBTE) is a regional partnership between ministries of education in Jamaica, Belize, and the Bahamas, the Institute of Education, the University of the West Indies, teacher organizations in the three countries, and independent individuals who contribute in various ways (Regulations for Teacher Certification, 2003). The Ministry of Education (Jamaica) has now declared that in the future, teachers will be tested in order to show that they deserve to maintain their initial teacher certification. The Ministry has also considering paying teachers according to their level of performance—again, part of the drive for accountability.

[6]The Ontario Ministry of Education suspended its teacher test in 2005, citing the need for the development of an evaluation process that better reflects teacher competence. They have introduced a 1-year mentoring and on-the-job induction and evaluation program that they expect will boost new teacher competence to work in the province's schools.

## REFERENCES

Anderson, J. (1988). *The education of Blacks in the south, 1860–1935*. Chapel Hill: University of North Carolina Press.

Anyon, J. (1997). *Ghetto schooling: A political economy of urban educational reform*. New York: Teachers College Press.

Anyon, J. (2005a). *Radical possibilities: Public policy, urban education, and a new social movement*. New York: Routledge.

Anyon, J. (2005b). What counts as educational policy? Notes toward a new paradigm. *Harvard Educational Review, 75*(1), 65–88.

Apple, M. (1990). *Ideology and curriculum*. New York: Routledge.

Chasnoff, D., & Cohen, H. (Producers). (1997). *It's elementary: Talking about gay issues in school* [video]. San Francisco: Women's Educational Media.

Clewell, B., & Villegas, A. (2001). *Absence unexcused: Ending teacher shortages in high need areas*. Washington, DC: Urban Institute.

Cochran-Smith, M., & Dudley-Marling, C. (2001). The flunk heard round the world. *Teacher Education, 21*(1), 49–63.

Crosby, E. A. (1999, December). Urban schools: Forced to fail. *Phi Delta Kappan*, 298–303.

Erskine-Cullen, E., & Sinclair, A. M. (1996). Preparing teachers for urban schools: A view from the field. *Canadian Journal of Educational Administration and Policy, 6*.

Flippo, R. F., & Richards, M. P. (2000, September). Initial teacher certification testing in Massachusetts: A case of the tail wagging the dog. *Phi Delta Kappan*, 34–37.

Haberman, M., & Post, L. (1998). Teachers for multicultural schools: The power of selection. *Theory into Practice, 37*(2), 96–104.

Howard, J. P. F. (1998). Academic service learning: A counter normative pedagogy. In R. A. Rhoads & J. P. F. Howard (Eds.), *Academic service learning: A pedagogy of action and reflection* (pp. 21–29). San Francisco: Jossey-Bass.

Hunter Quartz, K., & The TEP Research Group (2003). "Too angry to leave": Supporting new teachers' commitment to transform urban schools. *Journal of Teacher Education, 54*(2), 99–111.

Kincheloe, J. L. (2004). The bizarre, complex, and misunderstood world of teacher education. In J. L. Kincheloe, A. Bursztyn, & S. R. Steinberg (Eds.), *Teaching teachers: Building a quality school of urban education* (pp.1–49). New York: Peter Lang.

McLaren, P. (1980). *Cries from the corridors: The new suburban ghettos*. Toronto: Methuen.

Miron, L .F., & St. John, E. P. (Eds.) (2003). *Reinterpreting urban school reform*. Albany: State University of New York Press.

National Collaborative on Diversity in the Teaching Force. (2004). *Assessment of diversity in America's teaching force: A call to action*. Washington, DC: National Education Association.

Noguera, P. (2003). *City schools and the American dream: Reclaiming the promise of public education*. New York: Teachers College Press.

Ontario Ministry of Education. (2001, October 15). *Candidates' information bulletin for the OTQT* [Ontario Teacher Qualifying Test]. Ontario, Canada: Author.

Ontario Ministry of Education. (2002, February 9). *Candidates' information bulletin for the OTQT* [Ontario Teacher Qualifying Test]. Ontario, Canada: Author.

Portelli, J. P., Solomon, R. P., & Mujawamariya, D. (2003). *A critical analysis of the Ontario Teacher Qualifying Test: Teacher candidates' perspectives*. Toronto: Ontario Institute for Studies in Education/University of Toronto.

Putman, R. (2000). *Bowling alone: The collapse and revival of American community*. New York: Simon & Schuster.

Reed, W.A. (2004). A tree grows in Brooklyn: Schools of education as brokers of social capital in low-income neighborhoods. In J. L. Kincheloe, A. Bursztyn, & S. R. Steinberg (Eds.), *Teaching teachers: Building a quality school of urban education* (pp. 65–90). New York: Peter Lang.

Runyan, D. K., Hunter, W. M., Socolar, R. R. S., et al. (1998). Children who prosper in unfavorable environments: The relationship to social capital. *Pediatrics, 101*(1), 12–20.

Shujaa, M. (1994). *Too much schooling, too little education: The paradox of Black life in White society*. Trenton, NJ: Africa World Press.

Watkins, W. H. (2001). *The White architects of Black education: Ideology and power in America, 1865–1964*. New York: Teachers College Press.

# THEORETICAL AND CONCEPTUAL FRAMING OF URBAN SCHOOLING

The three chapters in Part I clarify and lay the foundation for themes that are central to this volume. James-Wilson's opening chapter (chapter 2) is built around the distinct yet interrelated concepts of *representation*, *social justice*, and *power and/or knowledge*. She argues for the representation of voices traditionally excluded from teacher education discourse, and that both distributive and cultural justice must be the concerns of teachers for urban settings. An important insight of James-Wilson is her rejection of the notion of the inner-city as deviant and its reframing as spaces of variation and heterogeneity. In chapter 3, Daniel provides an analysis of the general and more specific application of the concept of *community* in various environmental and cultural contexts. Her focus, however, is on building a case for social relationships and interactivity as social capital in urban spaces. She explores divergent conceptions of community from the Aboriginal, African-centered, feminist, Freirean, and *Gemeinschaft* pespectives before developing her own conceptualization of community that has transformative potential. Daniel introduces the notion of educational collectives, or networks, and the ethic of caring in urban settings. In chapter 4, Weiner introduces the notion of gender and raises concerns about the ways in which its absence from the discourse and practice of urban school improvement has propelled teacher education toward a model of professionalism that is harmful to the respectful collaboration among teachers, families, and communities. She proposes redefinitions of *professionalism* so that it bridges the social distance between low-income parents and urban teachers, and eases the "tensions of women working with women." To conclude, Weiner offers recommendations for school–home collaboration in urban settings. These three chapters focus on conceptualizations of *represen- tation in educational discourse, community in cultural contexts,* and *home-school–relations in urban settings.* These themes permeate the chapters on preparing teachers for urban schools and doing relevant pedagogy in urban schools. The broad conceptual frameworks offered in this section are complemented by the concepts and theories that contributors use to inform their own pedagogical practices and to frame their written work. Indeed, such a theory–practice continuum invites critical reflection and action, and action that leads to transformation in urban settings.

# Chapter 2

# Using Representation to Conceptualize a Social Justice Approach to Urban Teacher Preparation

Sonia James-Wilson
*University of Rochester*

Nieto (2000) suggests that "when schools and colleges of education take a stand on social justice and diversity, they can better prepare teachers to work with students of linguistically and culturally diverse backgrounds" (p. 183). It is far easier, however, to assert rhetorical commitments than it is to transform them into pedagogy and curriculum. This task is further complicated by the fact that little is known about how to prepare teacher candidates to teach for social justice within relatively large teacher education programs (Zollers, Albert, & Cochran-Smith, 2000), and most college faculty have not had professional development or formal educational experiences that have prepared them specifically for this purpose (Bell, 1997).

In this chapter, I provide a theoretical framework for the development of programs focused on urban teacher preparation by drawing on key ideas from cultural studies, semiotics, feminist theory, and political philosophy. Here *social justice as representation* will be offered as a way to extend the conversation about social justice and education beyond a paradigm that advocates for the redistribution of goods and benefits as the primary solution to inequity. This chapter begins with a brief discussion about teaching for social justice and the distributive paradigm. I then introduce the notion of social justice as representation and describe its relationship to official and

**17**

subjugated knowledge about urban education. Finally, I provide suggestions for how to apply this perspective within the context of urban pre-service teacher education programs. As a point of clarification, the word "urban" has been used to describe schools and communities that are located in metropolitan areas where there is evidence of both affluence and poverty within the local geographic area surrounding the school. "Inner-city" on the other hand, is used to describe schools and communities located in areas where there is a high concentration of poverty and few or no signs of prosperity in terms of property, commerce, and human resources.

## CONCEPTIONS OF TEACHING FOR SOCIAL JUSTICE

The notion of social justice has many interpretations and is highly contested because it is embedded within discourses that are historically constituted and sites of conflicting and divergent political endeavors (Rizvi, 1998). The concept of *justice* has been associated with acts of punishment, retribution, and reconciliation, as for example in Judeo-Christian and Islamic texts, and with social, political and economic conditions. According to Novak (2000), the term *social justice* was first used in 1840 by a Sicilian priest, Luigi Taparelli d'Azeglio, in an appeal to the ruling classes for the support of displaced urban workers. Novak suggests that the birth of this concept coincided with two shifts in Western history, the "death of God" and the rise of the command economy after the Enlightenment when people began to seek answers to societal problems, not in religion but in science and reason. This increased sense of the capacity of humankind led intellectuals to try to construct a just social order, and in effect accomplish "what even God had not deigned to do" (Novak, 2000, p. 1).

The literature about teacher education for social justice tends to emphasize ways to support the exploration of what it means to pursue justice in the classroom for teacher candidates and faculty alike (see Beyer, 2001; Cochran-Smith, 1995, 1999; McIntyre, 1997, Russo, 2001; and Sleeter, 1995). Notions of what it means to "teach for social justice" find their origins in political, critical, social, and economic theoretical frameworks, and are reflected in libratory, antiracist, multicultural, and inclusive pedagogies. Each of these approaches (a) encourages the critique of educational systems, (b) acknowledges the structural inequalities embedded in schooling as one of the ways in which unequal access to learning opportunities is perpetuated, and (c) constructs teachers as change agents in and beyond education (Cochran-Smith et al., 1999).

In addition to theoretical and pedagogical traditions, the political struggles of groups fighting for basic human and civil rights have also had a powerful influence on the ways in which educators think about their role in the promotion of social justice. Kohl (1999) goes as far as to suggest that "educational leadership has never been known for its boldness or originality, in particular when it comes to issues of equity and justice," (p. 310), and that some of the most significant victories for marginalized groups have been won by progressive movements in communities or in the larger society. Two prominent examples that support this argument are the battle to desegregate schools during the Civil Rights Movement in the 1950s, which was spearheaded by the African American community and lawyers from the NAACP Legal Defense Fund, and the demand for community control of schools and culturally responsive curriculum which was made by parents and community leaders during the Black Power Movement in the 1960s and 1970s. Although I do not agree that "leadership in public education has never come from the universities or from the schools themselves" (Kohl, 1999, p. 310), it is difficult to deny the enormous influence social movements have had on the ways we think about the connections between social justice and education, and indeed on the theoretical and pedagogical traditions on which we have come to rely.

## DISTRIBUTIVE JUSTICE

In their experience of engaging in discussions with teacher education faculty about their understandings of social justice, Zollers et al. (2000) report "all participants agreed that fairness is the *sine qua non* of a socially just society"(p. 7; italics added). John Rawls is probably the individual most commonly associated with the ideal of justice as fairness within the Anglo-American tradition of political philosophy. Influenced by the social and political instability of the 1960s, he described his proposition as a political conception of justice that elaborated on ideas already implicit in constitutional democracies (Solomon & McMurphy, 2000). Rawls attempted to strike a balance between liberty and equality as reflected in the two principles that are fundamental to a justice-as-fairness approach; first, that each person is entitled to the most extensive basic liberty, and second, that all primary social goods should be distributed equally, except in cases where unequal distribution would favor the "least advantaged."

In his seminal work, *A Theory of Justice*, first published in 1971, Rawls (1999) argued that people are born into different life positions and have different expectations of life that are determined, in part, by their society's political system and their economic and social circumstances. Although these positions cannot be justified by merit or desert, he recognized that social institutions favor certain starting positions over others. Because of the inequality this creates, which he presumes is "inevitable in the basic structure of any society," (pp. 7–8). Rawls suggests that a conception of social justice is required in order to provide a standard against which the distributive aspects of the basic structure of society can be evaluated so that political and economic systems can be regulated accordingly. In education, the social justice as fairness perspective can be identified in the rationale for federally funded programs, such as Headstart and affirmative action, which recognize that students do not begin their schooling on an "even playing field."

## BEYOND THE DISTRIBUTIVE PARADIGM

Although the concern for distribution is crucial to any conception of justice, theories within the distributive paradigm tend to downplay or ignore the social structures and institutional contexts that often help determine distributive patterns in the first place. As a result, Young (1990) contends "a critical theory of social justice must consider not only distributive patterns, but also the processes and relationships that produce and reproduce those patterns" (p. 241). Further, Fraser (1995) suggests that "justice today requires *both* redistribution *and* recognition," (p.12; italics in the original), and that new conceptions of social justice need to theorize the ways in which economic disadvantage and cultural disrespect are entwined and reinforce each other dialectically because they are both rooted in "processes and practices that systematically disadvantage some groups of people vis-à-vis others" (p. 15).

In her paper, "From Redistribution to Recognition?: Dilemmas of Justice in a 'Post-Socialist Age,'" Fraser (1995) argues that heterogeneity and pluralism are the norms against which demands for justice are articulated, and that struggles for "recognition of difference" (p. 68) have motivated countless groups in their fight against discrimination based on nationality, ethnicity, race, gender, and sexuality. In education, these movements have often been galvanized in resistance to the status quo where students, parents, educators, and communities have insisted on accommodations or inclusion based on physical ability, or cultural, linguistic and religious differences.

## A SOCIAL JUSTICE AS REPRESENTATION
## APPROACH TO URBAN TEACHER PREPARATION

As previously mentioned, popular conceptualizations of teaching for social justice are rooted in traditions of political philosophy that propose ways to achieve a more just society through distribution. Although this approach is not disregarded within the recognition paradigm, the focus on economic inequities makes it inadequate as a way to theorize about forms of injustice that do not involve the distribution of goods or benefits. Drawing on Fraser's conceptualization of the *recognition paradigm*, in this chapter I propose social justice as representation as a framework for thinking about discourses and practices used to represent and understand urban students, families, and communities.

It is important to clarify that when using the term *representation*, I am not referring simply to the ways in which marginalized people are framed within the mainstream. These practices are critically important because, historically, this population has not had control over the production of images that portray them, or equal access to the media in ways that would allow them to "tell their side of the story" (McCarthy & Crichlow, 1993, p. xvii). The definition suggested here considers the ways in which bodies are represented in popular culture and interrogates the ways in which "the truth" about these groups is constructed and regulated though normalizing ideologies and the dynamic relationship between knowledge and power. This approach is designed to help candidates understand that what we believe is "reality" is mediated through representations and cultural practices. In the case of urban and inner-city communities, the focus on representation does not deny that some of the "texts" about these environments describe life in ways that would be validated by the people who live in them, but this approach does emphasize that "'the real' must be constructed continuously in order to be recognized as such" (Britzman, Santiago-Valles, Jimenez-Monoz, & Lamash,1993, p.192).

Like the focus on recognition, a social justice as representation framework is primarily concerned with symbolic injustice, including the influence of notions about urban students, families, and communities that frame them as deviant and pathological, or as the primary reason for "their problems." Fraser (1995) suggests that symbolic injustice requires symbolic change, including the revaluing of disrespected identities and their cultural products, and the "wholesale transformation of social patterns of representation, interpretation and communication" (p. 15). Rizvi (1998) presents these "social patterns" as semiotic in nature, and argues that because students develop a sense of self-worth as they learn the acceptable models of social communication through schooling, "the semiotic issues of representation, interpretation and communication are highly relevant to the concerns for justice in education" (p. 55). In this remark, he refers specifically to students with disabilities, but I believe this viewpoint can be applied more broadly. Efforts to achieve social justice must pay attention to "...the way things are named and represented, the manner in which difference is treated and the ways in which the values and significations and norms which govern life in schools are negotiated and established" (p. 55). The social justice as representation approach suggested here is an attempt to spotlight the ways in which the negative representations of marginalized urban families and communities, uninformed interpretations of their behaviors, values, and attitudes, and disrespectful communication with and about them provide fertile ground for underachievement, social isolation, civic disengagement, and economic disadvantage. Within this framework representation, interpretation and communication—as both social and semiotic practices—are of paramount importance.

## UNDERSTANDING REPRESENTATION

Human beings are born with the need to make sense of their environment and as we mature, our capacity to distinguish and respond to new stimuli helps us to interact with our surroundings. The product of this active relationship between ourselves and the world is often referred to as making meaning. A social justice as representation approach finds it origins in the fields of cultural studies and semiotics, the general study of signs in culture, where culture is understood: as the context within which meaning exists; the dynamic that stimulates the production and dissemination of new meanings; and, the process of meaning-making within social groups (Lewis, 2002). Those meanings, which are assembled together for a particular purpose within a particular historical context, are mediated through language, symbols, signs and "texts" that are formed within systems that are fluid and mutable.

Making meaning requires cognition, where objects, people, and events in the "real" world are correlated with concepts or mental representations in our minds. In this way, they are organized, arranged, and classified in order to establish the relationships between them, or to distinguish them from one another (Hall, 1997). Even though cognition is a function of the brain, it does not happen in a social vacuum; other people help to make up the environment within which learning takes place. As we develop, the sounds and gestures that we use to communicate our ideas and desires become more complicated until making meaning requires a common language through which concepts and ideas become associated with particular words or signs that are used to represent them.

As Hall (1997) explains, because a particular image or word stands for or symbolizes a concept, it functions as a sign—or signifier—that conveys meaning. What carries meaning is not the sign or the concept, but the difference between the sign and other signs. Further, because meaning is relational, it is not bound in the sign but in its symbolic function, and even these are not static. As a result, all signs are arbitrary, and there is no natural relationship between the sign and what it has come to mean. Signs cannot fix meaning because meaning depends on the socially constructed relationship between the sign and the concept. This relationship is fixed by codes, which help to make these links through the practice of interpretation, where information is encoded and meaning is derived as the person receiving it decodes or interprets it (Hall, 1980).

As social actors, we use the conceptual systems of our culture and language to construct meaning and to communicate about the world meaningfully to others (Hall, 1997). As a result, according to Ryan (1999), "the process of representation does not allow us simply to mirror the objects, events and people in our experience...this process is socially constructed, and because it is, it is always subject to the forces that shape our social reality" (p. 68). Representation then cannot be understood without paying attention to the interrelationships between discourse, knowledge, and power.

## DISCOURSES AND DISCURSIVE PRACTICES

*Discourses* are regulated systems of meanings and representations that produce knowledge about the world by situating these within a symbolic or discursive order. These orders also exclude alternative meanings and meaning possibilities (Lewis, 2002). Discourses involve a set of written and spoken statements, commonly referred to as *texts*, where formulative rules are determined by the interrelationships between speakers and the acceptable procedures and perspectives through which knowledge is appropriated (Alcoff, 1996). Because they also determine the roles that speakers can take and the subject positions the hearer may assume (Foucault, 1972), a discursive practice "sets out the legitimate perspective for the agent of knowledge" (Foucault, 1977, p. 199).

The ways of understanding social reality held by the dominant or privileged group(s) are often accepted as part of the natural order by all—including those who are disempowered or marginalized by those views. The result of this is a form of social inequity that is "woven throughout social institutions as well as embodied within individual consciousness" (Bell, 1997, p. 4), or what Gramsci referred to as hegemony (Ives, 2004). Further, hegemonic discourses become embedded within "regimes of truth" (Foucault, 1980) or networks of social and political control, and operate to oppress others by legitimating what can be said, who has the authority to speak, and what knowledge is accepted as truth (Kreisberg, 1992).

## OFFICIAL KNOWLEDGE

Although we don't often think of the urban education discourse as "hegemonic," it has at times taken on this character through the research and knowledge bases that support it. In some cases, published research becomes formal, or "official knowledge," whereas the practical and personal knowledge of school administrators, teachers, para-educators, parents/guardians, and students is often considered to be less reliable. It is the official knowledge then that becomes canonized and applied universally to teaching and learning situations in generalized ways.

"Official knowledge, coupled with the social and political power of those who produce it, not only assumes the authority of 'the truth,' but also has the power to *make itself true"* (Hall (1997, p. 49; italics in the original). Therefore, Foucault speaks of "truth," not in the absolute sense, but as a discursive formation that sustains a regime of truth (Hall, 1997). Knowledge is always "inextricably enmeshed in relations of power because it is always being applied to the regulation of social conduct" (Hall, 1997, p. 47). Through our work in universities, on research projects, or especially through publication and public speaking, the ideas, beliefs, and viewpoints of teacher educators and educational researchers have become a key source through which knowledge of the profession is gained, regulated, and sometimes used to regulate the conduct of others.

As social scientists, we have developed methodologies within the field that we use to generate knowledge about, and to some extent govern, the practices of teaching and learning. Ryan (1999) suggests that we have the ability to do this "at least in part, by virtue of the status of [our] claims, that is, through [our] appeals to truth" (p. 67). As professors of education, our positions in universities and research institutions situate us as professors of knowledge, and we are endowed with a certain degree of legitimacy that, at the same time, dictates the position of those outside of the academy. Few people are unimpressed by the academic qualifications that most university faculty have earned, and thus equate this with their level of expertise and command of their subjects.

The literature in the field of urban education has been dominated by two concepts: *crisis,* which is associated with failing students, schools, and communities; and *improvement,* where writings tend to focus on effective schools, leadership, intervention programs, school reform, and urban coalitions (Grace, 1994). Although some have criticized it as "unnecessarily limited" in its capacity to appropriately inform efforts to understand and improve the life chances of people living in urban and inner-city communities (Gordon, Miller, & Rollock, 1999, p. 172), educational researchers and scholars have had a tremendous impact on how we think about the schooling of marginalized and minoritized children nonetheless.

During the 1960s, cultural deficit theories were used to explain the underachievement of poor and minority children and determined that academic failure was caused by family structure, attitudes, and values (C. Deutsch, 1964; M. Deutsch & Brown, 1964; John & Goldstein, 1964). In some of these studies, signifiers that have been used over the years, including *ghetto schools, children of the street,* and *dysfunctional families,* have helped to pathologize urban and inner-city students, schools, and communities. When children are described as *minority, at-risk,* or *failures* in an effort to describe their status or potential, these labels also imply their place in the world and their subject position.

During the 1970s and 1980s, the focus shifted away from children and families to the processes of schooling and the school experiences of diverse racial, socioeconomic, and cultural groups. In this work, researchers turned to such factors as verbal and nonverbal interaction between teachers and students, conflicting patterns of cultural interaction or "cultural mismatch," and the content of the curriculum as a way to explain differential achievement (Anyon, 1981; Heath, 1983; Rist, 1970; Shannon, 1985). Others have devoted their attention to the social, political, and historical contexts within which schools function (Ogbu, 1981a, 1981b).

In their review of research related to effective instruction for students from low socioeconomic backgrounds, Brophy and Good (1986) reported that scholars recommended more control and structuring from their teachers; more active instruction, feedback, and redundancy; more review, drill, and practice; and more lower level questions. Teachers were also advised to expose students to less material, emphasize mastery, and "move them through the curriculum as briskly as they are able to progress" (Brophy & Good, 1986, cited in Knapp, Shield, & Turnbull, 1995, p. 183). According to Knapp et al. (1995), this emphasis on "learning deficits, tightly controlled direct instruction, repetitive practice, and the mastery of discrete 'basic' skills has held the status of conventional wisdom among large numbers of practitioners, bolstered by a good deal of research" (p. 183).

## SUBJUGATED KNOWLEDGE

*Subjugated knowledge* is that which has traditionally been de-legitimated by other, more dominant forms of knowledge that have dominated the discursive field. During the past 40 years, this de-legitimation has resulted in a body of knowledge about urban and inner-city schools that has been constructed largely by those outside of these communities. The marginalization of knowledge about pedagogy in urban and inner-city schools, and the limited recognition of those outside of the academy who have personal and practical knowledge about these settings (as evidenced by the limited representation of these voices in professional literature, educational research, and the teacher education discourse in general) constitute a form of symbolic injustice. When the knowledge that speaks directly to the education of children in urban settings is not considered to have relevance equal to more official knowledge, what can result is also a form of inequity, as this knowledge is not given equal time within teacher education programs and is included as "add-ons," to the curriculum.

Some efforts have been made to involve teachers and families in the process of institutionalized teacher preparation. For example, the professional development school (PDS) model was designed as a way to bridge the gap between schools and colleges/universities, and is advocated as a way to improve the preparation of urban teachers. Ideally, exemplary teachers mentor candidates during their field placements and these practitioners teach courses in the teacher education program. In addition, university faculty commit to working with the school in various areas including curriculum and professional development. However, even this model has been criticized by Murrell (1998) for reinforcing the "status and power inequalities between educational professionals and low-income parents," primarily due to its "ideology of professional control" (p. 393). These concerns have also been reiterated in the work of Lopez and Scribner (1999), whose review of the research on discourses about parent involvement suggests, "researchers and reforms have not generally accepted the notion that school people might themselves learn from poor parents of color" (quoted in Weiner, 2000, p. 393).

## FROM THEORY TO PRACTICE

Any social justice approach to urban and inner-city education should focus on the personal and professional development of beginning teachers, and help prepare them to work for equity and social justice as members of the profession and as active citizens. A social justice as representation approach seeks to include the perspectives, experiences, and expertise of those who learn, teach, live, and work in cities within the urban education discourse. It also encourages the critical examination of the ways in which urban children, families, and communities are represented in our society and in our minds. I now offer a few recommendations for the ways in which pre-service programs might incorporate this perspective.

Teacher education programs concerned with teaching for social justice should include teaching strategies and content that can help candidates understand that difference does not always mean deficit. Building on Young's (1990) notion of the "politics of difference," candidates should be provided with opportunities to conceptualize diversity as dissimilarity and not as deviation from a norm. Within such an approach, teacher candidates would be encouraged to avoid the use of generalizations about students' lives based on stereotypes of the linguistic, ethnic, cultural, or socioeconomic groups with which they are affiliated. Course work would also need to provide readings, activities, and assignments that help them recognize the dangers in practices that "locate problems or pathologies in individuals, families and communities rather than in institutional structures that create and maintain inequality" (Lubeck & Garrett, 1990, cited in Swadener & Lubeck, 1995, p. 3).

Building on the characteristics of successful urban teacher education programs, a social justice as representation approach endorses practices that (a) provide opportunities for candidates to be taught by members of the community and effective urban teachers through well supervised practicum experiences, (b) include and recruit community members as prospective teachers, (c) offer candidates the opportunity to take part in field-based experiences outside of the school building, and (d) value the knowledge that parents/guardians and community members contribute to their children's education.

It is important that candidates preparing to work in urban and inner-city schools do not develop a monolithic view of the nature of these settings. Field placements should provide candidates with first-hand experiences of people and places at opposite ends of the socioeconomic spectrum as a way to help them understand the complexity of urban environments. Teacher educators would need to encourage the direct interaction between candidates and others in the school and community through activities that are meaningful and that allow them to become members of a situated learning community where they can learn from more experienced others. Most importantly, candidates need to be taught how to be participant observers in settings that are unfamiliar and perhaps uncomfortable, and how to respectfully question practices within families and the local community that appear to be unfair or discriminatory.

A social justice approach to urban teacher preparation should view the development of teachers' attitudes and beliefs about urban teaching, families, and communities as a primary concern. As such, programs should expose candidates to practical strategies for engaging with all kinds of parents/caregivers as equal partners and advocates for their children. Further, a social justice as representation approach would help teacher candidates recognize that norms and expectations related to teachers' interaction with families are socially and culturally constructed.

## CONCLUSION

In the effort to make these or any other suggestions for practice a realistic goal, educational researchers have suggested that the teacher candidates learn about social justice issues integrated into their program and not isolated in a single course (Larkin, 1995; Larkin & Sleeter, 1995; Nieto, 1996). Further, they argue that groups of faculty, not just individual professors, should have enough knowledge and understanding of these issues in order to integrate them into their courses (Zollers et al., 2000). As Garcia (1997) proposes, teaching for social justice requires professional preparation that has the power to not only transform our thinking, but also our lives. Good intentions are not enough to prepare candidates who can "change the world."

Teacher education programs that claim to be committed to social justice must be willing and able to describe and defend the pedagogical and sociopolitical commitments on which they are built. These programs should be willing to move candidates to places outside of their comfort zones, and unabashedly admit that they have both an agenda and an ideology that are founded on a particular set of tenets, beliefs, and assumptions. Teaching for social justice, like other social movements, should create a collective identity among teacher educators and teacher candidates where together they can develop a different view of themselves and their world. Through a process of *rearticulation* (Omi & Winant, 1986), new subjectivities can be produced by making use of the information and knowledge teacher candidates already have, and introducing new representations of urban and inner-city communities that infuse their prior knowledge with new meaning.

## REFERENCES

Alcoff, L. (1996). *Real knowing: New versions of the coherence theory.* Ithaca, NY: Cornell University Press.

Anyon, J. (1981). Social class and school knowledge. *Curriculum Inquiry, 11,* 2–42.

Bell, L. A. (1997). Theoretical foundations of social justice education. In A. Adman, L. A. Bell, & P. Griffin (Eds.), *Teaching for diversity and social justice: A sourcebook* (pp. 3–16). New York: Routledge.

Beyer, L. (2001). The value of critical perspectives in teacher education. *Journal of Teacher Education, 52*(2), 151–163.

Britzman, D. P., Santiago-Valles, K., Jimenez-Munoz, G., & Lamash, L. M. (1993). Slips that show and tell: Fashioning multiculture as a problem of representation. In C. McCarthy & W. Crichlow (Eds.), *Race, identity and representation in education* (pp.188–200). New York: Routledge.

Brophy, J., & Good, T. L. (1986). Teacher behavior and student achievement. In M. Wittrock (Ed.), *Handbook of research on teaching* (3rd ed., pp. 328–375). New York: Macmillan.

Cochran-Smith, M (1995). Uncertain allies: Understanding the boundaries of race and teaching. *Harvard Educational Review, 65,* 541–570.

Cochran-Smith, M. (1999). Learning to teach for social justice. In G. Griffin (Ed.), *The education of teachers: Ninety-eighth yearbook of the National Society for the Study of Education.* (pp. 114–144). Chicago, IL: University of Chicago Press.

Cochran-Smith, M., Albert, L., Diamattia, P., Freedman, S., Jackson, R., Mooney, J., Neisler, O, Peck, A., & Zollers, N. (1999). Seeking social justice: A teacher education faculty's self-study. *Leadership in Education, 2*(3), 229–253.

Deutsch, C. (1964). Auditory discrimination and learning: Social factors. *Merrill Palmer Quarterly, 10,* 277–296.

Deutsch, M., & Brown, B. (1964). Social influences on Negro-White intelligences differences. *Journal of Social Issues, 20,* 24–35.

Foucault, M., (1972). *The archaeology of knowledge and the discourse on language* (A. M. Sheridan Smith, Trans.). New York: Pantheon Books.

Foucault, M. (1977). *Discipline and punish.* London: Tavistock.

Foucault, M. (1980). *The history of sexuality: Volume I.* New York: Vintage Books.

Fraser, N. (1995). From redistribution to recognition: Dilemmas of justice in a "post-socialist" society. *New-Left Review*, July-August, 68–93.

Garcia, S. S. (1997). Self-narrative inquiry in teacher development: Living and working in just institutions. In J. E. King, E. R. Hollins, & W. C. Hayman (Eds.), *Preparing teachers for cultural diversity* (pp. 146–155). New York: Teachers College Press.

Gordon, E. W., Miller, F., & Rollock, D. (1999). Coping with communicentric bias in knowledge production in the social sciences. In E. W. Gordon, *Education and social justice: A view from the back of the bus* (pp. 172–184). New York: Teachers College Press.

Grace, G. (1994). Urban education and the culture of contentment: The politics, culture and economics of inner-city schooling. In N. P. Stromquist (Ed.), *Education in urban areas: Cross national dimensions* (pp.450–590). Westport, CT: Greenwood.

Hall, S. (1980). Encoding and decoding. In S. Hall, D. Hobson, A. Lowe, & P. Willis (Eds.), *Culture, media, language* (pp. 128–138) London: Routledge.

Hall, S. (1997). *Representation: Cultural representations and signifying practice*. London: Sage.

Heath, S. B. (1983). *Ways with words: Language, life and work in communities and classrooms*. Cambridge, England: Cambridge University Press.

Ives, P. (2004). *Language and hegemony in Gramsci*. Winnepeg, Manitoba, Canada: Fernwood.

John, V., & Goldstein, L. (1964). The social context of language acquisitions. *Merrill Palmer Quarterly, 10,* 265–275.

Knapp, M. S., Shields, P. M., & Turnbull, B. J. (1995). *Teaching for meaning in high poverty classrooms*. New York: Teachers College Press.

Kohl, H. (1999). Social justice and leadership in education: Commentary. *International Journal of Leadership in Education: Theory and practice, 2*(3), 307–311.

Kreisberg, S. (1992). *Transforming power: Domination, empowerment and education*. Albany: State University of New York Press.

Larkin, J. M. (1995). Current theories and issues in multicultural teacher education programs. In J. M. Larkin & C. E. Sleeter (Eds.), *Developing multicultural teacher education curricula* (pp. 1–16). Albany: State University of New York Press.

Larkin, J. M., & Sleeter, C. E. (1995). Developing multicultural teacher education curricula. Albany: State University of New York Press.

Lewis, J. (2002). *Cultural studies: The basics*. London: Sage.

Lopez, G. R., & Scribner, J. D. (1999, April). *Discourses of involvement: A critical review of parent-involvement research*. Paper presented at the annual meeting of the American Education Research Association, Montreal.

Lubeck, S., & Garrett, P. (1990). The social construction of the "at-risk" child. *British Journal of Sociology of Education, 11*(31), 327–340.

McCarthy, C., & Crichlow, W. (1993). Introduction: Theories of identity, theories of representation, theories of race. In C. McCarthy & W. Crichlow (Eds.), *Race, identity and representation in education* (pp. xiii–xxix). New York: Routledge.

McIntyre, A. (1997). *Making meaning of Whiteness: Exploring racial identity with White teachers*. Albany: State University of New York Press.

Murrell, P. C. Jr. (1998). *Like stone soup: The role of professional development schools in the renewal of urban schools.* Washington, DC: American Association of Colleges for Teacher Education.

Nieto, S. (1996). *Affirming diversity: The sociopolitical context of multicultural education* (2nd ed.). White Plains, NY: Longman.

Nieto, S. (2000). Placing equity front and center: Some thoughts on transforming teacher education for a new century. *Journal of Teacher Education, 51*(3), 180–187.

Novak, M. (2000). Defining social justice. *First Things, 108*, 11–13 [Web version]. Retrieved October 20, 2005, from http:firstthings.com/ftissues/ft0012/opinion/novak.html

Ogbu, J. U. (1981a). *Minority education and caste: The American system in cross-cultural perspective.* New York: Academic Press.

Ogbu, J. U. (1981b). School ethnography: A multilevel approach. *Anthropology and Education Quarterly, 12*, 3–29.

Omi, M., & Winant, H. (1986). *Racial formations in the United States: From the 1960s to the 1980s.* New York: Routledge.

Rawls, J. (1999). *A theory of justice* (Rev. ed.). Cambridge, MA: The Belknap Press of Harvard University Press.

Rist, R. (1970). Students, social class and teacher expectations: The self-fulfilling prophecy in ghetto education: *Harvard Educational Review, 40*, 411–451.

Rizvi, F. (1998). Some thoughts on contemporary theories of social justice. In B. Atweh, S. Kemmis, & P. Weeks (Eds.), *Action research in practice: Partnership for social justice* (pp. 47–56) London: Routledge.

Russo, P. (2001). *Using technology to support teaching for social justice in a pre-service program.* In M. Justice (Ed.), Proceedings of Society for Information Technology and Teacher Education International Conference, Orlando, Florida, March 5–10. (ERIC Document Reproduction Service No. ED475 823)

Ryan, J. (1999). *Race and ethnicity in multi-ethnic schools.* Clevedon, England: Multilingual Matters, Ltd.

Shannon, P. (1985). Reading instruction and social class. *Language Arts, 72,* 604–613.

Sleeter, C. (1995). An analysis of the critiques of multicultural education, In J. A. Banks & C. A. Banks, *Handbook of research on multicultural education* (pp. 81–96). New York: Macmillan.

Solomon, R. C., & Murphy, M. C. (2000). *What is justice?* (2nd ed). New York: Oxford University Press.

Swadener, B. B., & Lubeck, S. (Eds.). (1995). *Children and families "at-promise": Deconstructing the discourse of risk.* Albany: State University of New York Press.

Weiner, L. (2000). Research in the 90s: Implications for urban teacher preparation. *Review of Educational Research, 70*(3), 369–406.

Young, I. M. (1990). *Justice and the politics of difference.* Princeton, NJ: Princeton University Press.

Zollers, N. J., Albert, L. R., & Cochran-Smith, M. (2000). In pursuit of social justice: Collaborative research and practice in teacher education. *Action in Teacher Education, 22*(2), 1–12.

# Chapter 3

# Developing Educational Collectives and Networks: Moving Beyond the Boundaries of "Community" in Urban Education

Beverly-Jean Daniel
*York University*

The literature on teacher education is replete with references to the term *community* (Zeichner & Hoeft, 1996). What has become increasingly evident, however, is the fact that the concept is seldom defined, and its contemporary manifestations continue to exist within theoretical and esoteric realms.

This chapter provides an analysis of the usage of the term community in general, but specifically engages its applications within the realm of urban teacher education. I question the current usage of the term on two primary fronts: (a) the terminology is seldom defined within the context of teacher-education programs, thereby limiting its possible reification; and (b) the possibility of developing a sustainable, actualized community among teachers and students given the multiple interests that are represented among given groupings of people in an urban setting.

These points of interruptions of the term facilitate the asking of questions such as: What is the concept of community with which the teachers enter an urban school environment? Who is considered to be a member of the community? How are the boundaries of community determined? And what are the factors that determine membership in particular urban school communities?

I placed the term *community* in italics in this instance to indicate that this is not the taken-for-granted conception of the term. Rather, the community to which I refer is a group of persons wherein the members remain aware of the intersections of oppressions, the multiple relational dynamics inherent in that space, and are continually working at making the community a comprehensive learning space for all of its members. Further, the members of the group are able to identify common goals and objectives that are designed to benefit the members of the group.

This notion of community is not based on homogeneity or communities of intentional sameness (Kailin, 1999), or within the communities that employ various methods of social geography (Frankenberg, 2004) to demarcate and maintain racialized public spaces. Rather, I draw from the work of Audre Lorde (1990), in which she indicates that:

> Too often, we pour the energy needed for recognizing and exploring into pretending those differences are insurmountable barriers, or that they do not exist at all. This results in a voluntary isolation, or false and treacherous connections. Either way we do not develop tools for using human difference as a springboard for creative change. (p. 114)

Lorde goes on to say, "our future survival is predicated upon our ability to relate within equality...we must recognize difference...and devise ways to use each others' difference to enrich our visions and our joint struggles" (p. 122). Within urban schooling environments, it is central to the development and functioning of students and teachers that their differences be recognized and incorporated into the process of schooling on a daily and integrated basis.

## WHAT IS AN URBAN SCHOOLING ENVIRONMENT?

According to Louis Seashore, Kruse, and Bryk (1995), there are specific socioeconomic, political, and organizational challenges that are faced within urban settings. Urban school environments are often regarded as a microcosm of many societal ails, and within that space, multiple social issues become magnified and contained within a confined geographic location, that is, the school (McGaughy, 2000; Walker & Gutmore, 2002). Issues of racism, poverty, and gender dynamics are often visibly heightened within this urban space. Furthermore, urban settings tend to be a magnet for immigrant groups, which contributes to the already unsettled space.

Many immigrant groups come to these urban spaces and must contend with issues of language, cultural diversity, economic instability, and a wide range of educational experiences. All of these factors, like all forms of experiential knowledge, are embodied; therefore this knowledge enters the classroom with every student who occupies that space.

Murrell (2001), citing Orfield et al. (1997), indicates that urban school environments are plagued by several factors that contribute to the continued difficulty that students experience: (a) Highly qualified teachers tend to gravitate toward geographical areas with higher income levels; (b) board incentives focus on remediation programs rather than investment in quality schooling; (c) the number of school and peer-based initiatives tend to be lower in urban areas; and finally, (d) parents, community members, school boards and students tend to hold a pejorative view of the quality of schooling offered. Murrell indicates also that children and youth of color are the most negatively affected by the various forms of dysfunctional practices evident in urban school settings.

Urban spaces are also marked by different value systems embedded in economic power bases. An urban space that is considered to be financially viable, for example, Wall Street in the American context and Bay Street in the Canadian context, is highly valued urban property. Therefore, when we talk about urban spaces, we have to also preface it by indicating that these urban school environments are the ones marked by processes of "devalorization" (Sassen, 1998). According to Sassen, "forms of devalorization…are partly embedded in the demographic transformations evident in large cities. The growing presence of women, immigrants, and people of color in large cities along with a declining middle class have facilitated the operation of devalorization processes…" (p. 87). This means that the value placed on a particular geographical location is related to the economic viability of that space and its racial and gendered demographics. The value placed on a particular urban space is also dynamic, as evidenced in urban renewal projects. However, these projects tend to be primarily aimed at reclaiming the physical landscape while simultaneously displacing the human bodies within those spaces. Therefore, these urban renewal projects continue to place limited value on people, thus creating a further sense of chaos and instability that marks lower income urban spaces, which also become replicated in the schools.

When all of these factors are considered, along with the multiple social factors of diversity based on race and gender, the urban school environment becomes a difficult space within which to educate children. These issues underscore the importance of employing creative and innovate ways for working with students in urban schools.

## HOW AND WHY IS THE NOTION OF COMMUNITY IMPORTANT IN URBAN SETTINGS?

The notion of community becomes increasingly important in urban settings primarily because of the multiple issues evidenced in those spaces.

For the members of an urban space, their existence and survival is intricately connected in a myriad of ways. The connectivity among the teachers and the students influences the quality of teaching and learning that occurs in the classroom; the relationship among the staff members affects the sense of commitment and morale; the nature of the relationship between the parents and staff affects the level of parental involvement and support for school-based initiatives. Therefore, each person's success is based on and connected to the performance and functioning of the other members of that space. The notion of individualism within urban settings can result in anomie, which then impacts on people's ability to develop meaningful relationships with each other. Oliver (1976), for example, indicates that within the context of employing communitarian principles to the experience of schooling, improving the quality of life for the group should come before individual growth.

To some degree, one can state that the level of connectedness within such an environment is significantly more vital than that in other school settings. In suburban schools, for example, which tend to be better funded, the fact that the staff and students have the necessary environment and materials to facilitate their success may serve to curtail the need for a strong sense of community. However, in the urban setting, the very survival of the school is tenuous, and the continued cries for increased funding places the members in a very shaky and volatile situation of great interdependence. Therefore, in order for the urban unit to experience some degree of success, the members of that space must be committed to each other and to the larger social goal (Calderwood, 2000).

Haig-Brown, Hodgson-Smith, Reginer, and Archibald (1997), in their research project examining the working of an urban Aboriginal school program, also highlight the importance of connectedness among the members as a variable for success. Quoting one of the parent participants, they indicate "[w]ith us, everything is connected and interconnected, whether you are talking about rehabs...the sun, the rain everything...is interconnected and we try to use that method to teach our kids"(p. 96) The authors go on to state that the notion of community within this school environment is not based on a common culture or language. They indicate "[w]hile this is not a community defined by common culture, land base, or language, it is one defined by the common experience of being Aboriginal people living in this city... [T]here is a common bond of commitment to improving educational opportunities for Aboriginal youth in the city..." (p. 96). Therefore, the members of this school employ the notions of community and connection as important elements that foreground the effective education of their children.

## UNDERSTANDING COMMUNITY

According to Abercrombie, Hill, and Turner (1994), although the term community is very elusive, it is thought to contain three primary elements: (a) a collection of people that share a particular social structure, (b) a sense of belonging, and (c) all of the daily activities and routines are performed within a particular self-contained geographical area. A community may have one or more of these characteristics. Kendall, Murray, and Linden (2002) state that a community is "a society in which social relationships are based on personal bonds of friendship, kinship and intergenerational stability, such that people have a commitment to the entire group and feel a sense of togetherness" (p. 626). The German term *Gemeinschaft* (Tonnies, 1940), which means "to commune," has been used. However this concept of community had primarily been attached to rural and preindustrial societies, members of which tend to be homogenously based on race, language, customs, kinship, and membership that is prescripted at birth. Movement in and out of such communities tends to be minimal, and the core values of the group are seldom challenged.

In contrast to the notion of *Gemeinschaft*, the concept of *Gesellschaft*, which means "association," has been used to describe the nature of social relations in urban and industrialized settings, which tend to be limited, impersonal, specialized, with limited sense of consensus. According to Hale (1995), this form of community refers to

> An association of people based on principles of contract and exchange...an artificial society that is transitory and superficial. It emerges out of competitive struggles among individuals who do not feel themselves bound together by kinship or religion. People are geographically mobile and hence, tend to be heterogeneous with respect to racial and ethnic origins and religious beliefs. (p. 64)

Urban schools are highly reflective of these particular factors. Community requires a degree of intimacy that must be based on a shared sense of commitment or shared goals. In the case of the Joe Duquette High School (Haig-Brown et al., 1997), the shared goal was ensuring the best educational opportunities for their children and the intimacy that emerged out of their shared identification as Aboriginal peoples.

Oliver (1976), for example, stated that there are two primary foundational bases for societal development: the technological and the moral order. Therefore, as schools become more technologically ordered, the moral order on which notions of community are based is sublimated. The technological base in Western societies is linked directly with the system of capitalism, and therefore, the focus on the individual accumulation of wealth remains severed from the notions of intimacy and togetherness. Furthermore, schools closely mimic the sense of alienation as they have developed as sites of technological preparedness for the larger social structures (Oliver, 1976). This sense of alienation can become even more prevalent in urban settings in which issues of race, class, and the deficit in educational and curriculum funding are factored.

What then can we consider the factors that underscore the moral order of schooling? Inherent in the act of teaching and learning should be an act of caring and purposefulness. Teaching and providing information for its own sake, particularly considering that much of the information in the current curriculum continues to exude Eurocentrism, is of limited viability. The curriculum continues to remain disconnected from the majority of students whose lives form a landscape that limits active learning. Knowledge that remains disconnected from the lives of students provides limited opportunities for developing a sense of connectedness to community.

If communities are based on common rituals, these rituals must also have some degree of shared meaning. How do we begin to identify these rituals when by their very nature, urban schools have developed as repositories of social differences? The presence of these differences, though a unique site of learning, knowledge and experiences, are often constructed as problematic (Walker & Gutmore, 2002), and the concept of *the urban school* has remained firmly entrenched in notions of deficit and pathology. In order for us to begin to envision communities within an urban space, a different imaginary needs to be used so we can see beyond the difficulties and focus on the possibilities. What is also evident in urban geographic locations is that although the rural sense of homogenous communities may not be very visible, there are strong support networks that develop within those spaces, even within transient and impoverished populations such as the homeless or street youth. Based on such practices then, one can surmise that some type of network development is also possible within the school environment.

## COMMUNITY AND FREEDOM

According to Birt (2002), the search for community is also about the search for freedom. Therefore, the development of community in diverse spaces begins with a collective identification of a common freedom among its members. In the classroom, would teachers regard the success of all students as a source and symbol of freedom? Would students regard their personal and communal success as a mark of freedom? Perhaps the first type of freedom that would be important in an urban setting is freedom from the negative labeling so pervasive in the literature and research on urban settings. In order for that freedom to be experienced on an individual level, freedom also has to be based on a shared commitment to that change in the marking of the urban settings. Birt (2002) indicates

> Inasmuch as the struggle for freedom is social, it seeks a liberated social condition. It seeks to alter radically our way of being-with-others, to liberate us from self-estrangement and reified social relations. Yet, the surpassing of self-estrangement and social reification is possible only through an upsurge in common freedom. To the extent that we give social form to this upsurge we thereby create community. One cannot be self without others, but is always an existing individual in relation to others. (p. 88)

Birt goes on to say, "Our freedom—hence our very being—is active in relation of self to others and the world" (p. 88). Therefore, inasmuch as freedom is an individual experience, it can only be experienced in relations within a social context.

Calderwood (2000) identifies several markers of community, including a belief in shared identity, recognition, and reconciliation of difference, celebratory events, and competence. It is interesting to note that although Calderwood identifies the pitfalls inherent in making claims to community, she fails to move beyond the continued undefined adoption of the term. She employs the idea of "moments of communion," in which she discusses the importance of a communal sense of belonging and interaction, but also questions whether "these moments of communion produce resilient and enduring community" (p. 263). One can also question whether those moments of communion can produce the positive relational outcomes that can facilitate the development of community within urban school environments.

What is the relation of the teacher to the students, and the students to the teachers? Within indigenous forms of education, focused on the concept of *learning as a holistic process*, life and relationships in and of themselves were cyclical, the relations between people were clearer. Within a hierarchical, capitalist society, the notion of relation of self to others tends to be based more on utility; relationships are based on a series of manipulations to ensure that the individual is propelled higher up on the academic/economic ladder. Therefore, schooling that is constructed within capitalist systems is contraindicative to the notion of freedom and therefore community. Therefore, the concept of community and the praxis of community appear to be diametrically opposed within the current structure of schooling in North America, particularly within urban settings. In every utilitarian act, one person wins at the expense of another. Therefore, the sense of sharing and understanding within such relations of dominance and oppression is lost or marginalized, and another opportunity to experience a sense of freedom passes.

According to Freire (1998), it is interesting to note the way in which teachers protest against the perceived challenges to their freedoms, whether from the administration, parents, or the government. He asks, "[w]hat can be expected from teachers who protest against the administration's restrictions on their freedom to teach but who at the same time dishonorably restrict the freedom of the learners?" (p. 55). Freire believes that it is difficult to predict the outcome of such scenarios because of the role of human agency. But he states that students will experience less confusion if there exists a minimal discrepancy between teachers' goals and practices and the expectations and practices that inform their engagement with students. According to Freire (1998),

> Fortunately, on the human level, no mechanical explanation elucidates anything. We can not declare that the students of such an educator will necessarily become apathetic or live in permanent rebellion. But it would be much better for them if they were not subjected to such discrepancy between what is said and what is done. And of the testimony of saying and the testimony of doing, the stronger is doing because it has or can have immediate effects. The worst thing, however, for the training of the learners is that in the face of contradiction between words and deeds the learner tends not to believe what the educator says. If the educator makes a statement, the learner waits for the next action to detect the next contradiction. And this destroys the image that educators construct of themselves and reveal to the learners. Children are very sensitive to teachers who do exactly the opposite of what they say. (p. 55)

Stating an interest in equity and ensuring that all students succeed, while simultaneously engaging in acts that are contraindicative to those goals are discrepancies to which children are acutely attuned. I have consistently said to teachers that children are much more attuned to their environment and nonverbal cues than we give them credit for. They are very aware of the ideologies and values that teachers may be trying to hide from them. In my work with students, I have heard them very clearly elucidate the problems inherent in such contradictions. The students are able to identify which teachers they believe are "fake," and they can also provide specific examples of incidents that have led them to that assessment. They can identify which teachers are pretending to like them and which ones actually do. They are also extremely aware of the teachers they regard as biased, whether based on race, gender, class, or sexuality. The common response of the students is that they have no respect for those teachers. Every student is acutely aware (a) if teachers are not genuinely connected to the community in which they teach; (b) are not committed to ensuring the success of every student in that classroom; (c) consider themselves apart from the communities in which they work and can express limited identification with the parents, staff, and children in that schooling environment; and (d) are counting the minutes to when they can return to the panacea that suburbia provides.

According to Solomon and Levine-Rasky (2003),

> In-service teachers have forged a somewhat tenuous relationship with communities served by their schools. They often "invite" selected community groups into the school on special occasions and for particular activities. But the extent to which teachers get involved in the social, cultural and political life of the community is debatable. Teachers' roles as members of a dominant group, middle-class professionals, often separate them from the urban, working-class, inner-city, culturally diverse communities in which they work. (p. 129)

Considering the aforementioned, and the fact that the teachers' involvement in the communities within which their schools are located are representative of life experiences that are unfamiliar, it becomes important to envision a different conception of community involvement. With the increasing demands placed on teachers' time, and the increasingly diverse needs of the students in the classroom, teachers' involvement in activities outside of their school activities is yet another demand. This is not to say that those areas are not extremely important. However, is it a realistic expectation that the teachers will be able to engage with community groups at this level if they have not bonded with the students in the classrooms who are members of that community?

## EDUCATIONAL COLLECTIVES OR NETWORKS?

How do we begin to build communities in schools? Perhaps this is not the focus; perhaps a collective or network lends itself more effectively to the goals and objectives I have been highlighting. A *collective* can be defined as a group of persons working in cooperation. The term *educational collectives* can be employed where the primary goal is ensuring the education, training, and development of all of members within a geographically defined space. The notion and understanding of the term *education* also requires clarification. This application of the notion of education moves beyond its overapplication to specifically highlight the importance of the transfer of knowledge between parties, not simply a trickle-down, hierarchically organized process from teacher to student or the typical "banking" methodology (Freire, 1990). Education must be holistic and humanistic, at all times inclusive of learning and knowledge that can feed the entire human being.

Education must move beyond the dissection of people's lives into separate and disjointed identities—with home, school and spirituality all regarded as distinct. No teacher enters the classroom without a historical grounding that has informed his or her particular ideological base and particular worldview. According to Murrell (2001), in order for a teacher to effectively contribute to the development of students in a communal space, the teacher must have a clear sense of identity and the way in which that identity relates to the students in the community within which they work. In much the same way, no student enters the space of a classroom with simply the school personality in the knapsack; their identity significantly informs their interaction with the environment. The focus therefore on the schooling of the child results in a mental division of the person and their identities, thereby creating a partial person. True education ensures that the multiple selves remain interconnected and at all times aware of the condition of the integrated self.

Krishnamurti (1981) argues:

> In our present civilization we have divided life into so many departments that education has very little meaning, except in learning a particular technique or profession. Instead of awakening the integrated intelligence of the individual, education is encouraging him to conform to a pattern and is so hindering his comprehension of himself as a total process.... The individual is made up of different entities...education should bring about the integration of those separate entities—for without integration, life becomes a series of conflicts and sorrows. (pp. 11–12)

It is for these reasons that I use the term education. Schooling in its present context is simply designed to prepare workers who are disconnected from their work. In contrast, if education is appropriately conducted, it creates a sense of humanity and connectedness to others in both our environment and on a global scale. Aboriginal groups use the notion of the sacred circle to highlight this notion of connectedness, interdependence, and balance (Haig-Brown et al., 1997).

Krishnamurti (1981) also indicates that "Education is not merely a matter of training the mind. Training makes for efficiency, but it does not bring about completeness. A mind that has merely been trained is the continuation of the past, and such a mind can never discover the new" (p. 13). The current practices in schooling that represent a simple replication of dominant ideology do not foster the development, understanding, or application of new knowledges. Khalil Gibran (1951) believes that as adults, we need to prepare children for the world of tomorrow, not for the world of the past, because they will never be able to enter that world, and that we can merely visit the future through children. Therefore, to simply train students to replicate the histories and ideologies of the past is to limit their ability to effectively grow in the future. The teacher must also experience education if he or she is to effectively engage in educating children.

And education must be experienced as part of the person rather than separated from the self. Teachers must implicate themselves in their teaching and understand the ways they are intimately connected to the environment in which they work.

## EDUCATIONAL COLLECTIVES AND THE ETHIC OF CARING

Collins (2000) identifies the characteristics that define an ethic of caring within communities. These include the importance of individual uniqueness developed within a communal space wherein which no individual suppress or dominates the other. Their sense of individuality is experienced in harmonious and complementary ways and relations. Second, there is the importance and appropriateness of engaging emotions in relating to others, thereby creating a bridge between emotional and intellectual pursuits. The third characteristic of this ethic of caring involves the ability to empathize with others.

In developing a sense of community or an educational collective in the schools, I believe that the ethic of *caring* must foreground all interactions and relationships among the parties present in that space. Contemporary school relationships are often characterized by a sense of competition for grades, recognition, and the attention of the teacher. Schooling in capitalist societies replicate the interaction patterns evident in the larger society; therefore, the competition for individual wealth building and power are similarly reflected in schools. The students are seldom prepared to experience their success as part of a larger group.

Even in the act of identifying individual students who perform well academically, this action sets up relations of dominance and marks some people as worthy and others as unworthy. This is not to say that the students should not be recognized for their achievements, but there are other forms of achievements that can be celebrated that do not serve to pit the academically gifted against the students whose talents may not lie within an academic realm. Instead, it becomes integral to the act of education that teachers identify the other gifts and talents that students may possess.

The act of caring therefore requires an emotional investment and an ability to move beyond the limits of a technocratic model of schooling. However, if we were to conceive of that emotional investment within a collectivist environment, that caring can be demonstrated in specific acts of engagement such as the time and space a teacher provides to engage with a student by having that student ask a question. However, the manner in which the teacher responds if they model respect can be conceived as an act of caring. Inherent in the nature of the response are markers of equity, an underscoring of the importance of listening and learning, and an investment in the future of the child. Inasmuch as we are aware that respect is something that must be earned, there appears to be a sense within the classroom that simply by having the moniker "teacher," one is immediately afforded respect. Perhaps in areas that reflect traditional values and where respect is shared among all members of the space irrespective of age, a teacher is regarded as a central member of that community.

It is clear, however, that many students today do not believe this, and will indicate that they respect the teachers who treat them with respect. It is unrealistic and for teachers to expect that this attitude will differ simply because one has entered a building with the title *school*. We continue to mark social relations quite distinctly from the relations in the classrooms when classroom interactions merely mirror the larger social systems, structures, and relationships.

## EDUCATIONAL COLLECTIVES AND TEACHER EDUCATION

Abercrombie et al. (1994) regard community as a highly elusive term, but set out three elements they believe may be intended in its usage. According to the authors, communities can be regarded as groups of people within particular social structures with a sense of belongingness to the group and whose activities occur within specific geographical boundaries. The community is also regarded as having a shared culture based on language, attitudes, symbols, and behavioral systems. The cultural practices are reinforced by institutional and social controls such as the desire for acceptance and inclusion (Hale, 1995).

Daniel (2003) examined the notion of community within a cohort of teacher candidates enrolled in a 9-month teacher education program at an urban university. There were several interesting insights that emerged from that project, which underscore the difficulty of developing communities within schools. Based on the results of the study, this development of a sense of belongingness is a Herculean task, given the multiple interests and, at times, conflicting ideological bases that are represented within that geographical space.

This movement toward the development of a connection to a group or community underscored the shift from the individual nature of teacher education toward the cohort model in an attempt to create a sense of connection beyond the individual self. However, an analysis of the responses in the study indicated that although the teacher candidates within the teacher education cohort had a common focus on social justice, the projection of those issues to the larger world around them limited their personal investment in developing community within the group. This was further underscored when the teacher candidates were placed in a context where they would have to make personal choices that would affect their level of comfort. This distancing of social justice issues served as a buffer that prevented them from addressing their own complicit role in the development of a community. At the same time, however, the focus on a particular politically based activity still provided a common goal from which they could develop a sense of connectedness to the larger group (Daniel, 2003).

According to Benammar (1994), this striving for community may actually indicate an "absence of community." The author posits that the search for community is a political activity, an ideology reflected by the participants who indicated that the presence of other members of the cohort precipitated their engagement with issues that would have been difficult to address in their absence. Therefore, the importance of identifying a specific goal or objective for the school emerges, even if that activity is politically motivated. An example of a politically motivated activity is the coordination of the annual Terry Fox Run, a Canadian fundraiser for cancer research. The culture of the school becomes preoccupied with ensuring that the particular financial pledge is met. Would it be possible, therefore, for schools to begin to identify a goal for the education of their students? Is it possible for a school environment to work toward ensuring that every member of that school achieves and experiences some degree of success and accomplishment?

Within African-centered feminist traditions, the community is regarded as a source of support and serves as an impetus for engagement in political activity designed to improve the condition of the larger communal group. The focus is on the macrosocial structures rather than ensuring the upward mobility of a specific sector. Notions of community therefore must be grounded in actual practice and move beyond the theoretical realm, as is often the norm within academia. This leads one to question whether the metaphorical or theorized community functions in the same or similar ways as the actualized community, and what such actualized community would look like. In Daniel's (2003) study there was the sense among the members of the cohort that they were more similar or likeminded to each other than the other teacher candidates, not only in terms of their belief and values, but also in terms of their practices and their understandings of issues of equity and diversity.

The marking of a group as distinct provides the basis for cohesion to some particular principle or assumed ideological similitude. For example, the use of the terms *woman* or *gender* in feminist studies is replete with notions that are presumed to be indicators of shared experiences. However, simply being labeled woman is at best a superficial basis for creating a sense of identification to not only the term, but also an attempt to create a sense of community among those who are assumed to be included within this particular trope. In much the same way, therefore, simply attending or working at a particular school does not provide similar enough experiences to enable the members of that geographical space to become a community. The factors that can be considered appropriate markers of inclusion within particular communities tend to be very clearly delineated within its cultural markers, thereby informing people's experience of a particular discourse. However, those experiences can provide them with a certain degree of commonality that can allow them to engage in collective action and goals.

The internal dynamics of a school can facilitate and contest the development of the notion of community among the members through their interactions, the amount of time spent together, and their belief in having similar values and goals.

## IMPLICATIONS FOR THE DEVELOPMENT OF EDUCATIONAL COLLECTIVES

This chapter has been primarily theoretical, which points to the importance of developing research projects that examine the issue of community within schools. However, it has highlighted several possibilities that could be explored. The following are some suggestions that have emerged out of the literature that could be employed in the process of developing collectives in the school environment.

As a starting point, we must initiate actions that would change the social construction of the image of urban schools. As discussed earlier, the idea of an urban schooling environment is replete with negative connotations based on pathology and deficit. Those who live and work within these spaces are not immune to the negative effects of this labeling. To begin with, we must start by constructing urban schools as "spaces of possibility," thereby ensuring that the members of that space are also regarded as people with possibilities, talents, and capabilities.

The identification of common practices is important. These should be separated from values and ideologies because all people come into the space with differing histories, beliefs, and ideological bases, and it is difficult if not impossible to chose which values one should privilege within the school collective. Therefore, it becomes a more productive approach to identify socially just and democratic common practices that everyone in the school can identify with and abide by, which can then promote a sense of cohesion among the members of that geographical space (Fung & Wright, 2003). One example of this could be that older children take responsibility for ensuring that younger kids are safe on the playground, or helping them with their schoolwork by becoming readers for the classrooms. Such common practices can benefit the overall school environment while avoiding a hierarchy of acceptable versus unacceptable cultural values.

There are multiple benefits to teachers of adopting a collective or networking approach to education. Such an approach can serve to minimize power dynamics while maintaining and supporting the role of the teacher without structuring it as a dominant–subordinate relationship. Such a relationship would be based primarily on negotiation rather than control and power, thereby resulting in fewer challenges to the teacher and a more harmonious working environment.

In terms of the benefits to the students, they will be better prepared to interact with the teachers on a more respectful and equitable basis given that they will see those practices modeled by their teacher, and the actions of the teachers will be in alignment with their words. Such exposure also teaches the students appropriate means of interacting among themselves. Therefore, the students can focus on the identified personal goals and larger school goals rather than attempting to mark spaces and interactions within the schools where they can claim some level of control and dominance.

Finally, there are larger social implications for developing the school as a network or collective. The school is one of the first places where society's citizens learn their social roles and the skills to interact with diversity and difference. The messages that they learn in the schools, if the interactions with their teachers and peers are based on the notion of collective organizing, will also be carried out to the larger society.

## CONCLUSION

In this chapter, I examined the meaning of the term community and examined its application within urban school environments. I have argued that the term community, built on notions of belongingness and intimacy, is an unrealistic goal given the multiple interests that are evidenced in such a heterogeneous environment. Instead, I have offered the terms *education collective* or *network*, which move beyond the notion of connectedness to encompass an identification of the primary goals and objectives for the school. Furthermore, the notion of the educational collective does not require an investment in dominant–subordinate relations of particular ideological beliefs and values. Rather, such an environment focuses on concrete, measurable, and achievable standards of practice and goals that can be met regardless of one's religious, cultural, or ethnic affiliation. The movement of the term from an esoteric to a concrete, grounded space requires a reconfiguration of the concept as well as a sustained investment from the multiple stakeholders.

Therefore, as teacher educators, particularly those of us who are involved in preparing teachers to work in urban environments, it becomes important to begin to enact our understanding of community within the classroom. If we are asking teachers and teacher candidates to become part of a community, or in this case an educational collective or network, that expectation should be embedded in the practices, curriculum, and interactions of the members of the community.

## REFERENCES

Abercrombie, N., Hill, S., & Turner, B. S. (1994). *The Penguin dictionary of sociology.* Toronto: Penguin Books Canada Ltd.

Benammar, K. (1994). Absences of community. In E. M. Godway & G. Finn (Eds.), *Who is this 'we'?: Absence of community* (pp. 31–44). Montreal, Quebec: Black Rose Books.

Birt, R. E. (2002). Of the quest for freedom as community. In R. E. Birt (Ed.), *The quest for community and identity: Critical essays in Africana social philosophy* (pp. 87–104). Lanham, MD: Rowan & Littlefield.

Calderwood, P. E. (2000). When community fails to transform: Raveling and unraveling a "community of writers." *The Urban Review, 32*(3), 263–292.

Collins, P. H. (2000). *Black feminist thought: Knowledge, Consciousness and the politics of empowerment.* New York: Routledge.

Daniel, B. M. (2003). *Cohort group membership and individual agency in teacher education: Implication for addressing issues of race, gender and class.* Unpublished doctoral dissertation, University of Toronto.

Frankenberg, R. (2004). Growing up White: Feminism, racism and the social geography of childhood. In A. Prince & S. Silva-Wayne (Eds.), *Feminisms and womanisms: A women's studies reader* (pp.139–165). Toronto: Women's Press.

Freire, P. (1990). *Pedagogy of the oppressed.* New York: Continuum.

Freire, P. (1998). *Teachers as cultural workers: Letters to teachers who dare to teach.* Boulder, CO: Westview Press.

Fung, A., & Wright, E. O. (2003). Thinking about empowered participatory governance. In *Deepening democracy: Institutional innovations in empowered participatory governance* (pp. 3–44). New York: Verso.

Gibran, K. (1951). *The prophet.* Toronto: Random House of Canada Ltd.

Haig-Brown, C., Hodgson-Smith, K. L., Reginer, R., & Archibald, J.-A. (1997). *Making the spirit dance within: Joe Duquette high school and an Aboriginal community.* Toronto: James Lorimer & Company.

Hale, S. M. (1995). *Controversies in sociology: A Canadian introduction.* Toronto: Copp Clarke.

Kailin, J. (1999). How White teachers perceive the problem of racism in their schools: A case study in "liberal" Lakeview. *Teachers College Record, 100*(4), 724–750.

Kendall, D., Murray, J. L., & Linden, R. (2002). *Sociology in our times.* Scarborough, Ontario: Nelson Thomson Learning.

Krishnamurti, J. (1981). *Education and the significance of life.* New York: Harper Collins.

Lorde, A. (1990). Age, race, class, and sex. Woman redefining difference. In R. Ferguson, M. Gever, T. Minh-ha, & C. West (Eds.), *Out there: Marginalization and contemporary cultures* (pp. 281–288). Cambridge, MA: MIT Press.

Louis Seashore, K., Kruse, S., & Bryk, A. S. (1995). Professionalism and community: What is it and why is it important in urban schools. In K. Louis Seashore (Ed.), *Professionalism and community: Perspectives on reforming urban schools* (pp. 3–22). Thousand Oaks, CA: Corwin Press.

McGaughy, C. (2000). Community development and education: A tripod approach to improving America. *The Urban Review, 32*(4), 385–409.

Murrell, P. C., Jr. (2001). *The community teacher: A new framework for effective urban teaching.* New York: Teacher's College Press.

Oliver, D. W. (1976). *Education and community: A radical critique of innovative schooling.* Berkeley, CA: McCutchan Publishing.

Sassen, S. (1998). *Globalization and its discontents.* New York: The New Press.

Solomon, R. P., & Levine-Rasky, C. (2003). *Teaching for equity and diversity: Research to practice.* Toronto: Canadian Scholars Press.

Tonnies, F. (1940). *Fundamental concepts of sociology* (C. P. Loomis, Trans.). New York: American Book Company.

Walker, E. M., & Gutmore, D. (2002). The issue of civic capacity in urban educational reform: The case of New Jersey's thirty poorest districts. *The Journal of Negro Education, 71*(1–2), 60–76.

Zeichner, K. M., & Hoeft, K. (1996). Teacher socialization for cultural diversity. In J. Sikula, T. J. Buttery & E. Guyton (Eds.), *Handbook of research on teacher education* (pp. 525–547). New York: Simon & Schuster.

# Chapter 4

# Gender, Power, and Accountability in Urban Teacher Education: Tensions of Women Working With Women

Lois Weiner
*New Jersey City University*

In the past decade, reforms to improve urban schools have focused on improving teacher quality and bringing schools of education into the process of school reform. This development has been accompanied by reduced attention to parents' contribution to schooling (Lopez & Scribner, 1999). Parental beliefs, values, and knowledge about what constitutes sound educational practice may vary considerably from those of education professionals (Giles, 2001; Xu, 1998), yet initiatives to improve urban schools through a focus on teacher quality are most often based on a paradigm that ignores this disparity (Murrell, 1998, 2001; Peressini, 1996).

Controversy over the role that parents and communities might play in the process of deciding who becomes an urban teacher and what urban teachers need to know and do is rooted in contradictory epistemological and political stances. As Welker (1992) explains, one perspective is that teacher education is the responsibility of experts who can transmit to novices the knowledge base that has been delineated. A different perspective is that what teachers need to know to work well with all students cannot be answered primarily through referral to a knowledge base codified by research and the expertise of elites. Rather, the knowledge that what teachers need to know should be understood as contested terrain, in part due to differing epistemologies of parents and citizens (Murrell, 2001; Smagorinsky, 1999).

My analysis assumes this latter stance and proceeds from a perspective that programs of teacher preparation, no less than public schools, represent "sites of constant political and cultural struggle...over resources, ideological commitments, and the meaning of the school" (Anderson, 1998, p. 591). One of those struggles is the directionality of accountability, the extent to which teacher education is and should be answerable to people directly served by schools, in particular, families and communities. My thoughts in this chapter are based on the notion that accountability should be understood as the responsibility of individuals and institutions to students, families, and citizens. The term *responsibility* is personal and connotes the moral dimensions of decision making. Conversely, the concept of *accountability* represents an impersonal, seemingly objective process. The dominance of the notion of accountability and its correlate of "performance-based" or "evidence-based practice" is related to the ascendancy of neoliberal politics. As Davies (2003) observes, the rhetoric about outcomes and "evidence-based practice" contains "an invisible sleight of hand" that "makes invisible the managers and policymakers who will select what is relevant, and who will dictate how it is to be audited and deemed to have been put into practice" (p. 101).

I explain elsewhere why urban teacher education should be understood as requiring the knowledge that parents and communities, especially those that have not been served well by public schools, bring to school people, including teachers (Weiner, 1993, 1999). In this chapter, I extend my earlier analysis to suggest the ways in which gender's absence from the discourse and practice of urban school improvement has propelled teacher education toward a model of professionalism harmful to the respectful collaboration among teachers, families, and communities. I analyze how teaching's historical construction as "women's true profession" (Hoffman, 1981) cannot be separated from the hierarchical notions of accountability that have characterized educational change since the creation of urban school systems more than a century ago (Tyack, 1974), and those Davies (2003) identifies in contemporary reforms. I propose how we might redefine *professionalism* so that it bridges the social distance between low-income parents and urban teachers, and I sketch a few illustrations of how my thinking can be applied to programs of urban teacher education.

## GENDER'S INVISIBILITY IN THE DISCOURSE OF REFORM

Analysis of why gender has been missing in talk about school reform in the United States (Blackwell, 2000) and in urban teacher education (Weiner, 2002) goes beyond the scope of this paper, but one fundamental concept needs to be explained. From the vantage point of traditional sociology, "work," or paid labor, has been defined as contrary to the unpaid labor in "family" and "home" (Biklen, 1995). Therefore, work, or paid labor with children, falls into a figurative and literal "no-man's land." In her ethnography of the elementary school attended by her child, Biklen observes that relations between parents (mostly mothers) and teachers (mostly women) are strained by the shared desire to have their work with children respected and validated. Teaching and mothering, Biklen (1995) observes, are "women's work," and as such are not considered work at all by the traditional standards in sociology. Biklen's analysis is supported by historical examinations of ways in which professionalizing education provided the rationale for the gendered and hierarchical power relations in schools (Grant & Christine-Murray, 1999; Herbst, 1989; Tyack, 1974).

Noting professionalism's appeal to both middle-class teachers and mothers, Biklen (1995) argues against professionalism as it is generally constructed, observing that parents are excluded from decisions about their children's education for precisely the same reasons that women's concerns are hidden: Women's work is not valued. "The professional model is a gendered model of privilege," Biklen (1995, p. 41) concludes. The professional model obscures the ways that mothers and elementary teachers share social and gendered positions because of their relationship to children and their desire, held in common, to increase social recognition for their work with children. Interaction between parents and teachers is primarily one of women working with women, though this dimension of parent involvement is seldom named or explicated (Biklen, 1995). Grumet (1995) also argues from a feminist perspective against the "false dichotomy" of home and classroom that has historically driven attempts to transform teaching into a profession like the archetypal professions, law and medicine.

Biklen (1995) notes that her analysis is configured by her own race and class, acknowledging that some of her generalizations about the ways teachers conceptualize their work do not necessarily hold for the African American community today, nor have they historically.[1] Because they were frozen out of other occupations, teaching was one of the few jobs to which educated African American men and women could aspire, and it was an occupation that held considerable respect in their communities (Tyack, 1974; Walker, 2001). To some extent, African American teachers are still viewed as respected and important members of their communities, as Foster's (1994) interviews reveal. Gordon's (2000) investigation of how teachers of color view their occupation simultaneously complements and complicates Biklen and Grumet's construction of the relationship between gender and notions of professionalism. To investigate why more members of minority groups are not choosing to enter teaching, Gordon interviewed teachers of color about their perceptions of the occupation.

Her categorization of *teachers of color* includes individuals who self-identify as such and are accepted by their employing school districts as belonging to one of four ethnic groups: Latino/Hispanic, African American/Black, Asian American, and Native American. Gordon found that ideals of professionalism varied between the groups. For example, Latino teachers took considerable pride in their work and sensed respect for it among the immigrant communities from which they came. African American teachers were more likely than teachers from the other groups to think that their work was not valued or appreciated, even by their African American students. She found that teachers of color, parents, and community members, especially the African Americans whom she interviewed, tended not to encourage youth to enter the field of teaching. Based on the data, which she cautions involved relatively small numbers of teachers in a few locations, Gordon hypothesizes that negative attitudes toward teaching and a lack of respect for teachers among working-class communities of color increase with their sustained contact with the values of middle-class White America. To address this problem, Gordon (2000) advocates a definition of professionalism that entails "service for youth, student outcomes, and presentation of a professional self in school" and a "concept of professionalism that contributes to their [students'] welfare and to the welfare of their [students'] family and community" (p. 105).

Thompson's (1998) critique of "colorblindedness" in the literature on caring in education can be applied to the dominant notion of professionalism as well. She observes that theories about caring have an assumed "Whiteness" in their "political and cultural assumptions" that limits understanding of other perspectives that can inform educational practice (p. 522). She cautions that there is "no uniform perspective automatically shared by all members of a group," but insofar as "members of a culturally and politically identifiable group share a situation…a particular cultural set of values passed on by the community, it is possible to speak of shared assumptions that make up an identifiable cultural perspective" (p. 526). She concludes that the nature of the individual's connections to the community and perception of their situation determine whether the assumptions are shared.

Taken together, Thompson and Gordon's work exposes the limitations of the "colorblind" definition of teacher professionalism that is often used to support improvements in working conditions in schools or increases in teacher salaries. In the 1960s, when the modern teacher union movement developed in the United States, its definition of professionalism promoted the idea that in order to improve schools, teachers should be treated better as workers. This definition of professionalism was sometimes fused to a commitment to unionism as a defender of equality and social justice in the larger society (Golin, 2002). But neither of these constructions of professionalism appealed to teachers who understood their work as serving particular children and families—unless they agreed that the well-being of the particular children they were dedicated to serve could be advanced by the growth of a politically progressive union movement. As Golin (2002) found in his interviews, African American teachers whose personal experience of unions had been primarily that of exclusion did not easily accept the argument that the union movement was a natural ally in struggles for equality and justice.

Tensions arising from competing notions of professionalism are widespread (Grant & Christine-Murray, 1999) but I contend the conflict is most intense in city school systems. The tension of how to define one's professional responsibility is exacerbated by the hierarchical and impersonal conditions in urban schools because successful teaching anywhere requires personal attention to children as individuals. Hence the conditions in urban schools subvert the aspects of teaching that are most critical to a teacher's success, especially with a diverse student population. Severe contradictions arise (a) between teachers' personal and individual responsibility for children, (b) the ways their work continues the functions of the family and (c) the location of these functions in a bureaucracy as paid labor. Although this contradiction is exacerbated by conditions of scarce resources, it is not eliminated entirely even when financial support for schools is ample. This tension emerges most pointedly in conflicts over nonclassroom duties such as supervising children at lunch or on the playground.

For those who wish to professionalize teaching, to make it more like law or medicine, more like work and less like home, duties like supervising lunch are unprofessional. However, if we view schools as extensions of the family and home, then being with children at lunch is part of children's socialization and therefore very professional. In city schools, activities like lunch and recess are made to fit into a bureaucratic school structure so they resemble more what occurs in prisons and factories than in homes. What if schools were organized more like homes, so that lunch and play were times for human interaction between adults and children? What if teachers had lunch with kids but also had time away from the classroom for planning or socializing with other adults? My questions point to the ways that structures and conditions in urban schools heighten the tension over what it means to be a professional, forcing teachers to make difficult decisions about their moral and political responsibilities.

In addition, these conditions complicate teachers' involvement in teachers' unions, especially insofar as the unions accept the gendered definition of work and teaching as a job like any other. A union is obligated to take up problems that occur as a result of the school system's hierarchical arrangements, such as protection of teachers' salary and benefits. And whereas the union's efforts to defend teachers' professional interests do not address the tensions that unionism generates for teachers who view themselves in service to communities, the union reinforces a definition of professionalism that can lead to bitter divisions between White and African American teachers and parents. This occurred in Newark, New Jersey, during the violent, bitter strike in 1971, from which the city and union have barely recovered (Golin, 2002).

Unfortunately, although Gordon (2000) looks at constructions of professionalism through the lens of race, her analysis does not address feminist critiques of the professional model. She mentions gender only once, observing that "children's needs have historically been perceived as appropriate for non-professional service and mostly unpaid female service as well" (p. 24). However, she observes that among African American teachers, "confusion pervaded the conversations when we discussed attitudes of professionalism and why some jobs are rewarded more than others" (p. 24). Introducing the gendered construction of schooling, which Gordon alludes to in her redefinition of professionalism, is why the African American teachers she interviewed experience their devaluation by the greater society, and hence by the African American community as it acquires mainstream attitudes.

Here I should note that much feminist scholarship about school reform rejects hierarchical relations for professional staff but implicitly accepts the professional model vis-à-vis parents, placing mothers outside of the collaboration about children's education. Scott and McCollum's (1993) explanation of the dangers of top–down reform exemplifies this stance:

> Fundamental reform…cannot be achieved through administrative fiat. Top–down efforts in this direction are likely to be resisted; results will be superficial and short-lived. Ideally, teachers should work together, explore their own strengths and weaknesses, and collaborate in developing plans to realize high expectations for all students. (p. 185)

Acker's (1999) examination of teachers' work is explicit about the problems parents bring, warning that they can be unmindful of teachers' hard work and sacrifice.

We see the same tendency to invoke a definition of professionalism that excludes parents in Blackwell's (2000) summary of attitudes of selected teacher educators, teachers, and university administrators concerned about gender's invisibility in educational reform. They agree, unanimously, that "female teachers in schools must and should be treated as professional women, who are themselves sources of knowledge, expertise and wisdom about their jobs" (p. 8). They note that educational reform should begin with teachers rather than being on or about them, explaining that the kind of changes in curriculum "held so dear by education reformers are, in fact, positions that have long been endorsed by feminist pedagogy that advocate student-centered education, personal connection and involvement, problem-solving, and interactive learning" (Blackwell, 2000, p. 9). The participants note that major reports call attention to the salience of race, ethnicity, and culture, whereas gender imbalance in the profession is often ignored. However, they "were extremely uncomfortable...addressing gender in the absence of culture and race" (Blackwell, 2000, p. 11).

If we compare the responses in Blackwell's report to those of the teachers whom Gordon (2000) studied, we find that both groups are concerned with the absence of respect paid to teaching in mainstream American society. They differ, however, in identification of the cause of this lack of respect. I suggest that both desire a "concept of professionalism that contributes to their [students'] welfare and to the welfare of their [students'] family and community" (Gordon, 2000, p. 105). Professionalism in teaching, then, should be projected as paid service to particular children as well as to communities and the broader society.

This redefinition of professionalism, which rests in part on the feminist critique of professionalism as a gendered model of privilege, is especially important in altering relations between parents and teachers in urban schools, and in urban teacher education. Parental intervention is viewed with suspicion in many schools (Lareau, 2000), and with caution by researchers (Casanova, 1996), but I suggest that apprehension about parent involvement is most dangerous in urban schools and programs of teacher education that provide pre-service and in-service education for urban teachers. We know from historical accounts of the creation of urban school systems in the United States that they were intentionally organized as bureaucracies to address the political dilemmas that arise from schooling's role in a meritocracy (Tyack, 1974). The sociocultural gaps between teachers and families that occur in many school systems are reinforced by urban schools' insularity from the communities they are supposed to serve, an isolation intended to take politics out of education (Kaestle, 1973; Tyack, 1974). White, middle-class cultural norms of schools (Ogbu, 1995a, 1995b), often tacitly enlarge the already considerable social distance between White, middle-class teachers in urban schools and low-income, minority parents with little formal education (Gay, 1993; Knapp & Associates, 1995). Urban schooling's bureaucratic norms and culture make development of alternatives to the "structured and predictable" (Smrekar, 1994, p. 58) exchanges between parents and teachers that occur in most schools exceedingly difficult. Regulation of interaction "militates against enduring, honest, and understanding relationships" (Smrekar, 1994, p. 58), the sort of relationships that are essential for teachers and mothers to work through the inevitable strains that arise in collaborations across race. As O'Connor (1998) found in her study of parent participation in a White, urban school, this includes social class. In urban schools, minority teachers realize the definition of professionalism that I put forward when they serve as bridges to the community or as proxies for the low-income parents (mothers) whose participation is needed but not readily available.

## PARENTS AND SCHOOLS: NATURAL ENEMIES?

An unmistakable, if sometimes unarticulated, element in sociological research that examines how parents influence children's academic achievement in critiques of schooling's reproduction of social inequality, is the notion that parents are the "natural enemies" (Lareau, 2000) of schools and teachers.[2] Reay's (1998) ethnography of two schools in London, one serving middle-class families and the other working class, presents a more complex reality. Her study concludes that the White, middle-class women "queried neither the status quo nor the inequalities it produced" (Reay, 1998, p. 132). When they saw inequality, it was in relation to their position vis à vis other middle- class families. They redefined inequalities so that they were cast as disadvantaged. Her critique of these mothers is pointed, and she comments that in

> monopolizing scarce resources within the state sector, deploying financial resources to secure children's educational advantage, and drawing on useful social networks, which excluded working-class mothers, many of the middle-class women were ensuring that the outcome of the educational competition was resolved in their children's favor...not dealing with anything as ephemeral as the working-class women's hopes and desires. (Reay, 1998, p. 145)

With the exception of one middle-class mother who referred to her left-wing politics, only the Black women and a small number of White, working-class women viewed the educational systems as operating in ways that resulted in inequalities. Black women, regardless of social class, were all strongly committed to their children's academic success and placed a greater emphasis on it than White, working-class women. "Superficially, they seemed to be complying with discourses of meritocracy, in spite of their awareness of inequalities of 'race'" (Reay, 1998, p. 132).

Reay's findings confirm conclusions of another study in which authors interviewed, transcribed, and analyzed data from educated, middle-class mothers in a university town (Brantlinger, Majd-Jabbari, & Guskin,1996). Although the mothers viewed themselves as liberals who believed in integrated and inclusive education, they supported segregation and stratified school structures that benefited middle-class students. The authors analyze how the parents' ideology bridged the contradictions between their desired identity as liberals and their class position. However, Reay's (1998) analysis diverges from the depiction of parents, especially middle-class parents, as "natural enemies" of school people when she describes how mothers do the "dirty work of class" (p. 162). In a chapter on men's involvement, she notes that although there is very little research on fathers' involvement, "the little that does exist confirms that fathers are often distant from the day-to-day maintenance of home–school relationships" (p. 147).

"Maintenance" was a feature of the mothers' accounts that crossed class boundaries and consisted of tasks as unrelated as helping with homework to paying visits to teachers when problems arose about a child's safety or health. Reay (1998) argues that in doing "maintenance," the "dirty work of class," middle-class mothers are subject to different constraints than working-class mothers. "At the same time, the self-interest, instrumentalism and individualism which permeate many middle-class mothers' practices need to be analyzed in terms of their consequences for the less privileged mothers and their children" (p. 162). Reay also contrasts the reality of tensions and inequalities, among parents and between mothers and teachers, to rhetoric about "partnership," arguing that this "acts discursively to imply reciprocity and equality between parents and school" (p. 10).

## MAINTENANCE, ACCOUNTABILITY, AND TEACHER EDUCATION

Although a full exploration of how gender influences the status and position of teacher education within higher education would stray from the focus of this chapter, we need to acknowledge that pressures experienced by teacher educators for accountability are inseparable from the "raced," "gendered," and "classed" nature of higher education (Weiner, 2002). Teacher education occurs largely in institutions that do not grant doctoral degrees and do not produce research (Haberman, 1996). As a result, research that takes up policy in education, including how to conceive of and implement accountability of teacher education, may serve

> a surveillance function with the powerful, predominantly white and male researchers watching over the predominantly female, more ethnically diverse practitioners. The result is a lack of practitioners' trust of researchers and, by extension, of research, along with a distancing of practitioners from the research process and from decision making in research. (Campbell & Greenberg, 1993, p. 70)

There is a parallel between the power and status inequalities between parents and teachers, and teachers and administrators, and those of researchers and teachers, and teacher education faculty and colleagues in the liberal arts (Zeichner, 1995). The low status of education faculty in universities (Allen, 1998), and of teaching in higher education reflect the same devaluation of teaching—work associated with nurturing and women.

Reay's (1998) concept of *maintenance work*, uncompensated chores obscured from social view that must be done for children to succeed in school and for society to be reproduced, is seen in higher education as well as in families and N–12 schools. We might, for instance, understand advising students as a maintenance task that is an element of higher education. But where does student advising fall in the triad of service, teaching, and scholarship that are the requirements for promotion and tenure? Maintaining cordial relations with school people, such as occurs when visits are made to observe student teachers, or conferences between students and faculty that take up "personal" issues such as strained relations with a cooperating teacher, also constitute the maintenance performed by teacher educators. Yet reports and recommendations for the improvement of teacher education seldom acknowledge these labor-intensive and indispensable aspects of teacher education. The gendered, hierarchical notions of accountability that are hallmarks of the last decade of reform have no space or vocabulary for analysis of personal relations—of maintenance work.

In their structure and ideology, urban school systems and institutions of higher education subvert opportunities for women divided by roles—as parents, researchers, teacher educators, school administrators, and teachers—to meet as respectful equals. Circumventing those divisions requires that the notion of accountability be reconfigured as an ethos of responsibility that acknowledges the social distance between women, their division into hierarchical roles, and the tensions this creates. An ethos of responsibility parallels the reconfiguration of professionalism to mean service to children, communities, and citizens.

## "RESPONSIBILITY" IN URBAN TEACHER EDUCATION

How might the analysis I present be applied to teacher education? Whenever a flaw is detected in teacher education, often the first solution offered is to simply add new content. But there is no way around this particular addition, because one cannot fully understand why the voices of teachers—and teacher educators—are so seldom heard without taking gender into account (Weiner, Rand, Pagano, Obi, & Bloom, 2001). The notion of teaching as women's work must be integrated into course work, probably in social foundations of education courses. Examination of teaching as gendered work allows for parent involvement to be named for what it is most often: the socially-constructed demand for women to be responsible for children's school success.

In accepting certain responsibilities, it is critical to reject others: Teacher education cannot be held responsible for the social conditions, school structures, and organizational practices that create borders between families and schools. However, we in teacher education have a commitment to engage our students, and prospective and practicing teachers, in critiques of the seductive definition of professionalism, which elevates teaching's status in a social hierarchy that puts better educated —usually White women—in positions of power over women—mostly women of color—with less formal education.

One of the most common criticisms of social foundations coursework in teacher preparation is that students cannot see the implications or relevance of the texts and ideas. For that reason, I recommend adopting gender as a lens, along with that of race and class, to focus discussion of how teachers and prospective teachers' life experiences relate to their tacit cultural assumptions. In the United States, most pre-service candidates in programs of teacher education are young, White, monolingual females who live in small towns or suburbs and wish to teach children who are like themselves. The worldview of these candidates, which has been described as "parochial" (Zimpher & Ashburn, 1992), contrasts with the demographics of the student population in U.S. schools, now almost primarily not White and monolingual. They have entered teaching because they "love children" and aim to have children of their own.

The traditional teacher candidates in my classes are often angered when they read feminist critiques about teaching's low status because they are the first in their families to attend college and for them, teaching is a (relatively) prestigious career. Yet, when we consider representations of teachers in popular culture and analyze school reform strategies that de-skill teaching, their notions about their responsibilities as teachers shift. Many express anxiety about the newly discovered dilemma they will face when they have children of their own and must choose between doing maintenance work for their offspring, and maintenance work for the children in their classrooms. Their dismay at this realization, and the implications of their prior unawareness of what lies ahead in their lives as teachers and mothers, creates a disequilibrium that allows for the development of critiques of other assumptions, such as race and immigration–even the entire neo-liberal project.

My second recommendation is that teacher education programs invite representation of families and advocacy organizations, especially those in low-income communities, into advisory groups. External and community representation on teacher education advisory councils is often synonymous with administrative and corporate representation. The typical composition of advisory councils leads to a lack of critique of the epistemologies and assumptions of school personnel, university people, and the corporate sector, whose viewpoint is embedded in many reforms (Shipps, 1997). We know from research on innovative teacher preparation programs in the 1970s (Weiner, 1993) that parents are not interested in spending time on decisions that are administrative in nature, but can be tapped as informants about teaching decisions, bringing important information and insights about what teachers need to know (Giles, 2001; Murrell, 2001).

Another source of information and understanding of what families and mothers know about and want for their children are minority teachers with strong links to the communities, teachers who may not be active in school reform (Foster, 1994). Their participation should be actively sought in advisory councils and curriculum reviews. African American teachers who live in the city neighborhoods that schools are supposed to serve can illuminate and forestall disputes by conveying contradictory notions about projects that university faculty may not even imagine as problematic (Murrell, 2001). Although teachers of color are more accessible as sources of information and are more easily tapped than parents for participation in advisory councils, it is important to acknowledge that minority teachers may not represent all parents and that their viewpoint may not be the same as that of parents with little formal education. As Thompson (1998) and Giles (2001) warn, there is no uniform perspective shared by all members of a group, and minority teachers' ability to serve as bridges and proxies for minority parents depends on the presence of shared assumptions and connections.

Furthermore, teacher educators need to rethink the response to exclusion from state and national policies that are stratifying schools and schools of education in the name of improving student's academic performance (Weiner et al., 2001). One critical concern for teacher education is that maintenance work in teacher education is simultaneously being intensified and marginalized in terms of resources. Davies (2003) observes that under the evidence-based programs for accountability, "much of the resource base that was previously available to support professional work has been redirected into surveillance" (p. 94). As regulations about teacher education become more prescriptive and more restrictive (Bullough, Burbank, Gess-Newsome, Kauchak, & Kennedy, 1998), and neo-liberal reforms have diminished social safety nets, maintenance work with students about personal issues such as missing class to care for sick children or parents, or working an extra job to pay for tuition, becomes all more critical—and difficult to do well.

Finally, teacher educators need to make space to critique the notion of accountability. Davies (2003) contends that perhaps the most "devious" strategy in the dominant notion of accountability has been "the inclusion of equity discourses in the objectives that institutions were impelled to include" (p. 96). The competition for resources in the university needs to be understood as antithetical to feminist aims, even while allowing for the elevation of women into positions of authority.

To argue, as I do here, that tensions arising in women working with women in schooling must be the object of study in urban teacher education might be understood as essentializing gender or romanticizing women's collaboration. That possibility is certainly a danger, as Reay's (1998) insight about the obfuscatory quality of the concept of *parent and school partnership* reminds us. However, addressing the tensions of women working with women allows us to simultaneously acknowledge the divisions and inequalities among women while probing for the areas of common concern. Addressing both commonalities and differences is essential. Reversing the political forces that make teachers and teacher educators accountable for standards over which they have no say will require a significant mobilization of popular will. The insights and aspirations that contemporary feminism taps can help build a movement for social equality and improved schooling for all children. But for that to occur, we must be clear that the dominant definition of professionalization and notions of accountability are antithetical to our purposes.

## ENDNOTES

[1] I am grateful to several of my African American students, career teachers in public schools, especially Rosemary Flowers Jackson, for assistance in working through the ideas about professionalism.

[2] Lareau (2000) draws the term, *natural enemies*, from Willard Waller. My colleague, Bill Librera, has informed me that Waller also described family/school relations with the term, *perilous equilibrium*, although neither he nor I have found the location of the quote.

## REFERENCES

Acker, S. (1999). *The realities of teachers' work. Never a dull moment.* New York: Cassell.

Allen, H. L. (1998). *Faculty workload and productivity: Gender comparison* [ERIC Document No. ED416776]. The NEA 1998 Almanac of Higher Education. Washington, DC: National Education Association.

Anderson, G. L. (1998). Toward authentic participation: Deconstructing the discourses of participatory reforms in education. *American Educational Research Journal, 35,* 571–603.

Biklen, S. K. (1995). *School work. Gender and the cultural construction of teaching.* New York: Teachers College Press.

Blackwell, P. J. (2000). *Education reform and teacher education. The missing discourse of gender.* Washington, DC: American Association of Colleges for Teacher Education.

Brantlinger, E., Majd-Jabbari, M., & Guskin, S. L. (1996). Self-interest and liberal educational discourse: How ideology works for middle class mothers. *American Educational Research Journal, 33*(3), 571–597.

Bullough, R. V. J., Burbank, M., Gess-Newsome, J., Kauchak, D., & Kennedy, C. (1998). 'What matters most: Teaching for America's future?' A faculty response to the Report of the National Commission on teaching and America's future. *Journal of Education for Teaching, 24*(1), 7–32.

Campbell, P. B., & Greenberg, S. (1993). Equity issues in educational research methods. In S. K. Biklen & D. Pollard (Eds.), *Gender and education. Ninety-second yearbook of the society for the study of education* (pp. 64–89). Chicago: National Society for the Study of Education.

Casanova, U. (1996). Parent involvement: A call for prudence. *Educational Researcher, 25*(8), 30–32.

Davies, B. (2003). Death to critique and dissent? The policies and practices of new managerialism and of 'evidence-based practice.' *Gender and Education 15*(1), 91–103.

Foster, M. (1994). The role of community and culture in school reform efforts: Examining the views of African American teachers. *Educational Foundations, 8*(2), 5–26.

Gay, G. (1993). Building cultural bridges: A bold proposal for teacher education. *Education and Urban Society, 25*, 285–299.

Giles, H. C. (2001). Transforming the deficit narrative: Race, class, and social capital in parent–school relations. In C. Korn & A. Burstyn (Eds.), *Case studies in cultural transitions: Rethinking multicultural education* (pp. 130–159). Westport, CT: Greenwood Press.

Golin, S. (2002). *The Newark teacher strikes. Hopes on the line.* New Brunswick, NJ: Rutgers University Press.

Gordon, J. A. (2000). *The color of teaching.* New York: Routledge.

Grant, G., & Christine-Murray, E. (1999). *Teaching in America. The slow revolution.* Cambridge, MA: Harvard University Press.

Grumet, M. R. (1995). At home and in the classroom: The false comfort of false distinctions. In M. B. Ginsburg (Ed.), *Studies in education/politics: Vol. 915. The politics of educators' work and lives* (pp.55–71). Garland Reference Library of Social Science (Vol. 915). New York: Garland Publishing.

Haberman, M. (1996). Selecting and preparing culturally competent teachers for urban schools. In J. Sikula (Ed.), *Handbook of research on teacher education* (pp. 747–760). New York: Simon & Schuster.

Herbst, J. (1989). *And sadly teach.* Madison: University of Wisconsin Press.

Hoffman, N. (1981). *Women's 'true' profession.* New York: The Feminist Press.

Kaestle, C. (1973). *The evolution of an urban school system.* Cambridge, MA: Harvard University Press.

Knapp, M. S., & Associates. (1995). Introduction. In M. S. Knapp & Associates (Eds.), *Teaching for meaning in high-poverty classrooms* (pp. 1–10). New York: Teachers College Press.

Lareau, A. (2000). *Home advantage.* New York: Rowman & Littlefield Publishers.

Lopez, G. R., & Scribner, J. D. (1999). *Discourses of involvement: A critical review of parent involvement research.* Montreal: American Educational Research Association.

Murrell, P. C., Jr. (1998). *Like stone soup. The role of the professional development school in the renewal of urban schools.* Washington, DC: American Association of Colleges for Teacher Education.

Murrell, P. C., Jr. (2001). *The community teacher.* New York: Teachers College Press.

Ogbu, J. U. (1995a). Cultural problems in minority education: Their interpretations and consequences—Part One: Theoretical background. *The Urban Review, 27*(3), 189–205.

Ogbu, J. U. (1995b). Cultural problems in minority education: Their interpretations and consequences—Part two: Case studies. *The Urban Review, 27*(4), 271–297.

O'Connor, S. (1998). *Parent participation in a poor, White urban school*. San Diego, CA: American Educational Research Association.

Peressini, D. (1996). Parents, power, and the reform of mathematics education. *Urban Education, 31*(1), 3–28.

Reay, D. (1998). *Class work: Mother's involvement in their children's primary schooling*. Bristol, PA: UCL Press.

Scott, E., & McCollum, H. (1993). Making it happen: Gender equitable classrooms. In S. K. Biklen & D. Pollard (Eds.), *Gender and education. Ninety-second yearbook of the society for the study of education* (pp. 174–190). Chicago: National Society for the Study of Education.

Shipps, D. (1997, Fall). The invisible hand: Big business and Chicago school reform. *Teachers College Record, 99,* 73–116.

Smagorinsky, P. (1999). Standards revisited: The importance of being there. *English Journal, 88*(4), 82–88.

Smrekar, C. E. (1994). The organization of family-school interactions: A prelude to school-linked services [ERIC Document No. ED365373]. In R. A. Levin (Ed.), *Greater than the sum: Professionals in a comprehensive services model* (pp. 55–62). Washington, DC: ERIC Clearinghouse on Teacher Education.

Thompson, A. (1998). Not the color purple: Black feminist lessons for educational caring. *Harvard Educational Review 68,* 522–544.

Tyack, D. (1974). *The one best system*. Cambridge, MA: Harvard University Press.

Walker, V.S. (2001). African American teaching in the south: 1940–1960. *American Educational Research Journal 38,* 751–759.

Weiner, L. (1993). *Preparing teachers for urban schools. Lessons from thirty years of school reform*. New York: Teachers College Press.

Weiner, L. (1999). *Urban teaching: The essentials*. New York: Teachers College Press.

Weiner, L. (2002). Inquiry and evidence in teacher education: What's needed for urban schools. *Journal of Teacher Education 53,* 254–261.

Weiner, L., Rand, M., Pagano, A., Obi, R., & Bloom, A. (2001). Illuminating the relationships between state policies designed to improve urban schools and curriculum and instruction in programs of urban teacher preparation. *Educational Policy 15,* 644–673.

Welker, R. (1992). *The teacher as expert: A theoretical and historical examination*. Albany: State University of New York Press.

Xu, J. (1998, April). *Balancing home and school: Dilemmas of cultural interchange*. Paper presented at the American Educational Research Association meeting, San Diego, California.

Zeichner, K. M. (1995). Beyond the divide of teacher research and academic research. *Teachers and teaching: Theory and practice, 1*(2), 153–172.

Zimpher, N., & Ashburn, E. (1992). Countering parochialism among teacher candidates. In M. Dilworth (Ed.), *Diversity in teacher education* (pp. 40–62). San Francisco: Jossey-Bass.

# PRE-SERVICE TEACHER PREPARATION FOR URBAN TRANSFORMATION

Part II of this volume offers five chapters on pre-service teacher preparation for urban school transformation that transcend the geopolitical borders of Canada, the Caribbean, and the United States. Chapters 5 and 6 move beyond the traditional institutional boundaries of teacher education, and utilize the urban community as a rich learning environment for pre-service teachers. Chapter 5 (Solomon, Khattar-Manoukian, & Clarke) uses Henry Giroux's concept of *border pedagogy* to explore the learning experiences of candidates as they move across institutional, ethno–racial, sociocultural, and moral–political–intellectual borders to engage in community-service learning.

Smaller's chapter 6 focuses on "embedding" a teacher education program in an urban, inner-city, poverty-stricken neighborhood. Based on the principles and practices of university–community collaboration, this project demonstrates how teacher educators, school administrators, local teachers, parents, and community activists become integral to the development and implementation of this unique program. In chapter 7, Young's study analyses teacher candidates' pre- and post-course responses to the question "What does it mean to think outside the box?" posed in a multicultural teacher education course. She uses the theoretical underpinnings of critical pedagogy, multiculturalism, and culturally responsive pedagogy as a prelude to the race and ethnic discourses that emerged from "thinking outside the box." She offers suggestions of pedagogy to teacher educators engaged in the preparation of teachers who will work in racially diverse settings. In what follows, Hordatt Gentles' chapter 8 also uses the lens of critical pedagogy to analyse the preparation of

teachers in Jamaican teachers' colleges. Her research uncovers the reproduction of a negative authoritarian culture that leaves them ill-prepared
to cope as "migrant teachers" in the comparatively less restrictive, student-centered American urban schools. She proposes instead a critical
pedagogy approach to teacher preparation in Jamaica, one that embraces
social justice and democracy in both local and foreign classrooms. Chapter 9 also contextualizes teacher preparation in postcolonial Jamaica. In
this chapter, Evans and Tucker examine the role of teachers and their unstable identities that reproduce the colonial legacy of socioeconomic stratification and its detrimental impact on children in urban, inner-city
settings. Instead, the authors envision a more liberating, enriching, and
empowering curriculum and pedagogy that is rooted in students' own culture. To this end, they elaborate on a course titled The Emergent Teacher,
designed to help teachers in a postcolonial society come to grips with their
own sociocultural identity, and to develop the critical consciousness to
form affective social and pedagogical relationships with the economically
deprived urban students with whom they will work.

# Chapter 5

# Pre-Service Teachers as Border Crossers: Linking Urban Schools and Communities Through Service Learning

R. Patrick Solomon
Randa Khattar Manoukian
Jennifer Clarke
*York University*

Traditional teacher education is often characterized by isomorphism; cohorts of learners operating in the university domain or interned in practicum schools engage only superficially with communities in which their practicum schools are located. Representations of such communities are often developed from the perspectives of those with the power and authority to determine the status of these learning environments. In such configurations, urban, inner-city communities are often constructed in pathological ways—as sites of poverty, crime, limited resources, and cultural depravity. For middle-class schools, such communities become places from which needy children come, rather than where teachers go for knowledge and resources. Schools and communities, therefore, operate as exclusive domains.

Educational researchers and practitioners have recently proposed more progressive approaches to teacher preparation. Ladson-Billings (1995), Boyle-Baise (1998), Irvine (1989) and others have argued for the development of a culturally relevant pedagogy that utilizes the knowledge, values, and resources of communities from which children come.

They propose a school–community synchrony that fosters reciprocity between environments that are central to the learners' formative experiences. In this chapter, we utilize Giroux's (1992a) categories of *border* and *border crossing* as a way to reconceptualize teacher candidates' engagement with urban, inner-city communities as a dimension of their professional learning. Such categories extend teacher education beyond superficial understandings of the social, cultural, and economic forces that negatively impact schooling in urban contexts to provide insights into teacher candidates' (TCs)[1] interventions across different pedagogical dimensions of their teacher preparation. Simultaneously, conceptualizing teacher preparation in terms of border crossing provokes emancipatory possibilities and the work needed to achieve these possibilities. The chapter outlines the benefits derived by stakeholders and the challenges encountered by those who intervene morally, politically, and intellectually for social transformation in communities of practice.

## BORDER PEDAGOGY IN TEACHER EDUCATION

Giroux's (1992a, 2005) notions of *border, borderland,* and *border crossing* continue today to signal an important way of conceptualizing power relations in communities of difference. He argues, "[T]he category of border signals a recognition of those epistemological, political, cultural and social margins that structure the language of history, power, and difference" (p. 28). These are borderland margins whose topographical terrain might shift over time, as new historical and sociocultural challenges present themselves, but whose presence nevertheless continues to circulate and structure the very "language of power and difference" managing people's lives.

In educational contexts, Giroux (1992a) identifies the many ways in which domination of schools by those who control the social order (e.g., those espousing White, middle-class, patriarchal values) are manifested: (a) totalizing curricula and texts that exclude the experiences and histories of diverse student cultures; (b) pedagogical practices based on a knowledge-transmission model; (c) student–teacher relationships characterized by domination and hierarchy; (d) dominant group interests and ideologies that are pervasive in schooling; and (e) the marginalization of minority race/ethnic, social class, and gender groups. Yet despite a growing social recognition of the deleterious effects power struggles have on students' lives, teacher education programs tend to continue being insulated from a critical interrogation of the issues and practices that produce cultural hegemony. As a result of such superficial treatment of these important issues, many teachers working in working-class communities and with students from minority groups "lack a well-articulated framework for understanding the class, cultural, ideological, and gender dimensions that inform classroom life" (Giroux & McLaren, 1996, p. 316).

Through what Giroux calls "border crossing," pre-service teachers learn to challenge particular orders of domination that exist in any given context. In education, Giroux (1992a) notes that thinking in terms of borders:

> ...speaks to the need to create pedagogical conditions in which students become border crossers in order to understand otherness in its own terms, and to further create borderlands in which diverse cultural resources allow for the fashioning of new identities within existing configurations of power. (p. 28)

As border crossers, pre-service teachers become transformative intellectuals. They learn to read, challenge, and redefine different borderlines that have traditionally organized the access to power by the privileged. In this sense, they understand that as transformative intellectuals, they are de-centering organizational, political, and ideological parameters of power, personal identity, and history as they simultaneously remap their learning possibilities within the borderlands in which they engage. These borderlands are contested cultural terrains that have traditionally been premised on a practice of inequality, terror, and exclusion, while simultaneously presenting themselves under the hegemonic banner of the commonsensical. How may Giroux's concept of border crossing apply to teacher preparation for urban schools and communities? What challenges and possibilities manifest themselves when we think in terms of teaching as a practice in border crossing?

In this chapter, we analyze the impact of Giroux's notion of border crossing on teacher preparation, by exploring the four borderlands that teachers must learn to identify and critically interrogate (institutional, sociocultural, ethno–racial, and moral–political). We also describe ways that as transformative intellectuals, pre-service teachers might develop a language of possibility—that is, a "discourse of difference and voice" (Giroux, 1992b, p. 204). We further explore the different challenges TCs may confront working within and across these borderlands (see Table 5.1). To illustrate, we present how one unique teacher preparation program, grounded in principles of equity and social justice and premised on the importance of community involvement, provides TCs with the framework to become transformative intellectuals and border crossers.

To elaborate, the most obvious borderland category that TCs negotiate is the *institutional*. Those who receive their teacher education partly in university classrooms, and partly as interns in practicum schools, engage in institutional border crossing on an ongoing basis. As is well documented, the cultures of the university and that of public schools are quite different and

**TABLE 5.1**
**Border Pedagogy and Community Service Learning**

| Borderlands | Traditional Locations | | Progressive Locations |
|---|---|---|---|
| Institutional | University and practicum schools | ⟶ | Communities outside institutions |
| Ethno–Racial | Racial homophily and ethic encapsulation | ⟶ | Cross-race and/or ethnic relations and collaboration |
| Sociocultural | Pathological construction and marginalization of the poor | ⟶ | Democratic empowerment and integration of the poor |
| Moral-Political Intellectual | Charity and altruism | ⟶ | Social reconstruction and transformation |

*Note.* In reality, intersectionality and an on-going vacillation between traditional and more progressive locations is a feature of the above borderlands. *Straddling* borders is a more realistic way of thinking. Here, borderlands were categorized for explanatory purposes only.

often nonsynchronous. Baldwin's (1999) study, "When Public School and University Cultures Meet," points to the divergent perspectives, knowledge, and attitudes of each group. For example, the structures of authority and power hierarchies are quite different in each institution and this directly impacts professional and interpersonal relationships. The theory–practice divide appears to be riveted in the psyche of those entrenched in the university or the public school culture. To eliminate the borders, Baldwin advocates for professional development schools (PDS) as a cross-institutional approach to teacher preparation.

Miron (2003) raises yet another challenge for those seeking to operate in the interorganizational domain for the benefit of the residents they serve. He sees the relationship between politics and education as traditionally characterized by isomorphism and argues that "urban education can potentially cross the isomorphic borders of public schooling into interorganizational domain of the city itself, in particular, city government and its agencies" (p. 233). His vision of border crossing provides TCs the possibility of moving the educational process beyond the school boundaries and into government agencies' domain: to their social, cultural, and recreational resources.[2] TCs must therefore come to see their role as political—one of negotiating across borders to make government resources available for the development of communities.

Another rather obvious but rarely contemplated border category for educators to negotiate is that of *race and ethnicity*. Racially and ethno–culturally diverse societies are often characterized by "racial homophily" and "ethnic encapsulation" (Hallinan & Teixeria, 1987; Solomon, 1992; Tatum, 1997). Homogeneous racial and ethnic groups essentially operate within their own borders, rarely engaging voluntarily across borders in a meaningful, equalitarian, and sustained way. Teacher educators who have attempted to engage candidates in a critical interrogation of their worldview on racial/ethnic difference and its potential impact on teaching have faced resistance (Ahlquist, 1992; Solomon & Levine-Rasky, 2003). Pre-service teachers preparing to work in urban schools and communities characterized by diversity and difference must become aware of the challenges of crossing ethno–racial borders. A prerequisite for this engagement is the ongoing interrogation of one's own racial identity formation and the way this may potentially help or hinder working with difference in urban settings.

Regarding social class and schooling, border pedagogy is also concerned about the great divide that exists between schools dominated by middle-class structures and ideologies, and the working-class communities they serve. Haberman (1994), Kozol (1991), Yao (1997) and other critics have drawn attention to the gross inequities of schooling in economically poor communities and the tendency of these institutions to pathologize and blame the victims for their own poverty. This deficit model dominates the schooling process. Haberman (1994) argues that "the pedagogy of poverty requires that teachers begin their careers intending to be helpers, models, guides, stimulators, and caring sources of encouragement [but] they transform themselves into directive authoritarians in order to function in urban schools" (p. 308). He also added that teachers quickly give up the teaching of critical thinking, problem solving and creativity for ritualistic acts, and the performance of maintenance functions. Yao (1997) also implicates teacher education for its blind faith in, and unwavering reproduction and transmission of, the dominant middle-class values, knowledge, and ideology. Despite the exclusive borderlands already described here, Yao and others are hopeful that teacher education can prepare new teachers to engage in a kind of border pedagogy that would eventually transform urban schools. Indeed, urban schools and the communities they serve may well become sites of political, economic, and ideological struggle. Progressive teacher education programs must therefore prepare TCs to engage in the struggle.

A further significant border-crossing task for TCs is to move away from a charity or altruistic perspective toward a socially transformative approach to service learning. This is what Kahne and Westheimer (1996) conceptualize as crossing moral and political borders. Interrogating service learning more critically, Kahne and Westheimer perceive charity-oriented community service learning as one that values giving and altruism as civic duty and responsibility. What they advocate, instead, is a community change orientation that values understanding the reality of others through experience, and combining critical inquiry with political action for social reconstruction. Crossing these domain borders requires a major paradigm shift for TCs who had invested in simply providing service to those in urban, inner-city communities (Solomon, Khattar Manoukian, & Clarke, 2005). They must now develop a critical understanding of the social issues facing inner-city communities and the political will required to intervene.

This synthesis captures the multiple borderlands teacher candidates as transformative intellectuals must negotiate in their attempts to intervene constructively in the life of urban settings in which they are preparing to teach. This will indeed be a challenge for those from mainstream cultures without the lived experiences, critical knowledge, and political orientation to work with social difference in an urban landscape. In the next section, we introduce a unique urban teacher education program whose primary focus is to prepare pre-service teachers to work across borders by engaging with students and their families in urban settings.

## DESIGNING TEACHER EDUCATION FOR BORDER PEDAGOGY

The Urban Diversity (UD) Teacher Education Program at York University, Ontario, was developed in 1994 as a response to the urgent call to make teacher preparation programs more responsive and relevant to the diverse population they serve. Its curriculum creates the structure for candidates of various racial/ethnic, and other social differences to work collaboratively in practicum school settings. Such an opportunity for collegiality and collaboration across the racial/social divide is essential in a society that tends toward own-group cleavage. Informed by research on an interethnic contact model that reduces intergroup polarization, and negative stereotypes that reside in noncontact relationships (Lynch, 1987), this practicum design advocates the formation of cross-racial dyad partnerships and practicum school cohorts. The formation is facilitated by the recruitment of candidates from different group heritages in the Canadian population. The intake of the program represents such social group differences as race, ethnicity, immigrants, refugees, language, religion, and social class. The dominant White candidates include TCs of various European ethnic/national groups (e.g., English, Scotch, French, German, Italian, and other European groups), while the racial minority groups include such heritages as Asian (South, East, Southeast, and Middle East), African, South and Central American, and Aboriginal peoples. The UD program deliberately recruits candidates from social groups represented in the larger diverse Canadian population but are historically underrepresented in the teaching force (e.g., in one of the years of study, six persons with disability were recruited among other minority racial, ethnic, social groups), in order to ensure that wide representation of persons from different groups is maintained.

Specific objectives of the Urban Diversity program are to: (a) promote an environment in which TCs of various racial and ethno–cultural groups and abilities have extended opportunities to develop teaching competencies and professional relationships in a collaborative manner; (b) integrate issues of equity, diversity, and social justice into the curriculum and pedagogy of the teacher education program and in the classrooms of practicum schools; and (c) develop collaboration among practicum school staff, representatives of community organizations, teacher candidates, and teacher educators forming a "community of learners." Initial group-building activities enable candidates to build a strong cohort culture, helped along by assignments and activities that emphasize collaboration, team planning, and team execution. Beyond the university site and into the practicum school, small cohorts work across social differences in the pedagogical process, jointly planning, teaching, and debriefing learning activities. Such sharing of each other's cultural knowledge, experiences, and resources prepares them to move across institutional borders: from the university to the practicum school to the community.

The preparation of teachers to work across borders and through differences has always been a key dimension of the UD Program's methodological, theoretical, and logistical orientation. It delivers a synergistic approach of teacher education in which "learning to teach" experiences—in the university, in practicum schools, and in the community—reciprocally inform and transform each other (Howard, 1998; Solomon & Levine-Rasky, 2003). This pedagogical model is designed to promote in TCs a desire to recognize borderlands within which they can begin to interrogate not only their own racial formation, but also to critique and challenge the power relations, institutional structures, and organizing forces that come together within the borders of schools.

The program curriculum encompasses several pedagogical practices that together facilitate in TCs the ability to identify, negotiate, and straddle the different borderlands outlined earlier and to see schools as sites of political, social, and ideological struggle. Central to these practices is the program's service–learning focus. TCs are required to become involved in the community served by their practicum schools. Over the years, secondary and postsecondary institutions of learning have engaged their students in community-based service learning projects from which both students and communities benefit. Teacher educators have understood the pedagogical value of involving pre-service teachers in the life of communities (Guadarrama, 2000; O'Grady, 2000; Sleeter, 2000). As Giroux and McLaren (1996) note about the importance of service learning, engaging the community "enhances the possibility that prospective teachers will make critically reflective links between classroom practices and the ethos and needs of the surrounding social and cultural milieu" (p. 331). The UD curriculum provides a structure for sustained meaningful activity in the community in which TCs' practicum schools are located. This opening up of borders between school and community is based on three premises: (a) teachers who know students' communities intimately are most likely to engage in culturally relevant pedagogy; (b) those who interact with the community in a sustained way will audit and utilize its resources and its partners (e.g., social service personnel, cultural experts) in the schooling process; and (c) those who understand the configurations of power in urban communities wroth with inequities will likely engage politically in social transformation.

Each candidate is required to invest a minimum of 6 hours per month in a community-based project that we have categorized as *health and safety*, *educational*, *recreational*, and *political*.[3] Although some of the projects that TCs engage with are preexisting (some of which were developed by previous TC cohorts), often TCs develop novel programs based on their assessment of the community's needs and resources. Examples of health and safety activities include such projects as breakfast and snack programs that provide and emphasize nutritional meals for students. These programs give TCs the opportunity to interact socially and academically with students, teachers, and parents, while simultaneously becoming more aware of issues of poverty and social class and their role as border crossers. *Homework clubs*, *remedial clubs*, *tutoring programs*, *early literacy*, and *English-as-a-second-language* (ESL) programs are examples of projects under the educational category, whereas *arts and crafts*, *drama*, *sports*, and "*Cooking for Kids*" programs fall under the recreational category. A popular program under the political category is the *Women's Shelter* program, which has as its clients, women and children fleeing domestic violence. Here, candidates engage in a tutorial program for the children. Students' practicum placements are often in the city's most economically needy inner-city communities characterized by government-assisted housing, high unemployment, poverty, and a transient population. Because many of the projects TCs engage in are very-service oriented, we recognize that one of the challenges TCs must confront is overcoming the tendency to see their placement as an add-on to their already heavy workload or in terms of a charity orientation (for an elaboration of this argument, see Solomon et al., 2005). Indeed, negotiating this type of borderland is constitutive to their education as transformative intellectuals.

To enrich the community involvement focus of the program, an in-class forum is also constitutive of TCs' pre-service preparation. Here TCs engage with a variety of border crossing literacies designed to prepare them to learn to rewrite differences in ways that help them cross cultural borders (racial, ethnic, religious, moral, etc.). Through a variety of reflective, individual, and group activities consisting of rigorous discussions, reflections (both written and oral), and seminar presentations, TCs are provided with the opportunity to revisit their experiences on an ongoing basis, and engage in a guided critique of their own attitudes, beliefs, and perspectives on issues of race and racism, ethnicity and ethnocentrism, as well as other notions of social difference in Canadian society. TCs confront the social realities of racism, ethnocentrism, poverty, sexism, and homophobia, while exploring how their own social identities affect their interaction with urban communities. These practices expose TCs to the ways the act of naming defines what is named, but also how the act of naming as difference-making impacts on different forms of cultural productions (i.e., individual, cultural, ethnic, political, and ideological). Using the works of Helms (1995), Tatum (1992), Thompson and Carter (1997) and others who have developed and utilized models of racial identity formation, candidates go through a learning process designed to help them reflect on their own identity formation. Family, school, community, and media often emerge as powerful socializing agencies. Such a reflective self-study enables candidates to ascertain their level of personal awareness, knowledge, and antiracism education skills to negotiate race relations and racial difference.[4] The objective of such a self-study is to help candidates understand how their level of identity formation may impact their teaching and to develop a growth plan to move them to a higher level of competence for working across borders.

Along with this in-class forum, a third pedagogical practice for student inquiry is presented in an emphasis on teaching as research. Here, TCs are highly motivated to see every activity, event, and experience as an opportunity to do research. Based on this principle, a structure is provided for TCs to engage in observational research during their orientation into the community. Before commencing any observation and work in the community TCs are provided basic teacher-as-researcher skills that enable them to conduct basic demographic studies of the community served by their practicum school: auditing the cultural, recreational, and economic resources of the community, and assessing the needs that could potentially impact the schooling process. They learn basic data-gathering methods such as interviewing, observing, designing, and administering surveys, and document (archival data) analysis. Most importantly, they are urged to bracket their assumptions about urban, inner-city communities to ensure some measure of objectivity. In the communities served by their practicum schools, they explore the social, cultural, recreational, and economic resources from the perspectives of parents, social services agencies, school council members, students, business proprietors, and other stakeholders. In addition, the visit of social service agencies staff to TCs on the university campus provides information sessions on the unique programs and growth opportunities they provide TCs. Such an orientation provides the insights TCs need to make judgments about projects that are growth-producing for themselves, the students they teach, and the communities from which these children come.

Through various activities associated with these different critical forums, TCs work to develop a deeper understanding of their own assumptions and of the urban communities served by their practicum schools. Simultaneously, they move toward seeing themselves as transformative intellectuals and schools as sites of political, social, and ideological struggle, wherein they might become what Giroux (1991) calls border crossers who are educated "to explore zones of cultural difference by moving in and out of resources, histories, and narratives that provide different students with the sense of identity, place and possibility" (p. 341).

## BORDER-CROSSING EXPERIENCES

In this section, TCs utilize the principles and practices of community-service learning to engage in insightful reflections on their experiences as border crossers. Using the borderlands outlined earlier (institutional, race and ethno–cultural, socioeconomic, and moral–political), we analyze candidates' movement from traditional teacher education locations to more progressive positionings for community transformation. Although there are different points of intersection between and among these border categories (e.g., TCs often share experiences using multiple identities such as White, middle-class, female), for reasons of clarity, we deconstruct these experiences in distinct categories. The narratives that follow represent candidates' perspectives and experiences.

### Crossing Institutional Borders

The initial borderlands that teacher candidates find themselves negotiating are those of the institutional, particularly those of the university, the practicum schools, and the communities these practicum schools serve. As presented now, TCs reflect upon moving beyond such traditional borders of teacher education to engaging with communities in ways that are pedagogically and politically more democratic. Their reflections reveal how traditional modes of teacher education with a focus on relations between university and practicum schools often pervade TCs' attitudes and perceptions when they first begin their pre-service education. Additionally, their reflections illustrate how they struggle to position themselves simultaneously between three institutional spheres: the university, the practicum schools, and the communities their practicum schools serve, and begin to imagine how the democratic institution of schooling may become an integral part of the larger community. One TC relates this:

> Prior to becoming a teacher candidate, I had assumed that at teachers college I would learn how to create and deliver lesson plans, learn about curriculum and classroom strategies. I understood from speaking with educators that teacher education would be designed so that the university theory would be learned first and then we would go into the schools to practice what were taught. The UD Program and its community service learning component erased all of those ideas from my mind.

Similarly, another TC reflects on how traditional modes of education that focus on the relationship between the institutional borderlands of university and practicum schools stultify students' learning by explaining away their lived experiences and by ignoring their connections to the larger communities from which they come.

> Traditional notions of teacher education stress academic learning within a university classroom and practicum setting. They stop at the school doors as if the world with its problems and pressures does not enter along with the students. In my experience with social action and advocacy in the schools, it is difficult for some educators to learn the idea that schools are part of the larger community and that students come to school with baggage that must be unburdened before they can be free to learn.

As TCs begin to critically interrogate the traditional practice of pre-service education that operates exclusively between the walls of the university and practicum schools, they begin to imagine counternarratives that might resist the notion of conceptualizing school and community as nonsynchronous entities, and instead begin the process of building "bridges" that straddle these borderlands. Central to this process is a critical community involvement engagement. One candidate reflects on her role through her community service-learning placement in making this process possible.

> The benefit of uniting schools and community through community service learning is that it bridges gaps between the two spheres.... By locating myself within the community, I get a sense of what the community is like, what its needs are, who is there, and what these people are doing. I...[have] the privilege of meeting new people from backgrounds that are different from mine, and I am...enriched through what they share with me. I have the opportunity of meeting mothers, fathers, and other caregivers. I see where my students go after leaving school and at the same time I get a sense of fulfillment by providing a service for students who are having difficulty. I am learning about my school's community and becoming more aware of my students' diverse heritage, social differences, and concerns.

In each of the aforementioned interactions, TCs' subjective narratives were chosen for illustration because they point toward the role that institutions play in organizing people's lives. Border pedagogy, as a democratic educational practice, encourages TCs to read the institutional codes that inscribe power within traditional institutional structures that marginalize "communities of difference." As Giroux (1992a) explains, "Border pedagogy must take up the dual task of not only creating new objects of knowledge but also addressing how inequities, power and human suffering are rooted in basic institutional structures" (p. 29). By examining the ways these institutional structures reproduce oppression, TCs begin to interrogate the narratives that maintain "difference" as an exercise in exclusion. Their engagement in service learning helps them to begin to embrace counternarratives that recognize the limits of institutional walls and move beyond them toward more participatory and democratic modes of teaching. This is particularly important when dominant group institutions such as schools engage with disempowered communities of difference such as those found in urban, inner-city environments.

**Crossing Racial and Ethno–Cultural Borders**

In response to the increasingly heterogeneous context of urban North American societies, a prerequisite for working with diverse multicultural populations is engaging in educational practices that foster teaching for equity and social justice across racial and ethno–cultural differences. When TCs engage in service learning, they begin to negotiate racial and ethno–cultural borders, develop an awareness of their own assumptions, become sensitive to cultural differences, and foster knowledge about the communities from which their students come. This endeavor requires a conscious interrogation of inequities between dominant and minority cultures, particularly the privileged status of middle-class White teachers in relation to the "underprivileged" status of the students they often teach in urban, ethno–racially diverse environments.

When TCs are asked to interrogate traditional modes of teacher education that see race, ethnicity, and culture in insulated own-group ways, they are given an opportunity to become transformative intellectuals who are critical of the ways that power relations play out in classroom dynamics and to determine whose ethno–cultural histories, knowledge, and perspectives are represented and whose are marginalized. The reflections that TCs share show how they unpack power dynamics that are embedded in White privilege, how learning from students' lived experiences facilitates TCs' examination of their own cultural assumptions, and how such a conscious interrogation of personal assumptions might allow TCs to extend their understandings of race, ethnicity, and culture in their communities of practice. As one TC reflects:

> I have always thought myself to be a relatively unbiased individual, free of the bonds of racism and prejudice, but I have only recently started to come to grips with what it means to be a middle-class, White Canadian. I have neglected to recognize the power I inadvertently hold, and consequently the possibility that I might come to abuse it in my classroom.... Educators belonging to the White power structure must be ever vigilant about the subversive power they hold over their students. These teachers are in great need of making connections with their students and communities.

This TC's remarks are indicative of the dangers of racial and ethno–cultural encapsulation within (and outside) the classroom, where to be a middle-class White Canadian is a position of power that might be advertently or inadvertently abused. Inadvertent abuse is what King (1991) labels *dysconscious racism*. The TC's narrative points out that it is by moving away from a traditional position of racial and ethno–cultural insulation toward a more progressive location that one begins to cross such borders and engage in more democratic modes of teaching.

Another TC reflects on how power can be shared in the classroom by abandoning traditional authoritarian modes of pedagogy and crossing racial and ethno–cultural borders in order to learn from students:

> When I became less worried about "managing" the students and their homework, I was able to let the students teach me. They taught me about myself, and I now recognize how self-conscious I was about being Anglo, White, and middle-class—a member of the dominant society that marginalizes them and their families. Would I have any credibility? Would my "caring" be enough? I wondered how they would receive me, and I felt like an interloper. In order to connect with these kids, I had to recognize how my own cultural habits of English limit my interactions.

As TCs encounter different racial and ethno–cultural borders, they must interrogate their own assumptions about difference and "otherness." Giroux's (1992a) notion of *difference* is instructive here. He conceptualizes border pedagogy in ways that "provide the conditions for students to engage in cultural remapping as a form of resistance" (p. 33). Speaking about cultural difference, for instance, he remarks that it is important that "culture is not viewed as monolithic or unchanging" (p. 32). Rather, culture is more appropriately understood as a process of multiple and contradictory identifications that constantly shift with changing histories, language, and experiences.

As TCs grapple with the multiple understandings of culture, race, and personal identity, they begin to acknowledge the heterogeneity within themselves, an implicit recognition that might possibly, as Peck (1994) puts it, "bring into focus a human connectedness that recognizes cultural difference without essentializing it" (p. 119). This understanding might help move pedagogy in directions that rethink difference—not as that which disrupts learning, but rather as that which is necessary for learning and addressing the relations of power and/or knowledge that sustain discourses as stable, essential, and permanent.

**Crossing Socioeconomic Borders**

In urban city centers, TCs who have been traditionally positioned as middle-class professionals are likely to receive teaching appointments in working-class communities. These new teachers often enter the profession with the assumption that working-class communities are sites from which students need to "escape" rather than spaces that are progressive locations of democratic participation and communal dialogue. Through their community service learning, TCs grapple with the socioeconomic contexts of inner-city communities from which many of their students come and develop a deeper awareness of the cultural resources, knowledge, and partnerships communities can provide for teachers.

The TC narratives that follow flesh out some of the challenges that TCs face as they struggle to critically examine their experiences within working-class communities and the development of authentic relationships that have a positive impact on individual students. One TC has this to say:

> As teachers, it is imperative that we find ways to develop relationships with parents, families, and community members. Families, schools, and community organizations all contribute to student achievement. Students' backgrounds, economic conditions, and home environments all affect their adjustment to and performance in schools.... In order to learn about students, teachers need to be able to develop trusting relationships not only with their students, but [also] with the people who influence students' lives.

TCs also speak about the importance of community-based learning, which gives them the opportunity to understand the socioeconomic conditions under which their students live. They also learn to reflect on how this knowledge fosters relationships among teachers and students that transcend traditional classroom models of education. They "learn the language (street and body) of the students," deepen their awareness of the ways in which "a teacher's job does not end at the sound of the bell, or at the edge of the school property," and become sensitive to the ways in which "judgments and assumptions can be avoided because teachers are aware of where the students are coming from."

Another TC reflects on the value of having first-hand experience in dealing with poverty through his community service-learning placement:

> This [experience] made me realize how difficult it can be for a child coming from a lower income family to fit into a new school and deal with situations they have never been exposed to before. In teachers college, the inequities and the social injustices of society are constantly discussed in class, but until I saw this up close I did not know the struggle that these students face on a daily basis. This is where theory and real life experience actually came together.... [F]rom that point on, I found myself taking more seriously the circumstances and issues that lower income families encounter.

TCs' personal reflections of service learning in poor and working-class communities illustrate how they attempt to move away from traditional locations that pathologize poverty and disenfranchise students. A tension between the middle-class values of the school and the lack of resources in poor communities is central to the difficulties candidates face when asked to extend their vision of education beyond classroom walls to include the communities from which their students come.

Vital to addressing this tension is an understanding of the ways that socioeconomic privilege works to favor certain groups over others. At stake for democratic education today is not simply that certain groups are privileged materially and socially, but that the conditions that privilege these groups are the very "conditions that have disabled others to speak," explains Giroux (1992a, p. 27). In this sense, TCs engaged as border crossers must continuously interrogate not only the socioeconomic structures that marginalize particular communities, but also the structures that privilege others.

## Moral–Political Border Crossing

One of the most challenging borders for TCs to cross in their conceptualization and practice of community-service learning is from a posture of charity and altruism to one of social transformation (Kahne & Westheimer, 1996; Solomon et al., 2005). Crossing moral and political borders require TCs to move away from a charity-oriented, altruistic position toward a more political location where inequities are challenged. Here, community-service learning becomes more than an epiphenomenon attached to TCs' scholastic work, merely one more requirement with which they are burdened. Rather, TCs are involved in an active, concerted, and ongoing analysis of political structures and the ways power relations intersect to produce social injustice. Such a change in perspective opens up the necessary spaces for

TCs to become transformative intellectuals who work to combine critical inquiry with an understanding of diverse social realities, and to become involved in sustained meaningful action and social advocacy.

The reflections to come illustrate how TCs struggle to move away from a traditional charity and/or altruistic orientation toward more politically motivated and socially transformative locations. Their reflections reveal how their involvement in community life shifts their position from that of leaders to that of participants whose involvement becomes a vital part of a more broadly conceptualized social transformation.

As TCs begin to engage in their community placements, their involvement is often characterized by a charitable morality-bound orientation, that is, having "compassion for the less fortunate" (Kahne & Westheimer, 1996, p. 595). Such altruism is often seen as the "haves" giving back to the "have-nots." This commitment is evidenced in such TC comments as, "I'm seeing the benefit of giving back to my community.... I believe that it is important to be an example for others, to pass along the tools that have been passed on to me." Another TC remarks, "For some pre-service teachers I imagine the CSL [community service learning] provided them with a moment of epiphany." Acts of charity as an end in themselves are critiqued for providing a "within-border" engagement with no long-term transformative potential for economically depressed communities. Indeed, those TCs critical of community-service learning as charity argue that it is a top–down, neoconservative approach to giving that does not open up possibilities for participatory democracy. Communities that are economically poor and politically powerless have forms of charity imposed upon them instead of negotiated with them. One TC argues:

> I have been unable to determine how the community has been in dialogue with the Breakfast Club or has contributed to the form and functioning of the program. To not consult the community in this matter has a twofold effect: it re-inscribes a neoconservative model of accountability by reproducing a top–down approach to governance. This alienates the community that is being served and creates a situation that is fundamentally antidemocratic.

This TC brings to the fore a central tension that confronts educators who engage in community- service learning initiatives. Whether community projects are initiated by TCs or institutions that work with the community, it is often the case that initiatives are taken without direct negotiation with community members or social agencies that operate in the community. Such actions often alienate the very people they are supposed to serve. Moreover, they confirm suspicions that those outside the community who have little vested interest in the community can engage in actions that directly affect the community members without having to be accountable to the community.

Another TC reflects on the struggle to move away from an altruistic orientation to teaching toward a more politically and socially transformative space:

> My responsibility as an educator becomes political. When I learn about women and children's issues from my community work, I will not only be reminded…of my own experiences with patriarchy, but I will need to find ways to bring this knowledge into the classroom, school, and community in order to give this cause voice and educate toward a better understanding of these issues, and thereby bring change into the world.

As with many of the teacher candidates who engage in community-service learning initiatives, they often develop insights into how their roles within the community can become instrumental in sociopolitical transformation. This role—that of becoming transformative intellectuals —is one that they bring back with them to the classroom.

Giroux's position on border pedagogy as a political project reinforces the view that progressive educators can no longer see themselves as mere pedagogues, but must begin to embrace more socially transformative locations. This entails the proclivity "not merely to reaffirm difference but to also interrogate it, to open up broader theoretical considerations, to tease out its limitations, and to engage a vision of community in which student voices define themselves in terms of their distinct social formations and their broader collective hopes" (Giroux, 1992a, p. 35). In this way, future educators learn to engage in an ongoing interrogation of the power relations that privilege certain groups over others, to forge alliances and dialogue with communities about matters that affect the welfare of the community, and to value the political role they must assume as critical educators. These are practices that make possible education as a democratic project and teaching as a politically transformative practice.

## CHALLENGES FOR TEACHER EDUCATION

Giroux's discourse on border pedagogy signals the urgent need for teachers to move beyond their traditional borders of schooling and instead create more progressive institutional, race and ethno–cultural, socioeconomic, and moral–political borderlands. Throughout this chapter, we have dealt with synchronous and intersecting border categories and highlighted the salient factors that mediate power and power relations in urban, inner-city communities. But teacher movement, from the traditional to the progressive, will be fraught with challenges and contestation. At the institutional level, expanding the traditional locations of teacher education to integrate the urban community will provoke the traditionalist who perceives teacher education as residing only in sanctioned institutional settings of the university classroom and the practicum school. The struggle for progressive teacher educators will be to convince field-based teacher education partners that community-service learning will, in fact, contribute to the development of culturally relevant pedagogy.

Educating teachers to emerge from their race and ethnic cleavages and engage collaboratively in inter-race and/or ethnic environments will prepare them to work with competence and grace across borders. But breaking away from the bondage of identity and socialization requires teacher preparation that critically interrogates historically rooted hierarchies in multiracial societies, one that challenges underground discourses that reside within White and other dominant groups' borderlands, and one that challenges White privilege and other issues of social stratification. Teacher educators who have responded to this challenge have met with unrelenting resistance (Ahlquist, 1992; Roman, 1993; Sleeter, 1993; Solomon & Levine-Rasky, 1996). However, any significant movement across this divide will ultimately result from teacher education that critically interrogates the social, political, and ideological construction of race and ethnicity and its impact on the schooling process.

What are the likely challenges of teacher education that examines the socioeconomic construction of urban schools? What are the issues of moving away from the pathological construction and marginalization of the working-class and economically poor toward a more progressive integration into the democratic life of communities? In a society that operates on the myth of meritocracy and one that values competitive individualism, teacher beliefs and practices may well fuel the "deficiency theory," that those that live in poverty do not possess the competency to rise above poverty. Teacher educators are therefore challenged to explore the larger inequities of capitalist societies and their deleterious impact on the underprivileged.

Finally, within the moral–political borderland, teachers have traditionally felt altruistic, even civic, responsibility, for providing charity for communities that live in poverty. The Kahne and Westheimer (1996) model of moving from charity to the social transformation of communities is instructive here (see Solomon et al., 2005, for an elaboration of this model).

To conclude, for pre-service teachers to engage effectively in border pedagogy in their communities of practice, Giroux (2005) and Giroux and McLaren (1996) suggest that they must be prepared as transformative intellectuals, as cultural workers, and as strident pedagogues. To accomplish this important task, teacher education must itself be transformed into a political project!

## ENDNOTES

[1] In this chapter, we use pre-service teachers interchangeably with teacher candidates.

[2] There is the tendency for school boards and city governments to charge their constituents for the use of facilities or to reassign resources to the highest bidder. For example, the time and space allotted to inner-city youth for basketball would be bought out by organizations with disposable capital. This was the policy of some school districts during their perceived "financial crisis."

[3] For a number of reasons, TCs often cannot participate in their CI projects during the regular school day. When they participate after school hours or on weekends, they have the option of taking lieu time out of their practicum to a maximum of 6 hours per month. This arrangement is to ensure that TCs are adequately compensated for their personal time on the project.

[4] Such an identity audit may also be conducted on other social markers such as class, gender, sexual formation and so on.

## REFERENCES

Ahlquist, R. (1992). Manifestation of inequality: Overcoming resistance in a multicultural foundations course. In C. Grant (Ed.), *Researcher and multicultural education: From the marginal to the mainstream* (pp. 89–105). London: Falmer.

Baldwin, R. S. (1999). When public school and university cultures meet. In M. Wideen & P. Lemma (Eds.), *Ground level reform in teacher education: Changing schools of education* (pp. 77–94). Calgary: Detselig.

Boyle-Baise, M. (1998). Community service learning for multicultural education: An exploratory study with pre-service teachers. *Equity & Excellence in Education, 31*(2), 52–60.

Giroux, H. (1991). Democracy and the discourse of cultural difference: Towards a politics of border pedagogy. *British Journal of Sociology of Education, 12*(4), 501–519.

Giroux, H. (1992a). *Border crossings: Cultural workers and the politics of education*. New York: Routledge.

Giroux, H. (1992b). Resisting difference: Cultural studies and the discourse of critical pedagogy. In C. Nelson, P. Treichler, & L. Grossberg (Eds), *Cultural studies: An introduction* (pp.199–212). New York: Routledge.

Giroux, H. (2005). *Border crossings: Cultural workers and the politics of education* (2nd ed.). New York: Routledge.

Giroux, H., & McLaren, P. (1996). Teacher education and the politics of engagement: The case for democratic schooling. In P. Leistyna & A. Woodrum (Eds.), *Breaking free: The transformative power of critical pedagogy* (pp. 301–331). Cambridge: Harvard Educational Review.

Guadarrama, I. (2000). The empowering role of service learning in the preparation of teachers. In C. O'Grady (Ed.), *Integrating service learning and multicultural education in colleges and universities* (pp. 227–243). Mahwah NJ: Lawrence Erlbaum Associates.

Haberman, M. (1994). The pedagogy of poverty versus good teaching. In J. Kretovics & E. J. Nussel (Eds.), *Transforming urban education* (pp. 305–314). Boston: Allyn & Bacon.

Hallinan, M. T., & Teixeria, R. A. (1987). Students' interracial friendships: Individual characteristics, structural effects and racial differences. *American Journal of Education*, 563–583.

Helms, J. E. (1995). An update of Helms's White and people of color racial identity models. In J. Ponterotto, J. M. Casas, L. A. Suzuki, & C. M. Alexander (Eds.), *Handbook of multicultural Counseling* (pp. 181–198). Thousand Oaks, CA: Sage.

Howard, J. (1998). Academic service learning: A counter-normative pedagogy. In. R. A. Rhoads & J. Howard, (Eds.), *Academic service learning: A pedagogy of action and reflection* (pp. 21–29). San Francisco: Jossey-Bass.

Irvine, J. J. (1989). *Black students and school failure*. Westport, CT: Greenwood Publishing Group.

Kahne, J., & Westheimer, J. (1996). In the service of what? The politics of service learning. *Phi Delta Kappan, 77*, 593–599.

King, J. E. (1991). Dysconscious racism: Ideology, identity, and the mis-education of teachers. *Journal of Negro Education, 60*(2), 133–146.

Kozol, J. (1991). *Savage inequalities: Children in America's schools*. New York: Crown Publishers.

Ladson-Billings, G. (1995). Toward a theory of culturally relevant pedagogy. *American Educational Research Journal, 32*, 465–491.

Lynch, J. (1987). *Prejudice reduction and the school*s. London: Nichols Publishing.

Miron, L. F. (2003). Joint ventures between public schools and city government: Implications for community development. In L. F. Miron & E. P. St. John (Eds.), *Reinterpreting urban school reform* (pp. 229–247). Albany: State University of New York Press.

O'Grady, C. R. (Ed.). (2000). *Integrating service learning and multicultural education in colleges and universities*. Mahwah, NJ: Lawrence Erlbaum Associates.

Peck, J. (1994). Talking about racism: Framing a popular discourse of race on Oprah Winfrey. *Cultural Studies, 27*, 89–126.

Roman, L. (1993).White is a color! White defensiveness, postmodernism, and antiracist pedagogy. In C. McCarthy & W. Crichlow (Eds.), *Race, identity and representation in education* (pp. 71–88). New York: Routledge.

Sleeter, C. (1993). How White teachers construct race. In C. McCarthy & W. Crichlow (Eds.), *Race, identity and representation in education* (pp.157–171). New York: Routledge.

Sleeter, C. (2000). Strengthening multicultural education with community-based service learning. In C. O'Grady (Ed.), *Integrating service learning and multicultural education in colleges and universities* (pp. 263–276). Mahwah, NJ: Lawrence Erlbaum Associates.

Solomon, R. P. (1992). *Black resistance in high school: Forging a separatist culture*. Albany: State University of New York Press.

Solomon, R.P., Khattar Manoukian, R., & Clarke, J. (2005). From the ethics of altruism to possibilities of transformation in teacher candidates' community involvement. In L. Pease-Alvarez & S. Schecter (Eds.), *Learning, teaching and community:*

*Contributions of situated and participatory approaches for educational innovations* (pp. 171–190). Mahwah, NJ: Lawrence Erlbaum Associates.

Solomon, R.P. & Levine-Rasky, C. (1996). Transforming teacher education for antiracism pedagogy. *The Canadian Review of Sociology of Education, 35*(4), 337–359.

Solomon, R. P., & Levine-Rasky, C. (2003). *Teaching for equity and diversity research to practice.* Toronto: Canadian Scholars' Press.

Tatum, B. D. (1992). Talking about race, learning about racism: The application of racial identity development theory in the classroom. *Harvard Educational Review, 62*(1), 1–24.

Tatum, B. D. (1997). *Why are all the Black kids sitting together in the cafeteria? And other conversations about race.* New York: Basic Books.

Thompson, C. E., & Carter, R. T. (Eds.). (1997). *Racial identity theory: Applications to individual, groups, and organizational interventions.* Mahwah, NJ: Lawrence Erlbaum Associates.

Yao, F. L. (1997). *Inner-city schools, multiculturalism, and teacher education: A professional journey.* New York: Garland Publishing.

# Chapter 6

# Moving Beyond Institutional Boundaries in Inner-City Teacher Preparation

Harry Smaller
*York University*

> *School…is in origin quite alien to working-class life. It does not grow from that life; it is not "our school" in the sense that other schools can be spoken of by the folk of other classes. The government forced them on us…. School in working-class life expresses nothing of that life; it is an institution clapped on from above.*
>
> —Jack Common, son of a railway engine driver, 1938; quoted in Corrigan and Curtis (1985, p. 163)

This chapter provides a description of a new teacher education program, operated under the aegis of York University but situated in the middle of Regent Park, a large, government-owned, low-income housing project extending over several city blocks in downtown Toronto. The chapter begins with brief historical explorations of state schooling systems and teacher education programs followed by a description of the Regent Park community. However, the main portion of the chapter is devoted to a discussion of the ways in which this program differs from other teacher education programs in its attempt to help effect modest but "real" change in our seemingly impenetrable public school system. At the philosophical center of this innovative program is a commitment to grapple with the elusive notion of *community*—to ground teacher education in a fundamental exploration and understanding of what this concept might mean in a diverse, inner-city neighborhood. Linked to this approach is the belief that for inner-city schools, teaching and learning must all be similarly grounded if we are to be more successful in educating their young people than we have been to date.

Regent Park is a specific residential neighborhood, marked by poverty and racial and/or ethnic diversity, and located in a specific city in North America. To be sure, school regulations, policies, practices, funding, and governance differ from city to city, state to state. Similarly, teacher education and certification programs—university-based and otherwise—also vary widely. However, we would certainly argue that there are many ways in which the existing cultures of schooling, teaching, and learning in Regent Park schools can be generalized across inner-city schools in many parts of Canada and the United States, and therefore that generalizations might be made about ways in which these can be changed. In this regard, it is interesting to note the findings from a recent national study on alternative certification programs in the United States, in comparison to university-based teacher education programs. Their findings suggest that it is not at all the relative differences in the structures of the programs that make the difference, but rather "a function between the program *as implemented*, the school context in which the on-the-job training occurs, and the career trajectory of the individual participant" (Humphrey & Wechsler, 2005, p. 4; italics in original). Similarly, we argue that the lessons learned in the first 3 years of the York University–Regent Park Teacher Education program might also prove relevant to other United States and Canadian teacher education programs—certainly those that specifically express the intent of better supporting new teachers wishing to devote their lives to improving schooling for inner-city students.

## STATE SCHOOLING—WHAT IS IT ABOUT?

How did compulsory, centralized, public schooling systems come about? Why have they turned out the way they have? Why do they seem so resistant to change? To be sure, the stories and accounts over the years of their origins and development have been numerous, multifaceted, and often contradictory. On one hand, traditional schooling histories have tended to dwell only on the positive aspects of the "development" of public education. Stories are told of how schools have improved from distant, cold, poorly furnished, one-room schoolhouses, to modern, fully equipped, welcoming buildings located in every neighborhood. We are told that parents and other well-meaning citizens in every community across the land worked together selflessly and tirelessly to build and expand schooling, and to convince fiscally conservative community leaders that public schooling should be supported. Although there might have been rough beginnings, we are told that public schools have been increasingly successful in reaching out and educating more and more of the youth population, regardless of their social background. In short, the traditional story emphasizes how our public schools have come to serve as the universal institution in our society for providing social mobility to all young people willing to apply themselves (Fleming, 1972; Wilson, Stamp, & Audet, 1970).

More recently, however, many of these stories of "progress" have been challenged seriously by educational historians. For example, since the mid-1970s, Alison Prentice (1975), Ian Davey (1978), Bruce Curtis (1988), and many others have argued convincingly that it was not necessarily the "general public" who were responsible for conceptualizing public schools as we have come to know them. Rather, "school promoters," members of the 19th and early 20th century economic, political, and religious elite, were central in the planning and development of the compulsory, centralized, hierarchical state schooling systems we have today across the United States and Canada. In fact, over the past century, many parents and students, particularly of working-class, minority, and immigrant backgrounds, have attempted to resist or at least alter what they saw as foreign institutions being foisted on them. They opposed what seemed to be the dominant purpose of these settings—extinguishing their family and cultural backgrounds and beliefs in favor of promoting a specific dominant culture: ethnocentric, classed, raced, and gendered in "proper" adherence to the obedient Christian values espoused by the upper- middle-class elite of the times.

Given this disjuncture, it is certainly understandable why many educators, not to mention parents and students themselves, have argued that public schools have not served all students successfully. In fact, the evidence is very clear that significant proportions of students from certain class, ethnic, racial, and linguistic backgrounds were, and continue to be, systematically unsuccessful in public schools across the continent (Curtis, Livingston, & Smaller, 1994; Toronto Board of Education 1970, 1984, 1997). Some historians and sociologists even challenge the assertion that these schools were ever intended to treat all students equally. Rather, these researchers argue that they were established and run for the precise purpose of sorting and streaming youth so that they could successfully "find their proper place" in our hierarchical society (see, e.g., Ball 2003; Curtis, Livingstone, & Smaller, 1994).

Is it possible to draw on the empirical results of our school systems, to interpret what its actual goals might be, compared to what is claimed as their *raison d'etre*? Do public schools exist mainly for the enhancement of each individual student, to allow each to develop to his or her full potential? Do the public schools exist mainly to assist young people to become economically self-sufficient within our larger community? Or do public schools exist for the benefit of society and/or the nation as a whole—to de-

velop proper citizens who will help ensure the establishment and maintenance of a good society?

Some might argue that all three of these traditionally held objectives are,
or could be, met simultaneously in any given school. Others would suggest
that this is not possible, that these three objectives are in some respects mu-
tually incompatible or even contradictory. In addition to these traditional
views of schooling, more cynical objectives have been cited concerning the
existence of public schools and/or systems as we know them—such as for the
purposes of social governance and control in changing and/or global times
(Bloch, 2003; Popkewitz, 2000), and/or to maintain custodial functions and
"warehousing" of youth in times of high unemployment, shifting family
structures, and other forms of social change or unrest (Barakett &
Cleghorn, 2000). Whatever the analysis, it is certainly understandable why
Jack Common (quoted at the beginning of this chapter), among a myriad of
other working-class and minority students, would come to experience their
schooling as being "alien." It is also certainly understandable why a disproportionate number of students from backgrounds that are not dominant
have not been successfully served in our schools, and why this continues to
be the case (Dei, James-Wilson, & Zine, 2000). Where does this leave the
field of teacher education?

## TEACHER EDUCATION—WHAT IS IT ALL ABOUT?

> Underlying the public criticism [of teacher education] is an acceptance of
> the folklore and myths of institutional life. The discourse of our teacher ed-
> ucation is a celebration of existing institutional patterns. The discussion
> takes for granted that the problems of teacher education are improving the
> relation between theory and practice, and facilitating communication be-
> tween university and school.... The discourse of administrative change, ef-
> ficient procedures, and rational planning is made to seem as progressive,
> yet the practices conserve the power arrangements of schooling.
>
> The public discourse should be distinguished from the actual reform
> practices. Public language functions as a slogan system to develop a con-
> sensus about an agenda for schooling.... The public language, however,
> may have little relationship to the actual values that shape practice, the
> latter reflecting the working out of specific networks of power in the orga-
> nization of institutions. (Popkewitz, 1987, pp. viii–ix)

Given these historic and continuing tensions and contradictions over what
public schooling is supposed to achieve, it should not be surprising that this
dissonance spills over to the field of teacher preparation. One could right-
fully ask: How can we agree on what good teacher education is if we cannot
agree on what good schools should be about?

This dissonance has certainly continued throughout the history of teacher education, both in Ontario and elsewhere. For example, since the day that the Ontario Normal School opened its doors in Toronto in 1847, and for its entire 80-plus years of existence, it was fraught with dissent—from politicians, educators, the media, the pubic, and its own students alike—about how and what it was intended to accomplish (Prentice, 1990). Recent years have not shown any abatement in these tensions. In Ontario, the post-World War II era has experienced a plethora of royal commissions, government task forces, and government-funded studies dedicated partially or entirely to the question of teacher education, each one in turn beginning with a critique of the status quo and ending with a, mainly apocryphal, prescription for change (see, e.g., Fullan & Connelly, 1987; Ontario Department of Education, 1968; Ontario Ministry of Education, 1994). And this is hardly a phenomenon unique to Ontario, or Canada. For example, if the literally hundreds of panels and papers presented each year at the American Educational Research Association annual conference on the (desperate) need for change in teacher education is any indication, this tension and debate over the purposes and practicalities of teacher education occurs right across our continent.

## PHILOSOPHICAL FOUNDATIONS OF TEACHER EDUCATION

One way to look historically at the changes in teacher education is to examine the sometimes dramatic shifts in their philosophical underpinnings. During its early years, for example, the Toronto Normal School was obsessed with the task of molding and developing the moral character of the teacher, and this objective clearly served as the basis for this program. Applicants were required to submit a guarantee of good moral standing signed by an official of their particular (Christian) faith. Rigid rules governed their behavior during their participation in the program, and this behavior was closely monitored at the school, the community, and in their homes (Prentice, 1990). Significant parts of the curriculum and program were devoted to these myriad aspects of character development.

Judging from the extensive literature, these early moral foundations for teacher education were not dissimilar to those found in other jurisdictions in Canada, the Caribbean, and the United States. However well versed the candidates might have been in academic and pedagogical knowledge and skills, their future career hung on their morals, values, and behavior. The task of developing the "character" of student teachers remained a foundational objective; one that continues to this day, drawing heavily on the prescriptive aspects of professionalism.

Over the years, a number of other foundational objectives have been added as these state-sponsored programs expanded and became more sophisticated. At various historical points, curriculum and academic subject specialty often appeared as the most important objectives in the syllabi. At other times, this was replaced with a primary emphasis focused on the children, usually involving courses and fieldwork related to child psychology and human development. Another historical strand has been a focus on pedagogy itself—an attempt to elevate the technical and other aspects of teaching practice as the most important part of teacher education. More recently, in some jurisdictions at least, some programs have selected a different grounding in the social aspects of formal schooling. Often these programs would build from a close examination of the classroom and/or the entire school, as a social setting that must be explored and understood if new teachers are to be successful in acquiring skills, knowledge, and values needed to promote successful learning in their own classrooms.

Certainly, most or all of these themes and issues are important, and many teacher education programs over the years have attempted to include a range of objectives in their overall program. At the same time, however, one could argue that many or most programs still reflect an emphasis on one or two of these major philosophical footings. In addition, many argue that the vast majority of our teacher education programs continue to reflect the dominant White, middle-class, patriarchal, and heterosexual values of our society, and as result only help to perpetuate public schooling systems as we have come to know them.

By comparison with these other philosophical foundations for teacher education, the York–Regent Park teacher education program has been grounded on the belief that a knowledge and understanding of *community* constitutes a crucial entry point for becoming a successful teacher. To be sure, this is a complicated task. To begin, the concept of community itself is complex and can be read in many different ways—geographically, economically, ethnically, racially, and so forth. This becomes part of the investigation for student teachers—to explore these meanings, complexities, and nuances, and ways in which community interacts with schooling, so as to understand the ways in which this interaction can be supported and promote the most effective teaching and learning. This approach is most important in spaces where there is a wide diversity of residents, especially for schools where the teachers themselves reflect social and cultural backgrounds different from those of most of their students. These new understandings of community and social difference become the basis on which courses in child and youth development, and academic/social knowledge and pedagogy are explored.

## THE REGENT PARK COMMUNITY

The neighborhood known as Regent Park was developed in the immediate post-World War II period as Canada's first major, government-owned and maintained, low-income housing project. An existing working-class community extending over an area of about six square city blocks in the downtown core was razed and a total of approximately 2,000 housing units were constructed using two basic architectural styles—row housing units, and a number of apartment buildings ranging in height from 3to 12 stories. Originally promoted through the traditional liberal rhetoric of providing short-term accommodation for needy families in economic transition, the complex soon became a permanent residence for families unable to break out of a poverty cycle inherent for many of the working-class in the postindustrial economy of large urban areas. In the decades since the founding of Regent Park, the only major demographic change has been a very significant increase in representation by members of minority racial, ethnic, and immigrant groups, as these families also have come increasingly forced to occupy the lower rungs of Canada's class hierarchy. Today, an estimated 10,000 to 12,000 residents live in Regent Park.

Not surprisingly, given the disparities of opportunity for working-class wage earners, Regent Park demonstrates a marked contrast from the city as a whole, according to a number of social indicators. For example, there is 50% more unemployment there, and Regent Part wage earners earn under 50% of Toronto's average income. These disparities also exist in the overall educational attainment of the adult population in Regent Park compared to the rest of the city—twice the proportion of those without a high school diploma, and one quarter the proportion of university graduates. As discouraging as this picture is, the recent educational situation for many young people in Regent Park suggests little room for optimism about possibilities for long-term improvement in educational attainment. Recent dropout rates for students living in this area remain twice that of the overall city rate (56% as compared to 29% according to one report). Similarly, although the secondary school graduation rate across Toronto for immigrant students who have lived in Canada for less than 5 years was 69%, during the same period, only 30% of those from the Regent Park area successfully completed high school (Pathways, 2001). Clearly, in spite of the significant efforts of many teachers and educators working in the elementary and secondary schools in the area, much more is needed to transform this situation.

## BACKGROUND TO THE YORK–REGENT PROGRAM

The York–Regent program was initiated through the fortunate conflux of several structural and personal happenstances; most importantly, the arrival at York University of a long-time Regent Park teacher and principal for a 3-year secondment with the Faculty of Education. From the outset, Jeff began to lobby for the development of an innovative teacher education program based in Regent Park. Having attracted the commitment of a small group of community-based educators, activists, and parents, faculty colleagues at York, and the interest of the associate dean responsible for pre-service teacher education, discussions and planning began in earnest. Most importantly, a decision was made at the outset to keep the process "bottoms up"—working at all times through and against the knowledge of how the dominant culture of institutions usually works, and ever-conscious of Popkewitz's (1987) aforementioned observations of the institution's ability to "conserve the power arrangements of schooling" in order to "maintain specific networks of power in the organization of [teacher education] institutions" (p. ix).

Every step of the way has been marked with this important caveat. Although the program would follow the general overview of York's consecutive pre-service programs (a post-degree, 9-month, university courses and school practicum syllabus), there would definitely be significant differences. On numerous occasions when it became apparent during the planning process that institutional interests appeared to negatively impact the program (site location, staffing, curriculum, selection of candidates, involvement with the community, etc.), this was addressed openly and vigorously by the faculty at the York–Regent program. After considerable discussion and planning, the program opened its doors to its first cohort of 45 student teachers in late August 2002, in space located in the Regent Park Community Center.

Briefly, the program consists of three components, all of which generally occur on a weekly basis throughout the 9 months: 2 days of university courses held at the Center, 2 days of school-based practicum in Regent–Park schools, and weekly involvement in a community-practicum component. At various intervals during the year, students also engage in weeklong "blocks" of practice teaching in their practicum schools, for a total of about 9 weeks over the academic year.

The program has now graduated four cohorts of teachers. Although defining "success" for a teacher education program is certainly a complicated matter, it would appear that the program has indeed been successful. We have had more than our share of media attention and accolades from local school board and York University officials. However, the real test has been the responses of teachers and administrators of the local schools, Regent parents, and community activists, and particularly the student teachers themselves, both during and after completing the program as they themselves entered the classrooms of our increasingly diverse city. At the outset of each year's program, many students questioned why we were spending so much time on "the community" and issues of social diversity and difference; why they were required to take on a weekly volunteer engagement with a community organization; and why we insisted they spend the entire year of their practicum experience in only one school. However, as each year unfolded, most have come to see the purposes we had in mind, and to understand the importance of experiencing, questioning, unpacking, and synthesizing the crucial relationships between schooling, teaching, learning, and community—both conceptually and in the real world. Working-class and minority cultures were not entities to be ignored, denigrated, opposed, or overcome for the sake of "proper" schooling. The student teachers were not on a "mission" to "save" students from some incapacitating existence or ignominious fate. Rather, most student teachers came to see and understand rich community cultures, and learn ways in which to build on these cultures to ensure that their students succeeded academically.

## UNIQUE FEATURES OF THE YORK–REGENT PROGRAM

Although some or much of what happens may seem similar to other teacher education programs, there are certainly significant differences in the ways the York–Regent program was established and run. Some of these components may seem straightforward and common to other programs, yet it is difficult to overstate the crucial importance and interrelation of each of these themes in helping to ensure that the program is truly able to break away from the traditional networks of power in the organization of institutions and adopt alternative foundations for ensuring change.

### Community Collaboration and Engagement

The first stage in the development of the program involved a lengthy series of engagements in Regent Park itself. Following a sustained initial round of informal meetings and ad hoc discussions with parents, high school students, teachers, community activists, community organizations, and agencies extending over several months, several more formal sessions were planned and undertaken. Each of the parent–school councils in the four Regent area elementary schools was approached, and formal presentations and/or discussions were undertaken. Following these meetings, a crucial general meeting was held, attended by about 35 teachers, parents, older students, and community activists. At this event, random groups were formed and asked to brainstorm responses to two basic questions: What kind of teachers do you want in your schools? What could and should a community-based teacher education program do to help produce such teachers? Not surprisingly, virtually all of ideas and suggestions generated met with the approval of all those participating, and this chart formed something of a mantra for the program as it developed.

Another positive outcome from these community consultations was the insistence of a number of community members that engagement between the program and the community continue, to assist with the development of the program, and thereafter on an ongoing basis to help in its guidance and to oversee its activities. As a result, the Community Advisory Committee was established—an open-ended group of parents, teachers, and activists who have been meeting with the program staff and teacher candidate representatives on a periodic basis since that time. One of its first formal activities was to plan a community "welcoming" and "opening" event for the program—a wonderful afternoon ceremony held during its first week of operation attended by approximately 200 people, with welcoming speeches and cultural presentations by a number of community representatives.

In addition to the ongoing meetings of the Community Advisory Committee, the program also benefits from, and is directed by, the multitude of spontaneous, informal interactions with community residents and workers on virtually a daily basis—a continuous source of comment and feedback on the strengths and weaknesses of our program. Little happens in our program about which we do not receive ongoing feedback.

**Physical Location of the Program**

The planning group was adamant that the physical location for the program—classrooms, computer lab, meeting rooms, and work space—had to signal clearly our philosophical commitment to grounding the program in the community. It could not happen in a school or other institutionally oriented building. After some negotiation with residents and officials associated with a community center located in the middle of Regent Park, we were very fortunate in gaining the use of facilities in the building. This particular center (owned and operated by the Parks and Recreation Department of the City of Toronto) has always been a hub of community happenings, particularly after school and in the evening, a perfect situation that allowed our candidates to meet, get acquainted, and interact with residents of all ages on a daily basis. It also provided an opportunity for teacher candidates to learn about the larger community firsthand in a way that successfully cut across the traditional negative image that often afflicts communities like Regent Park. Only in this way have the student teachers been able to come to understand the strengths inherent in these families, the ways in which they individually and collectively live their lives, the ways in which they celebrate their successes, and the ways in which they struggle with poverty and other structural adversities in order to carry on.

Locating our program in the community and the community center provides benefits beyond just the student teachers and the program itself. Judging from the many comments of community members, having the university-identified program in the midst of their community is seen as a distinct advantage for several reasons. They see their children and the schools in the community benefiting from new teachers who have been educated in their community, and who have come to understand the community from the inside, rather than studying (and "othering") the inner city as an outsider. Indeed, some see their children as helping to support this special learning process for our candidates—in the community center, in the neighborhood, and in the schools where our candidates undertake their teaching practicum. In addition, many parents speak favorably about the visibility of a teacher education program in their community, and how it might serve as a model and incentive for young people in the community to continue their own formal education and consider teaching as a possible career choice.

## Staff Commitment to Collaboration and Community Involvement

The roles of the academic and support staff are also unique. In order to ensure the ongoing success of the program, the staff has committed themselves to a wide range of additional activities, both in the program and in the community, beyond their regular teaching and practicum supervision load. The entire staff meets approximately every 3 weeks to discuss, plan, and continuously evaluate all aspects of the program, including the progress of the individual candidates. Involvement in the larger Regent community happens in a number of different ways: (a) organizing and supporting education-related programs for local students, teachers and residents; (b) volunteering with direct-service groups; (c) sitting on local residents' boards and committees; (d) collaborating with residents and others in developing arts and recreation-based programs and activities in the community; and (e) organizing in-service workshops and courses for teachers working in schools in Regent Park and neighboring inner-city communities.

This is indeed a challenge for those involved with this teacher education programs as well as faculty in the larger university setting. In a university setting, the faculty is burdened with many other responsibilities; other teaching (undergraduate and graduate), graduate student supervision, research and development projects, university service, and so forth, not to mention the "publish or perish" syndrome. Clearly, a commitment to the overall work culture of a setting like the York–Regent program is not something that every faculty member can reasonably assume, even among those who might feel an affinity for its philosophical bearings.

## Diversity of Program Staff

Not every teacher is suitable for every teaching situation, and this maxim certainly applies to the particular community-based philosophical orientation of the York–Regent program. For this reason, the planning group was adamant from the outset that any and all decisions about staffing for the site must be made in consultation with the existing staff. Our judgments are as subjective as anyone's about whether the values, attitudes, knowledge, skills, and commitment of any given faculty member might adequately "fit" the "culture" of the Regent program. The degree of success the program has achieved to date clearly reflects the nature of the staffing.

A crucial decision made at the outset of the program was that the staff must be diverse, and that at least some must have roots in the community. To this end, this condition was "structured" into the program from the outset, ensuring that at least two staff members clearly reflect this background. First, one course director position (for the community development course) has been designated for a part-time, community-based instructor. This position rotates every 2 years, thus allowing the program to benefit from a variety of community representatives who both teach in the program as well as participate in its ongoing development. In addition, the permanent, part-time, administrative support position has been filled by a woman who was raised in the community, with deep knowledge and understanding of its residents (young and old), its programs, organizations, schools, and other institutions, in addition to its social history.

The remaining staff—faculty members who serve as course directors, supervisors of school and community practicum placements, and a site coordinator—are selected from both tenure-stream faculty and from "seconded" faculty at York. At the present juncture, three of these four faculty members were previously employed as public school teachers in the Regent Park area before joining York's faculty; the fourth was previously employed for many years with community agencies in the area. In addition, all brought strong backgrounds of volunteer work in the community (with direct service agencies, community development organizations, and local activist groups).

### Selection and Orientation of Teacher Candidate Applicants

York uses a number of criteria to evaluate applicants for admission: (a) their undergraduate grades, (b) whether they have a graduate degree, (c) experience working with youth in school or community settings, (d) reference letters, (e) a personal statement, and (f) an evaluation statement prepared following a personal interview. In addition, there is also a university Access Program, whereby applicants can self-identify for special consideration if they belong to one of four groups: Aboriginal, refugee, person of color, or person with a disability (physical, emotional, or learning). For their personal statements, Access Program applicants are also asked to discuss the structural ways that they may have been prevented from otherwise meeting any of the regular requirements for consideration.

Although these criteria are used in various ways by the faculty admission teams evaluating these files, there is no question that in the general admissions routines, university grades themselves often dominate these decisions. By comparison, the Regent Park team also place emphasis on what we believe to be other strengths, ones that might signal perhaps even more strongly, important preconditions for succeeding as good student teacher candidates and subsequent success as classroom teachers—particularly those wishing to work in diverse, multicultural communities. In particular, we look at the kinds of university courses applicants have taken (Do they reflect an interest in social diversity?), the community activities they have participated in (e.g., reflecting interests in equity and social justice), the ways in which their personal statements describe how they understand the school systems, and the reasons why they wish to become teachers. Is there some relationship between "scholarship" (as measured by GPAs) and "good" teachers and/or teaching? The research literature is very ambivalent on this, and there is certainly no consistent evidence to suggest that high GPAs necessarily lead to becoming or remaining good teachers (Caskey, Peterson, & Temple, 2001). Perhaps we are just as interested in why a potential applicant might not have placed (or been able to place) academic excellence at the top of his or her priorities while in the university.

Once the successful applicants have sent in their acceptance forms in the spring, they are enrolled on an interactive e-list. Before the program begins in late August, a series of program information updates are sent out and registrants are encouraged to ask questions, make suggestions, discuss concerns, and engage in discussion about such things as why they wish to become teachers and what they are expecting out of the program. Needless to say, this does much to help prepare candidates for the program.[1]

## Curriculum

Although the framework for the overall curriculum and course requirements for the teacher education program is determined centrally (through university regulations established by the provincial government and its agencies), we are committed to ensuring that the organization and content of the courses offered in the Regent program reflect its community orientation. For example, two of the official foundations courses, Communications and Human Development, have been amalgamated and refocused so as to begin from and build on the ways in which community in general, and Regent Park as an example, work to shape how we all develop and learn to communicate. Thus, this human and community development course includes a strong component of learning about the community and meeting with its representatives—parents, students, teachers, community activists, and so forth. Similarly, the two courses entitled Foundations of Education and Models of Education were amalgamated, and the broad themes that would be normally be included in these courses were introduced and examined, both through a wider overview and an examination of local community aspects of these themes. Thus, for example, exploration of the history of state schooling includes a larger provincial and/or national, and a local Regent perspective; sociological explorations of theory and data relating to social difference and social exclusion in schooling include both the macro and the local. Similarly, the curriculum and pedagogy courses—for example, language, literacy, and mathematics—were also developed based on community content and perspectives.

In addition to the formal courses, a number of other program components and activities also reflect our community foundation. For example, the first week of classes is constituted as a "community orientation week", with a series of visitors and speakers from the Regent community (parents, community leaders, activists, students, representatives from community organizations, etc.), intermixed with visits in the community—all leading to fruitful discussions on the students' reflections of these initial interactions with Regent Park. During the year, special attention is given to events that are happening in the community, and students are encouraged to participate in and assist in organizing such events.

**School Practicum Placements**

The school practicum (practice teaching) component engendered much discussion during the planning phases of the program, as we attempted to put into place a program that would balance two major objectives. We certainly wanted to meet candidates' perennial perceived needs and interests of gaining adequate classroom-based teaching knowledge and skills. At the same time, we wanted to ensure that the overall practicum experience reflected our concern that they gain a deep understanding of the broader relations of schools and schooling—in each classroom, but also in the halls, playgrounds, staff rooms, administrative offices, and neighborhoods of each building, as well as the crucial relations in extent between schools, parents, and families. For several reasons, this was particularly challenging. Given the seemingly universal penchant of many student teachers for the apprenticeship model ("less theory, more practice"), suggestions that they spend significant time in observing and questioning their surroundings were often initially resisted in favor of undertaking as much practice teaching as possible. To help ensure that their overall experience extended beyond the classroom—and as a result of examining all of the other spaces in which schooling interacts with students and families—a number of steps were taken.

First, with few exceptions, each candidate is assigned to one Regent school for the entire year's practicum placement, and they are expected to engage themselves throughout the year with all aspects of the school and its community: extracurricular activities, recess and/or lunch-hour duty, participating in staff meetings and other school functions, and with parents' meetings and school–community activities in general. In addition to host teachers, each host school also designates one teacher to serve as a coordinator for the student teacher placements in the school. Along with general coordinating routines, the responsibilities of this person include meeting with student teachers in the school on a regular basis to engage in discussion about their overall observations and experience, reflecting on the ways in which all of the schooling spaces and extended neighborhood also influence the ways in which students engage in their learning practices.

## Community Practicum

In addition to the other compulsory aspects of the program (university courses and school practicum), candidates also engage in a community practicum for a minimum of 2 hours each week throughout the academic year. During the first weeks of the program, candidates have an opportunity to hear from representatives from a number of organizations, agencies, and groups in Regent Park, and their possibilities for practicum placements. Potential settings involve working with people of all ages (from new mothers and babies, to teens and seniors programs), and although their choices extend across this range, most candidates understandably choose to undertake this volunteer work with school-aged children and youth. However, in order to promote their involvement in, and understandings of, the larger community, these volunteer assignments cannot take place in a school but rather must be situated in other community locales. During the year, the 45 student teachers are involved in a wide range of activities—tutoring or mentoring elementary and secondary school students, homework clubs, community sports programs, and so forth. These experiences, and the newly gained knowledge and understanding from them, are regularly discussed with their school practicum coordinator, and constitute a formal part of the weekly discussions held during their community development course. The final grade they receive on this course includes an evaluation of their practicum experience in the community.

## Teacher Candidates' Reflections on Experience in the Program

What are the challenges and implications for teacher education, and for teaching in urban schools, which emerge from our experiences in the York–Regent Park program? Do the candidates' experiences significantly differ from those of other teacher education programs? Will the ways in which they take up their responsibilities as teachers in urban classrooms differ significantly? Will they be any more successful than colleagues in other programs in working with social difference?

Reflections from the candidates themselves, after they have spent some time in the program, provide good insights into its impact. For many, their experiences in the program do seem to mark a significant change in the ways they have come to understand diverse inner-city cultures, and therefore the ways in which they see themselves and their responsibilities as classroom teachers. The narratives that follow are excerpted from their written reflections about 3 months into the program.

For most student teachers starting in the York–Regent program, the first false belief to be dispelled was one that many brought with them to the program—that Regent Park (and by extension, any inner-city, working-class neighborhood), was unknown, foreign, dangerous territory. Joanne's (all candidates' names are pseudonyms) initial concerns, as stark as they sound, were quite common among students when they first arrived (in fact, Joanne brought two friends along with her for her first trip to the site). "I must admit that when I first time heard I was going to a class in Regent Park, many of my friends tried to warn me of the dangers to my personal safety, which terrified me." However, she soon found herself within a "unique and special community." Similarly, Sam remarked, "since the very first meeting, I somehow felt very comfortable. I could see that there was no evidence to support the negative image given to this community by the media and other agencies." Maria added, "I never expected Regent Park to be such a warm, welcoming, and thriving community.... There is an immediate sense of togetherness, an unspoken bond that becomes visible as people nod, wink, or smile hellos as they walk by each other." To Mary, the process was clear: "The students I get to chat with in the community lunch room, the students I'm tutoring, people on the streets with whom I get into little conversations, and the staff at the community center, all are experiences that make me feel more comfortable every day."

Like Sam, this initial, positive experience allowed many students to reflect on all the ways in which their belief system had been wrongly influenced, and how it was that they had come to harbor such negative views. In addition to the obvious influences of the dominant media, Janet also quoted and reflected on earlier remarks of a teacher in a more upscale part of the city who had commented on her plans for joining the York-Regent program. "Teachers run away from that area, honey...I know people that have been stabbed and killed in schools in Regent Park. Believe me, teachers run from there...." Janet clearly came to see this "othering" process as being embedded even within the wide domain of public schooling itself, and caused her to wonder to what extent the structures of the school board itself played in maintaining this prejudice against poverty and social difference. Janet continues:

What the media said about the community didn't surprise me, but to hear a teacher, a role model in a school, speaking this way was shocking.... I am still wondering about my observation [concerning the lack of diversity among teaching staff], and if it relates at all to the bureaucratic systems within the school boards that are absent or not as prevalent in community-based organizations...

Other students reflected on how the program restructured the ways in which they understood social difference and their roles as teachers working in such cross-cultural settings. Mary noted that the program "allows outsiders to personally experience the community from within...[particularly for] individuals who have a passion for teaching, which means that they are willing to build relationships with children and learn from them.... We need to remain open and positive about people and things we do not understand." Similarly, Bill soon realized the ways in which he had to rethink his new role as a teacher:

I have learned that as a teacher I will be affecting the lives of people by the way I speak and act. From the students' perspective, I have realized that each individual learns in a different way, and has strong aptitudes in some areas and less in others. It is always an exciting challenge for me to create a situation with opportunities that maximize the potential for each individual's learning style and learning abilities.

Many candidates go through a difficult period of self-questioning, interrogating their own identity and position in this context. For example, several weeks into the program, Antonio questioned his role:

Poverty is one of the challenges that faces some of the residents in Regent Park. As an individual who has never experienced poverty, how can I connect with these students? I wonder how these kids look at us TCs [Teacher Candidates], and whether they harbor resentment toward us because we grew up under different circumstances. At times I feel inadequate because I did not experience some of the challenges in learning that they do. Does one have to be a Bill [pseudonym for his Black host teacher who himself was raised in Regent Park] to make significant impacts on an impoverished community, or can I make one too?

However, as each year progresses, candidates come to understand the complex contexts of Regent Park and the need to adopt something other than the traditional "top–down" approach to teaching in diverse communities. Not surprisingly, language encompassing the social relations of "power" soon enters the lexicon, as students come to see the nature of the relations—historical and contemporary—within traditional inner-city schooling arrangements. Jennifer explained how she had come to a "different understanding" as a result of being in the program and the community:

Because of my host school and my community practicum, I no longer see Regent Park from a "deficit" point of view.... Rather, I see how rich this community is, with committed, hard-working, decent people who unfortunately get a bad reputation from people who don't live and work in this community. Perhaps this is why some youth feel powerless....

Given his Caribbean background, Andrew understandably had an especially critical and adroit perspective on these relations of power:

Having been exposed to the ghettoes of Kingston, Jamaica, I was well aware of the media's need to exaggerate the nature of an underworld to sustain the status quo and create paranoia among the middle and upper classes. Hence, it was no surprise to me that when I came to Regent Park as a York University teacher candidate, there was a sense of open friendliness and communality so characteristic of so-called ghettoes and small villages in Jamaica.... [Very problematic are those teachers who] approach the area with the same manner of a Jane Goodhall or Louis Leakey anthropological expedition, portraying a genuine interest in the difficult ties affecting the area, but viewing the solutions with a missionary mentality. I believe that approaching education in an inner-city community with a neo-colonialist or neo-missionary attitude not only further perpetuates the "us and them syndrome" but also places the onus on the educator to be a "savior." [The] reality of educating youth in Regent Park is a far cry from some Hollywood melodrama of a "White liberal teacher" freeing inner-city children from ghetto despair; this is about recognizing the experiences of your students and how external factors affect and create barriers to education.

Perhaps Jane's reflections, coming from middle-class, middle-aged, White privilege, and penned even before the end of the first semester, might well serve to summarize and conclude this overall exploration—the reasons for envisioning a York–Regent Park Teacher Education program and the hopes of those who have worked to establish it.

The ten weeks I have spent in the Regent Park Community have had a profound impact on my professional life. I am infinitely grateful to this community for allowing me in as an accepted and integral member, and welcoming myself and my fellow classmates with open arms. I have been treated with warmth, understanding, and support.... What I am suggesting is that my sense of belonging in teaching reaches far beyond the basics of job compatibility and salary satisfaction. It extends to the very ideals that I hold in my heart. The community focus is exactly what I was seeking.... The time has come to deconstruct the stereotypes. Regent Park is a diverse, thriving community, with many talents and strengths, a true representation of our city. I will no longer be blind to White hegemonic thought. I have long considered myself to be a critical thinker, but how little I really knew or understood. Being a part of this powerful and wonderfully designed program is a privilege.

## SUMMARY DISCUSSION— LESSONS FOR URBAN [TEACHER] EDUCATION EVERYWHERE?

As noted in the introductory sections of this chapter, working-class and minority students have not been well served by many (if not most) schools across Canada and the United States. There are many reasons for this, but one crucial factor is the ways in which student teachers are (or are not) provided with the opportunity to explore these reasons in depth. To begin this discussion, starting with the concept of community provides possibilities for exploring, not only its own differential meanings, but also the ways in which our schools have not been successful up to now, in an manner that moves beyond the traditional "blame the victim" approach all too often in evidence.

To this end, the purpose of reproducing the aforementioned reflections of our student teachers is not to extol the virtues of the program per se. Rather, these comments have been reproduced in order to provide insight into how these candidates were able to "take up" a different vision about "inner-cityness,"—different than that which dominates the discourse of our North American culture, and, unfortunately, which also reflects the values and beliefs of too many (otherwise well-intentioned) teachers who work in the classrooms of poor and/or diverse neighborhoods across our continent.

To be sure, having different understandings of community is not sufficient in and of itself; our candidates and graduates continue to grapple with curriculum, pedagogy, school and/or school board rules, regulations and procedures, and with the dominant traditional, social, and authority relations within our public schools. However, many now do so with these different understandings in mind, and use these new values and beliefs to continue exploring alternative ways in which they and their colleagues can take up this responsibility more successfully. To this extent at least, it may be that the York–Regent Park program does have lessons that can be generalized across inner-city teaching and learning, wherever it is located.

## ENDNOTE

[1] In fact, in advance of the beginning of this year's program and following the e-discussions, one of the candidates arranged for those interested to meet at a downtown pub in early August—a wonderful event attended by a majority of the candidates and several faculty members!

## REFERENCES

Ball, S. (2003). *Class strategies and the education market: The middle classes and social advantage*. New York: Routledge-Falmer.

Barakett, J., & Cleghorn, A. (2000). *Sociology of education: An introductory view from Canada*. Scarborough, Ontario: Prentice Hall Allyn & Bacon, Canada.

Bloch, M. (Ed.). (2003). *Governing children, families and education: Restructuring the welfare state*. New York: Palgrave/MacMillan.

Caskey, M., Peterson, K. D., & Temple, J. B. (2001). Complex admission selection procedures for a graduate pre-service teacher education program. *Teacher Education Quarterly*, 28(4), 1–21.

Corrigan, P., & Curtis, B. (1985). Education, inspection and state formation: A preliminary statement. *Canadian Historical Review, 28*, 156–171.

Curtis, B. (1988). *Building the Canadian state: Canada west, 1836–1871*. London, Ontario: Althouse Press.

Curtis, B., Livingstone, D., & Smaller, H. (1994). *Stacking the deck: The streaming of working class students in Ontario schools*. Toronto: Garamond Press.

Davey, I. (1978). The rhythm of work and the rhythm of school. In N. McDonald & A. Chaiton (Eds.), *Egerton Ryerson and his times* (pp 221–253). Toronto: Macmillan of Canada.

Dei, G., James-Wilson, S. J., & Zine, J. (2000). *Removing the margins: The challenges and possibilities of inclusive schooling*. Toronto: Canadian Scholars' Press.

Fleming, W. D. (1972). *Ontario's educative society*. Toronto: University of Toronto Press.

Fullan, M., & Connolly, M. (1987). *Teacher education in Ontario*. Toronto: Government of Ontario.

Humphrey, D. C., & Wechsler, M. E. (2005). Insights into alternative certification: Initial findings from a national study. *Teachers College Record*. Retrieved September 9, 2005, from http://www.tcrecord.org

Ontario Department of Education. (1968). *Living and learning: Report from the provincial committee on aims and objectives of education in the schools of Ontario*. Toronto: Government of Ontario.

Ontario Ministry of Education. (1994). *For the love of learning*: *Report of the Royal Commission on Learning* (Ontario). Queen's Printer for Ontario, Toronto: Government of Ontario.

Pathways. (2001). *Background paper for pathways to education program*. Toronto: Pathways to Education.

Popkewitz, T. (Ed.). (1987). *Critical studies in teacher education: Its folklore, theory and practice*. London/Philadelphia: The Falmer Press.

Popkewitz, T. (2000). Reform as the social administration of the child: Globalization of knowledge and power. In N. C. Burbules & C. A. Torres (Eds.), *Globalization and education: Critical perspectives* (pp.157–186). New York: Routledge.

Prentice, A. (1990). "Friendly atoms in chemistry": Women and men at Normal School in mid-nineteenth-century Toronto. In D. Keane & C. Read (Eds.), *Old Ontario: Essays in honor of J. M. S.* Careless (pp. 285–317). Toronto: Dundurn Press.

Prentice, A. (1975). *The school promoters*. Toronto: McLelland & Stewart.

Toronto Board of Education. (1970). *Every student survey*. Toronto, Ontario: Author.

Toronto Board of Education. (1984). *Every student survey*. Toronto, Ontario: Author.

Toronto Board of Education. (1997). *Every student survey*. Toronto, Ontario: Author.

Wilson, J. D., Stamp, R., & Audet, L -P. (1970). *Canadian education: A history*. Toronto: Prentice-Hall of Canada.

# Chapter 7

# Thinking Outside the Box: Fostering Racial and Ethnic Discourses in Urban Teacher Education

Patricia A. Young
*University of Maryland Baltimore County*

The ability to differentiate instruction and teach a range of children is essential for in-service and pre-service teachers (Eisner, 1983). However, nurturing and developing pre-service teachers to teach in urban schools and communities requires additional tutelage. Teachers must know how to think critically, solve multifaceted problems, master content knowledge, and then transfer these skills to children. They must know what they know, be able to articulate that knowledge to children, and acquire knowledge they do not themselves possess. The role of a teacher dictates that they (a) provide a variety of instruction to meet content area, individualized, and group needs; (b) facilitate, monitor, record, assess, and evaluate the learning goals of each child; (c) manage classroom actions and activities; (d) handle the needs of students (physical, behavioral, emotional, mental, social, cultural, racial, ethnic, and linguistic); (e) and walk in the shoes of children.

Given these challenges, screening those who want to become teachers is imperative. The demand for teachers has brought forth people from all disciplines of life: retirees, career changers, bright-eyed recent graduates, and young adults who became captivated while in high school. This variety of applicants still remains homogeneous by racial and ethnic distinctions. Given this dilemma, educating pre-service teachers about the racial, ethnic,

**109**

cultural, and linguistic needs of children is imperative. These factors must be embedded as these candidates develop and engage in the art of teaching (Darling-Hammond, 1999, 2000; Darling-Hammond & Berry, 1999).

As the only African American female professor in a large elementary education department at a comprehensive state university, I was one of several minority faculty members hired to teach the multicultural education course. My role would be to unlock the knowledge, research, and practice within multiculturalism, and to make it palatable for a mostly White, upper-middle-class female student body. This task was further contextualized by the need to address the predominately Latino, Spanish speaking, urban communities where these pre-service teachers would begin their careers. Balancing the needs of pre-service teachers, the university, the community, program accrediting agencies, and my philosophy of educating the whole person became the challenge in administering this practitioner course. Most of my pre-service teachers had never been exposed to this curriculum. Occasionally, a student verbalized his or her unfamiliarity with this "new" knowledge and why such knowledge was excluded from their educational experience. I offered feedback, extrapolated where I could, and then redirected the students to further literature. What I appreciated most was the candidates' commitment to become teachers; this commitment was one thing of which they were sure. My job would be to educate pre-service teachers in a dose of reality.

This study examined whether the combination of critical pedagogy and culturally responsive pedagogy would aid in the development of transformative educators who could teach culturally and linguistically diverse children. Through the examination of pre-service teacher's responses at the beginning and end of the semester to an open-ended question, "What does it mean to think outside the box?," students' perspectives, knowledge, and growth are analyzed and articulated. This is an examination of one professor's lived experience and interpretation.

## COMBINING CRITICAL PEDAGOGY
## AND CULTURALLY RESPONSIVE PEDAGOGY

According to Biesta (1998), in the 1980s, critical pedagogy experienced a shift from the importance of class to that of race and gender. In the 1990s, other shifts emerged such as culture in and out of the classroom, identity and identity politics, and multicultural education. Biesta suggests that critical pedagogy has also engaged on a theoretical level with feminism, postmodernism, and poststructural and postcolonial theories. However, the effects of critical pedagogy on practices in the classroom have been debated (Biesta, 1998; Ellsworth, 1989). This study seeks to broaden the theoretical and practical underpinnings of critical pedagogy, multiculturalism (Ball, 2000; Obidah, 2000; Sleeter & McLaren, 1995), race, and ethnicity (Omi & Winant, 1994), and culturally responsive pedagogy (Gay, 2000) as a prelude to racial and ethnic discourses in urban teacher education. If all of these disciplines are aligned, then classrooms should be open for discourses in social, historical, political, racial, ethnic, cultural, and all other contexts. Thereby, pedagogy is transformed and the learner more informed.

Culturally responsive pedagogy seeks to analyze what we do as practitioners and how we think as educators. It is a place to look at "education for critical consciousness" (hooks, 1994, p. 36). This type of reflective analysis is consistent with what practitioners are required to know and to do as part of their work. Culturally responsive pedagogy is about "teaching, and the teaching of concern is that which centers classroom instruction in multiethnic cultural frames of reference" (Gay, 2000, p. xix). The critical components are "*cultural self-awareness* and *consciousness-raising* for teachers" (Gay, 2000, p. 71). Therefore, the focus of this pedagogical act is to create culturally responsive and critically conscious practitioners.

Like multiculturalism, discourses on culturally responsive pedagogy should always be seen through the lens of race and ethnicity (Ladson-Billings, 1996a, 1996b; Ladson-Billings & Tate, 1995; Mattai, 1992; Milner, 2003; Young, 2001). By racializing culturally responsive pedagogy, ideology doesn't fall victim to "Toon Towning"[1] the reality of race and racism in schools and schooling. That is, the articulation that "race" matters as a socially constructed phenomenon must be authentically represented in all contexts, particularly "culture-centered frameworks" (Lynn, 2004, p.160). To speak and act for children and communities of color and not acknowledge the impact of race and racism is to engage in "cartoonish" discourses about educating other people's children and perpetuate the "dominant racial ideology" (Omi & Winant, 1994, p. 86).

Critical pedagogy, as a historical, sociopolitical, and educational practice becomes transformative when it reciprocates through professor and pre-service teacher interactions. Theorists of critical pedagogy value the practitioner or teacher as a social and moral agent, a transformative intellectual, and a cultural worker (Giroux, 1998; hooks, 1994; McLaren, 1991, 1994). Thereby, pre-service teachers' culture, identity, and experiences are the foundation for their learning (Giroux & Simon, 1989).

Given the challenges of schools and educating children, teachers need to (a) be versed in the socially constructed experiences of their students; (b) understand how schools reproduce inequality; (c) acknowledge how the dominant society oppresses subordinate cultures; and (d) advocate against disempowering children, schools, and their communities (Giroux, 1988). At question is the connection of what teachers do and how they perceive, react, and articulate. In terms of educating future teachers who will, in turn, educate poor and minority children, there is much knowledge to generate, translate, revise, and discard.

Pre-service teachers should understand how the dominant culture denounces the cultural ways of being, doing, and seeing expressed by minority groups. They must investigate their own "cultural capital"[2] and explore their cultural histories and cultural experiences (Giroux, 1988, p. 7). These majority-raced pre-service teachers have to acknowledge and understand the power and privilege they possess; that as gatekeepers to knowledge, their cultural, racial, and ethnic dispositions can enhance or inhibit the academic achievement of underrepresented groups. Critical pedagogy asks pre-service teachers to expose the system that supports their economic, political, social, and educational well-being. They must see and understand domination, and refuse to be an active member in the oppression of others. This is a difficult task for the young and privileged.

Broadening critical pedagogy and culturally responsive pedagogy enables the flow of critical analyses in race, ethnicity, class, power, gender, and language within the context of schools and schooling (Gay, 1995; McLaren, 1994). Without the uniting of culturally responsive pedagogy, critical pedagogy remains an intellectual interpretation of the elite rather than a practical application for the masses.

## RACIALIZING CULTURE AND CRITICAL PEDAGOGY IN CONTEXT

African American women scholars and educators have been articulating their experiences in the academy (Benjamin, 1997), particularly the linkages between multiculturalism, race, and critical pedagogy (Ball, 2000; Gay, 1995; King, 1991; King & Ladson-Billings, 1990; Ladson-Billings, 1996a, 1996b, 1998; Obidah, 2000). Ladson-Billings (1996b) proposes that leading student discussions about race can be a conduit for discussions about oppression and marginalization. Students in her graduate course wrote short essays examining their identities. The students of color were quickly able to articulate their ethnic identities; however, White students were reluctant to respond, or chose other essay topics. Those White students who chose the topic *Identity* produced longer and more in-depth papers about "self" and other forms of oppression that they had experienced. These graduate students soon found an inclusive space for discussions of race, rather than focusing on perspectives of White guilt.

Ball (2000) and Obidah's (2000) research utilized critical pedagogy as a theoretical frame through which to articulate the empowerment of the individual and its transformation as they acquired a cultural knowledge base. Specifically, Ball (2000) focused on how three African American female in-service teachers implemented critical pedagogy to help children transform their lives. Each teacher participated in community-based classrooms where 98% of the children were African American. Ball found two key concepts prevalent in the instruction of these teachers. First, the teachers emphasized an *understanding of themselves* to all the children, who then reflected on perceptions of self in the context of society. Second, the teachers wanted their students to *be proactive in their interactions with the world*. Ball (2000) illustrated through the examination of "discourse patterns and pedagogical practices" the execution of critical pedagogy as a theory that converts into practice (p. 1006).

Obidah (2000) engages in a reflective study of her own classroom (a college level course titled *Education and Culture*), where she took on the role of a "critical multiculturalist," or one who understands the need to analyze multicultural education from a theoretical and practical perspective (p. 1036). Obidah framed her study in the research on critical pedagogy and multiculturalism. In a class of 29 (5 males and 24 females; 11 White, 9 African American, and 2 biracial), students began learning how to critically reflect on their ideologies about culture and education. Obidah used a variety of teaching strategies and tools (small- and large-group discussions, films, presentations, etc.). Through the promotion of liberatory pedagogical practices, students began to reveal themselves through discourses on identity and race. Obidah found that course content and pedagogy focusing on race, ethnicity, class, gender, and other forms of multiculturalism can be challenging to mediate within the class structure. Furthermore, as her professorial authority was questioned and challenged, she realized that there must be a negotiation of comfort zones by professors and teachers. Obidah (2000) carefully characterizes her experience in the role of a critical multiculturalist as "moments of resistance, reflections and revelations" (p. 1042).

King's (1991) research advocates that pre-service teachers develop "self-reflective," "critical," and "transformative emotional growth experiences" (p. 134). She taught a graduate Social Foundations of Education course that provided White students with a "liberatory pedagogy," focusing on issues of oppression in society and students' ideologies about diversity and inequity (p. 144). King situates her findings in what she describes as "dysconscious racism," a type of racism that implicitly accepts the norms and privileges of the White dominant culture. This dysconsciousness is further described as "an *impaired* consciousness or distorted way of thinking about race" (p. 135). King (1991) had 57 students respond to an open-ended question about the inequities between Black and White infant mortality. She found that students responded in uncritical and restrictive ways, thereby exhibiting this dysconscious racism. King suggests that teacher education needs a form of "cultural politics" that addresses the "cultural rationality of social inequity in modern American society" (p. 143). In this way, students can move toward a liberatory pedagogy.

This study, like Ladson-Billings', Ball's, Obidah's, and King's, expands the research of African American female scholars and the field of teacher education by offering insight into Black women's pedagogy, challenges, triumphs, and personal reflections in the academy. Moreover, it provides practical implications for actualizing a liberatory pedagogy, cultural self-awareness, consciousness raising, critical pedagogy, and racialized discourse—all of which are needed to educate urban teacher educators.

The work is more broadly situated in the theoretical framework of critical pedagogy as it seeks to learn about the relationship between pedagogy and power (McLaren, 1994). As future educators, these pre-service teachers are the purveyors of knowledge and power, and they must understand these issues from a macro- and microlevel. Through the analysis of pre-service teachers written discourse, an understanding of how power relations are shaped and transformed is revealed (Fairclough, 1995a). To become a transformative educator, pre-service teachers must rethink their individuality and engage others in inclusive ways.

## METHODS

According to Denzin and Lincoln (2000), qualitative research has evolved over time, and we are presently in the "seventh moment," in which the fields of social science and the humanities are "sites for critical conversations about democracy, race, gender, class, nation-states, globalization, freedom and community" (p. 3). This study operates within this traditions' attempt to engage pre-service teachers in critical conversations—discourses from pre-service teachers about racial, ethnic, social, economic, and political issues related to teacher education, and to thereby prepare candidates for urban schools and communities.

### The Course and Its Content

This research began at a comprehensive state university on the west coast with a population of 33,000 students. The teacher education program offered teaching credentials and master's degrees. The education program was accredited by the National Council for Accreditation of Teacher Education (NCATE), and state certified. The multiple subject teaching credential program for elementary teachers served over 1,000 full-time and approximately 40 part-time candidates per school year. Most of the candidates engaged in a year-long program of course and fieldwork resulting in an elementary education teaching credential.

I taught a prerequisite course in multicultural education titled Cultural Pluralism in Elementary Schools. The goals of this course were to (a) help pre-service teachers examine their beliefs and values, (b) explore the history of ethnic and racial groups, (c) expose pre-service teachers to classroom practices and materials that promote equity, and (d) demonstrate strategies for learning about children. This was one of three courses that focused on diversity, equity, urban schools, and children of color. The other two "diversity" courses, offered in the 1-year program, focused on educating second-language learners.

As a prerequisite course, Cultural Pluralism in Elementary Schools was offered during the fall, spring, intercession, and smmer sessions. During the semester, 8 to 10 sections of the course were offered. Given the number of professors, lecturers, and adjuncts who taught the course, quality control was an issue. Therefore, all course instructors used the same text: *Comprehensive Multicultural Education: Theory and Practice,* by Christine I. Bennett (1999). Some of the topics this text covered were (a) Multicultural Schools and Teaching, (b) Themes of Assimilation and Pluralism,(c) Theories of Learning Style and Multiple Intelligence, and (d) Multicultural Curriculum Development.

Through this process, it was hoped that all pre-service teachers would be exposed to the same curriculum content. I added supplemental readings to my course that provided a more in-depth examination of issues critical to educational research and educating culturally and linguistically diverse populations. For example, I incorporated a reader containing articles such as: Lisa Delpit's (1988) *The Silenced Dialogue*; John Ogbu's (1990) *Minority Education in Comparative Perspective*; Donaldo Macedo's (2000) *The Colonialism of the English Only Movement*; William Watkin's (1994) *Multicultural Education: Toward a Historical and Political Inquiry*; and Richard Valencia's (1997) *The Evolution of Deficit Thinking*.

## The Pre-Service Teachers

This study examined student responses from seven cultural pluralism courses I taught during the years 2000 and 2001. Five courses were taught in 2000 and two in 2001; four courses during the semester, one during intercession, and one during the summer. The racial and ethnic make-up of the pre-service teachers was 87% White, 7% Latino American, 2% African American, 2% Asian American, and 2% other.

## Pedagogical Strategies

Given that the course was designed to increase pre-service teacher's knowledge of diverse cultures in their schools and communities and to help them develop a multicultural perspective, a variety of pedagogical strategies were used throughout the course. In particular, the class assignments included lectures, discussions, group activities, student presentations, fieldwork, and opportunities for critical analysis of attitudes and beliefs. Student assignments included (a) weekly critical response journals, (b) cultural group presentations, (c) a multicultural children's literature project, (d) a case study of a second-language learner or a speaker of a dialect, and (e) the final research paper. There were additional assignments and activities that could not be mentioned or included. This analysis focuses on one culminating activity: "thinking outside the box."

**Data Collection and Analysis**

Pre-service teachers were administered an open-ended question—"What does it mean to think outside the box?"—in order to assess their responses on the first (pre-course) and last (post-course) day of the class. From the seven courses (spring 2000, intersession 2000, summer 2000 [two classes], fall 2000, summer 2001 [two classes]), 158 pre-course responses and 158 post-course responses were collected from participants. Responses without "pre" and "post" course answers were discarded.

Critical Discourse Analysis (CDA) was the method of analysis adopted because it "studies both the power in discourse and power over discourse" (Titscher et al., 2003, p. 146). The texts are analyzed using a variety of ways and means (Fairclough, 1995a). First, student responses were typed and categorized by session and date. Then the responses were examined for their "thematic structures" or their associations in terms of topics or themes (Fairclough, 1995b, p. 29). From the pre-responses, the following thematic structures began to emerge: single-dimensional perspective, bi-dimensional perspective, multidimensional perspective, and metamorphosis. Thereafter, the responses were coded according to these thematic structures. The same process of analysis proceeded for the post-course responses. The thematic structures retrieved from the post analysis became awareness and transformative perspectives. Once thematically structured, the most representative samples were included in this chapter. Explanations of the themes came from the analysis of the responses; thereby the analyses yielded definitions of each theme.

If texts are indicators of social change, then through Fairclough's (1995a) discourse analysis, changes in the text should be revealed through the thematic structure. That is, the text should exhibit changes from the pre-responses to the post-responses. The pre-responses should provide samples of pre-service teacher responses before instruction, and the post-responses should reveal teacher responses after a variety of instruction, facilitation, and assessment.

Participants responded to the question as an in-class, nongraded activity. They were told that there was no right or wrong answer to the question posed, and were asked to write their names on the paper so that their responses could be returned at the end of the semester. I informed participants that I was very interested in what they were thinking. I believe the question was nonthreatening, and that it was viewed by pre-service teachers as a typical class activity.

Generally, student evaluations from these courses were highly rated at 85% or better on a 100% (excellent) scale. The evaluations asked for student responses to the instructor's teaching, expectations, feedback, knowledge, preparation, clarity, responsiveness, and professionalism.

## Thinking Outside the Box: Pre-Course Responses

Giroux and McLaren's (1992) analysis of language and experience might best serve to describe the pedagogical strategies that translated from university professor to pre-service teacher. In this case, the majority of the pre-service teachers are from the dominate culture; therefore their learning must be that of agent, transformer, and activist. First, pre-service teacher's knowledge is viewed as a primary source and is validated within the context of the class. Second, they are provided with the space to critically analyze their lived experiences and how they perpetuate dominate forms of knowledge. Third, pre-service teachers are provided with spaces to articulate and reconceptualize their developing critical literacy.

Given that the pre-service teachers in this course were either recent college graduates or career changers, no assumptions were made regarding what they did or did not know. On the first day of class, I review the syllabus and take any perfunctory questions. During introductions, I instruct candidates to interview the person sitting next to them and then tell us something interesting and memorable about their new peer. At the end of the first day of class, I write the question "What does it mean to think outside the box?" on the blackboard, and distribute blank sheets of 8½ × 11 paper, allowing unlimited space for student responses. If time permits, students discuss their answers within a small group and then respond in a whole-class discussion. Through this process, student's knowledge is validated within the context of the class (Giroux & McLaren, 1992). Lastly, I collect the one-page responses with the intention of revisiting this question at the end of the course.

Although the question posed does not clearly define a direction, considering that the question was asked in a multicultural course, students connected their content specific responses to the course and/or knowledge they already possessed. I found students to be quite curious in this process.

The pre-course responses yielded thematic structures (Titscher et al., 2003), including single dimensional, bidimensional, multidimensional perspectives, and metamorphosis. The single dimensional perspectives focused on what the individual should do or be able to do with the knowledge they possess. Most of these responses were written in the third person; hence pre-service teachers distanced themselves from the topic or the class. The single dimensional perspectives presented a narrow point of view and demonstrated that further thinking in this area was required in order to understand one's cultural capital or acquire a critical consciousness. Alternatively, it could also indicate an answer provided simply to satisfy the participation requirements of the course. For example, many students responded that to think outside the box meant simply to "be open-minded." For example, Nikki G. exhibits this single dimensional perspective in her response:

> Thinking outside the box, means opening your heart and mind. This takes place when you are secure and love yourself first. To think outside a box is opening your eyes from the blur of convictions, prejudices, and stereotypes. To respect and forgive is how to think outside the box. (spring 2000)

Nikki G. uses the pronouns "you" and "your" to focus on what the individual should do. In this case, the individual should open his or her heart and mind. How a person does this is not articulated; however, it is assumed that the reader would know what this means. Nikki G. suggests loving and feeling secure about oneself. Therefore, the way outside of the box is a way that must be tackled internally rather than externally. A person should take off their "rose colored" glasses or un-blur their own prejudices and stereotypic dispositions, and show respect and forgive. It is not totally clear what Nikki G. poses here; however the mention of respect and forgiveness could suggest that this is what the person must do for his or herself and others. So the focus of the single-dimensional perspective is the improvement of oneself without outside interference. Change is, therefore, thought to come without external interference or interventions.

The bidimensional perspectives offered an interpretation that included individual focus and also a consideration of other groups of people. These responses demonstrated thinking into and through the question posed: these responses seek to provide some meaning and context for their answers. In this example, Angela H. contemplates the condition of thinking outside the box:

> Thinking outside the box is being able to see life from someone else's point of view. My "box" is White, American, middle-class, female. I think outside that box only when I can experience or attempt to experience what someone else's view may be that has a different box. Thinking outside my box is not an easy task; often some people never can, while others choose to think that getting to know someone different and experiencing

their culture, perspective, and life, in a nonjudgmental situation is help-ful. However, I do not believe one could ever *truly* think outside their own box, because it is within that box that they view and experience other's boxes. (intercession 2000)

Consistent with the bidimensional perspective, Angela H. begins to consider other people in her response, hence demonstrating thinking "into" and "through" the question posed. Angela H. personalized her re-sponse by race, class, nationality, and gender —a White, middle-class American female. She wanted the reader to know the position in which she was historically, personally, economically and socially rooted—that her identity was that which constructed herself and her response. Angela H. acknowledges that she has a choice whether to experience "someone else's view," and that this is not an easy task for a White, female, mid-dle-class American. However, others choose to engage "other" people because they find it helpful. This nonjudgmental engagement with "oth-ers" and their lives and culture is difficult for Angela H., and not some-thing she would do voluntarily. Angela H. ultimately sees her biased view of the world as one that will not change, because she is permanently af-fixed in her box and beliefs.

The multidimensional perspectives offer more complex responses that focus on the individual and group, movement beyond the box, and the box itself. These responses were more inclusive insofar as they spoke to both the individual and the group (e.g., one person, many people, one's own mind). There is a freeing or freedom of thought and space that is also articulated. The pre-service teachers describe it as being "free of judg-ments," "encountering new ideas," and "to stretch one's mind." The re-sponses specifically indicated how one can move outside the box (create new ideas or philosophies, dream, hang out with a different crowd, go to a new church). The box is quantified, qualified, and personified as that which isolates or traps a person. Participants describe this condition in terms such as *boundaries, limitations, glass ceiling, personal bias, identity, envi-ronment, language/dialects, social space, geographic space, ethnic space,* and *way of life.* In contrast, to be outside the box means that one may feel uncom-fortable or feel the need to be defensive. Judy K. exemplifies a multidi-mensional perspective in the following response:

The box represents the space one lives in—social space, geographic space, and ethnic space—anything that is familiar to oneself. To think outside the box is to go beyond what is familiar and comfortable, and to stretch one's mind. In other words, to step outside of the box and see what's out there. Perhaps it's something uncomfortable or disagreeable, but it's there! So thinking inside the box is like living inside the box and knowing only the rules and way of life as it is inside. (spring 2000)

For Judy K., the box represents the multiple spaces a person encounters in their lifeworld. The familiarity makes that space comfortable and safe. Thinking outside the box forces one to see in a new way. Judy K. views living inside the box as a way to isolate or separate oneself; this seems to represent a developing perspective counter to isolation.

The metamorphosis perspective demonstrated a focus on the individual, the group, and a knowledgeable interpretation of the question. This survey of responses indicates that participants considered both the individual and the group. They interpreted the question to mean that the individual or group must move either physically or mentally. Specifically, they defined this as: "transport myself," "imagine myself," "removing myself," and "thinking outside society." Given that the responses began to consider others in the context of self, they experienced a metamorphosis. For example, Carol S. writes the following:

> To transport myself outside of my own comfortable life that is filled with the expectations I have for myself, as they pertain to me and those around me. To engage in alternative thoughts and ideas that confront me that I may not have acknowledged, understood, believed, or to which I would not readily conform. To stop and imagine myself in these new or alternative situations, and begin to envision or exercise my role from outside my box. (summer 2000)

Carol S. demonstrates a metamorphosis perspective as she considers herself in the world of others, and a letting go of the box in which she isolated herself. Through her willingness to explore and learn, Carol S's interactions with this outside world shifts her thinking, and she begins to engage in a vicarious exploration of this new world. This new world is where Carol S. readily stays and chooses to participate in a role. Given Carol S's newness to the field of education, she continues to experience a metamorphosis, but does not grow intellectually.

As indicated by these four thematic structures, pre-service teachers provided multiple responses based on their existing knowledge base. These responses indicate that pre-service teachers sought to move their thoughts beyond the box; however, they did not have the words, context, or knowledge to expand their understanding. That is, they could not grow in thought or knowledge without acquiring new information or knowledge to build upon what they already knew. To grow or expand as human beings entails a process of establishing a foundation, and then allowing the learner to construct and reconstruct his or her own knowledge, thereby combining both knowledge and power (McLaren, 1994). I do not believe participants sought to give the professor what they perceived she wanted to hear. Further, the range in themes speaks to the necessity to refine student thinking to become that of an educator.

These pre-course responses revealed that a depth of knowledge and critical consciousness needed to be developed throughout the content of the course. Specifically, the pre-service teachers needed to move toward a more culturally responsive and critically conscious knowledge base about themselves and the people in their social spaces. They needed to examine their cultural capital as it related to the content of the course. Furthermore, I needed to help those who see the world from a myopic perspective to expand their view. My goal was to provide an environment where multiple perspectives from culturally diverse peoples could be heard, and to provide enough research where candidates could make decisions about what they felt was true or not. In my courses I believe that if pre-service teachers come to this knowledge themselves, then they are more likely to remember the content, more likely be able to translate it to others, and then finally be competent enough to teach it to others. I never simply pour information into their heads, but rather allow students the time to come to the knowledge on their own. I provide the artifacts and then ask students for a critical and/or reflective interpretation of the data. Through the content of the course, pre-service teachers are challenged to "move beyond" their comfort zone (hooks, 1994, p. 201). Ultimately, they must decide whether to move into, through, or beyond their box.

## THINKING OUTSIDE THE BOX: POSTCOURSE RESPONSES

On the last day of the course, participants again respond to the question "What does it mean to think outside the box?" Their responses are thematically structured as awakening and transformative perspectives. The *awakening perspectives* all reveal additive knowledge acquired through critical content reading and written evaluation, interactive class participation, active listening, conscious engagement, repetitive assignments, and high expectations for learning and/or the acquisition of knowledge. Participants demonstrate a desire to be aware with phrases such as: "I realize," "I now understand," "I felt," "I find," "I really consider," "I have come to realize," and "I was unaware." Here the word "I" is used in a self-reflective rather than egocentric manner. To transform self-reflection is one of the first steps. Candidates' responses also indicate that they now consider others on a physical, mental, and emotional level. To connect with people physically, mentally, and emotionally, pre-service teachers suggest the following: "Walk in another person's shoes and imagine or internalize their feelings..." (Natalie B., summer 2000); "Consider a person' cultural background and their reasons why they are who they are..." (Candice M., summer 2000); "Take the time to understand other cultural backgrounds..." (Kelly M., fall 2000); and "Extend far out of the box...learn about other cultures..." (Terry S., fall 2000). These excerpts illustrate an investment of time and energy in getting to know people who are different than themselves. In these examples, participants grapple with giving some aspect of themselves to get back knowledge, recognition, or personal satisfaction. This is the reciprocal nature of transformative educators. All these responses offer solutions or results-oriented reactions based upon their new knowledge. Pre-service teachers write, "If we expect to find solutions to the inequities that exist in society...this is even more crucial for future teachers..." (Natalie B. summer 2000); "Consider a person's cultural background... It's really a much more exciting way of life." (Candice M. summer 2000); "Coming to understand others is a step up to changing myself..." (Kelly M. fall 2000). Terry S. describes her awakening as follows:

> After learning the information I have through class texts, and hearing about experiences of classmates regarding multicultural education (and the need for it), I have come to realize that I have lived inside "the box." I felt I was open-minded and educated about aspects of other cultures, but I have learned that that is not enough to be multiculturally educated—enlightened. I am going to have to extend far out of the box by taking it upon myself to learn about other cultures rather than wait for the information to come to me—like the information that has come to me because I was required to take this class. I don't want to think inside the box. I was unaware, until later into this course, that I was in it. (fall 2000)

For Terry S., her interactions with multicultural research literature and ethnically diverse pre-service teachers have helped her to discover the sheltered reality of her box. Her enlightenment begins with her willingness to explore others cultures and their lifeworlds.

Terry S. feels responsible to take an active role in her learning. This type of active responsible learning is that which awakened educators must possess to become culturally competent and critical conscious educators. An awakening begins the process of transformation.

Transformative educators consider others before themselves, and this consideration is compassionate, caring, and critical. They use phrases like, "I found," "I feel," "someone else's," and "our." These transformative educators seek to understand all that people are and can be, and have already made a personal and professional commitment to improving themselves and the lives of others. They are selfless insofar as they critically understand, interpret, and postulate the differential world of others and themselves, and incorporate an intellectuality that transcends "into, through and beyond." For example, Cassay J. exhibits "into, through, and beyond" as she describes her emotional connection with others:

> Thinking outside the box means to live, experience, and understand someone else's perspectives in order to be agents of transforming lives

into a better one. Thinking outside the box means loving people, having a commitment to people, believing and having faith in people's capabilities, and being humble to not impose our own views and perspectives on others. Thinking outside the box means finding a common ground to be on along with various people with various backgrounds and beliefs. (summer 2001)

Cassay J. exhibits qualities of a transformative educator in her desire to emotionally and spiritually connect to "other" people. Her selflessness reflects her willingness to put aside her own views in order to learn about and from others. This "common ground" is what makes students, teachers, and communities transform. Cassay J., like other respondents, speaks to pieces of this transformation; however, the transformation of the human spirit is manifested collectively:

> . . . having knowledge of other cultures is not thinking outside the "box." Having the knowledge, along with a realistic view of their social standing, historical context of culture, political fights, and endured oppression begins to go outside the "box." Just understanding these things is not enough. You have to take it a step further. You must embody this information and make it available to others. (Steven M., intercession 2000)

Transformative perspectives of pre-service teachers alter self and critically construct and reconstruct knowledge. They hypothesize about the "what ifs," and create new knowledge. Transformative perspectives revamp the self in the process of their own learning. Educators that transform, like Steven M., are also keenly aware of those who don't get it. As agents of change, we must also engage and help inform those who haven't acquired a critical consciousness or examined their cultural capital. This is the knowledge of empowerment. "To discover another's truth…" (Joanna N., summer 2000); "to be agents of transforming lives into a better one…" (Cassay J., summer 2001); "jump out of our own mindset and find the key to theirs…" (Lynn S., fall 2000); these are statements of transformative thinking. They exemplify a consideration of others in all ways; that as educators, we are responsible for active participation in the process and end products, and that we must be locksmiths rather than gatekeepers of knowledge.

Transformative perspectives demonstrate a reinvention of knowledge other than that taught in the classroom. Pre-service teachers in this course discover their own "ah ha," and thereby the knowledge becomes an organic growing entity in itself. This representative sampling of responses demonstrates that through a series of culturally responsive, critically conscious (Swartz, 2003), self-reflective, and race-based activities (Milner, 2003; pre-service teachers can begin to examine their cultural capital and move toward culturally responsive thinking, doing, and being. The hope is that these pre-service teachers will be more likely to critically analyze the macro- and microperspectives as they pertain to issues such as urban schooling, the hidden curriculum, standardized testing, race-based educational agendas, social inequities, and the like. Essentially, transformative teachers see the world for what it really is; they are not tenants of Toon Town.

## CONCLUSION

I did not realize the complexity of what a transformative educator should possess until the final analysis of the theme: transformative perspectives. My definition of *transformative educators* reads as follows: Transformative educators critically understand, interpret, and postulate the different worlds of others and themselves, and incorporate an intellectuality that transcends "into, through, and beyond"; their practice is always culturally responsive and critically conscious. McLaren (1994) and Giroux (1988) understand the transformative intellectual as the teacher who engages in a special social or political practice. Gay (2000) argues for the transformation of student thinking; and hooks (1994) advocates for a classroom where "transformative pedagogy" takes place (p. 39). The transfer of emancipatory knowledge can only happen when teacher educators and pre-service teachers work together in the transformation process. Thereby, an understanding of the relationship between power and knowledge can be realized on macro- and microlevels (McLaren, 1994).

The transformative educator is an individual who can take the knowledge they acquire along the way and extrapolate the good, critically analyze the bad, and then teach others the rewards and repercussions. These educators are not static beings; they are always learning and relearning. They speak from informed perspectives, and guide others to new knowledge. They transform human beings in an effort to change the world for the better.

Transformative educators have lifelong awakenings that transcend them as human beings. They continue to strive toward cultural consciousness, to search for meaning. Transformative educators never cease to amaze themselves; they are always creative, critical, conscious, and crazed about the work they do. To transform means to reinvent oneself and the knowledge that an individual possesses. A transformative educator is active and visionary.

## THE PRACTICE

When teaching a multicultural education course, it is imperative to use a variety of instructional strategies that focus on enhancing and altering candidate's perceptions and ideologies. Throughout this course, participants were exposed to racially, ethnically, historically, and culturally specific curriculum content with the goal of developing a racialized lens in which to begin seeing the world. Through the analysis of self, culture, race, and language, they learn how to relate better with people who are socially different (Gay, 2000). Thereby, pre-service teachers are "developing sociocivic skills for effective membership in multicultural [urban] communities" (Gay, 2000, p. 20). Ultimately, the goal should be to get pre-service teachers to reflect on their beliefs, values, perceptions, prejudices, and biases, and to reevaluate inaccurate and negative assumptions. They must critically analyze the knowledge they acquire and disseminate.

In order to create racial and ethnic discourse in the teacher education classroom, I suggest the following:

- Have pre-service teachers acknowledge their ethnicity and engage in some discussion of cultural capital. They must invest in discovering their ethnic origins, so have them share their own ethnic and racial experiences. Invite yourself into the conversation only after participants have shared their experiences or when needed, but keep it brief. Connect your discussions to those of participants, and avoid the limelight.
- Create an environment where student's knowledge, experience, and histories are validated and supported.
- Provide a variety of assignments and activities where pre-service teachers discover their biases, dispositions, attitudes, and feelings. Create conditions for those with ethnocentric attitudes and behaviors to self-discover. In doing so, students will hopefully engage in introspection and evaluate whether teaching culturally and linguistically diverse populations is within their capacity.
- Facilitate discussions, activities, assignments, and so forth. It is best not to overlecture in these types of courses; this allows the group to construct and generate their own knowledge. If pre-service teachers generate knowledge themselves, they retain it longer.
- Allow a variety of activities where pre-service teachers can voice their opinions and engage in fact-finding, and stimulating awakenings. An awakening is more conducive to retention than those ideas and concepts that are memorized. Be a resource, not a road map; let candidates find their own awakenings. An awakening is a lifelong journey, not a semester's event.

## COMBINING CULTURALLY RESPONSIVE AND CRITICALLY CONSCIOUS PRACTITIONERS THROUGH RACE

Combining culturally responsive pedagogy and critical pedagogy seeks to help pre-service teachers develop "critical knowledge" (Giroux, 1988, p.

8). The knowledge acquired through the implementation of culturally responsive pedagogy and critical pedagogy develops an educator who is prepared to teach diverse, urban populations. "Schools need prospective teachers who are both theoreticians and practitioners, who can combine theory, imagination and techniques" (Giroux, 1988, p. 8). Therefore, combining these practices can provide pre-service teachers with the comprehensive critical content needed to move their perspectives from single dimensional, through metamorphosis to awareness, and finally, evolving transformative educators.

Pre-service teachers must be taught to "think racially." As some teachers, professors, politicians, and policymakers see learning about multiculturalism as a necessity, discussions about racism are seen as the unnecessary evil. Many "White pre-service teachers" denounce the history of racism in the United States as not their problem, and refuse to see how the past informs the present. This suffering, and the knowledge that it brings, must be acknowledged by all. hooks (1994) argues there is a "particular knowledge that comes from suffering" (p. 91). I would add that those who don't know of this suffering must use their experiential concepts of *suffering* to step out of themselves and understand the suffering of others. Consequently, they must engage in a vicarious, spiritual form of suffering—of consciousness to be able to transform the lives of poor and minority children.

## ENDNOTES

[1] Toon comes from the word, "cartoon." *Toon Towning* is a metaphor for engaging in acts of colorblindness, racial oppression, racial discrimination, racial profiling, and so forth. Therefore, the enactment means that the purveyor ignores reality and engages in a cartoonish representation of reality. Toon Town is the place where toon towning manifests.

[2] *Cultural capital* is when a society "distributes and legitimates certain forms of knowledge, language practices, values, modes of style" (Giroux, 1988, p. 5). Those forms that receive high value are deemed legitimate where others are seen as inferior. Cultural capital in schools can also be defined as ways groups socialize, walk, talk, act, move, dress, and behave. Schools are the place where class distinctions and the dominant societies culture are defined, articulated and enacted (Giroux, 1988).

## REFERENCES

Ball, A. F. (2000). Empowering pedagogies that enhance the learning of multicultural students. *Teachers College Record, 102*(6), 1006–1034.

Benjamin, L. (Ed.). (1997). *Black women in the academy: Promises and perils*. Gainsville: University Press of Florida.

Bennett, C. I. (1999). *Comprehensive multicultural education: Theory and practice* (4th ed.). Boston: Allyn & Bacon.

Biesta, G. J. (1998). Say you want a revolution . . . suggestions for the impossible future of critical pedagogy. *Educational Theory, 48*(4), 499–511.

Darling-Hammond, L. (1999). America's future: Educating teachers. *Education Digest, 64*(9), 18–24.

Darling-Hammond, L. (2000). Recruiting teachers for the 21st century: The foundation for educational equity. *Journal of Negro Education, 68*(3), 254–274.

Darling-Hammond, L., & Berry, B. (1999). Recruiting teachers for the 21st century: The foundation for educational equity. *Journal of Negro Education, 68*(3), 254–280.

Delpit, L. (1988). The silenced dialogue: Power and pedagogy in educating other people's children. *Harvard Educational Review, 58*(3), 483–502.

Denzin, N. K., & Lincoln, Y. S. (2000). Introduction: The discipline and practice of qualitative research. In N. K. Denzin & Y. S. Lincoln (Eds.), *Handbook of qualitative research* (2nd ed., pp. 1–28). Thousand Oaks, CA: Sage.

Eisner, E. (1983). The art and craft of teaching. *Educational Leadership, 40,* 4–13.

Ellsworth, E. (1989). Why doesn't this feel empowering? Working through the repressive myths of critical pedagogy. *Harvard Educational Review, 59*(3), 297–324.

Fairclough, N. (1995a). *Discourse and social change.* Cambridge: Blackwell.

Fairclough, N. (1995b). *Media discourse.* London: Edward Arnold.

Gay, G. (1995). Mirror images on common issues: Parallels between multicultural education and critical pedagogy. In C. E. Sleeter & P. L. McLaren (Eds.), *Multicultural education, critical pedagogy, and the politics of difference* (pp. 155–189). Albany: State University of New York Press.

Gay, G. (2000). *Culturally responsive teaching.* New York: Teachers College Press.

Giroux, H. A. (1988). *Teachers as intellectuals: Toward a critical pedagogy of learning.* New York: Bergin & Garvey.

Giroux, H. A., & McLaren, P. (1992). Writing from the margins: Geographies of identity, pedagogy and power. *Journal of Education, 174*(1), 7–24.

Giroux, H. A., & Simon, R. I. (1989). Popular culture as pedagogy of pleasure and meaning. In H. A. Giroux & R. I. Simon (Eds.), *Popular culture, schooling and everyday life* (pp. 1–29). New York: Bergin & Garvey.

hooks, B. (1994). *Teaching to transgress: Education as the practice of freedom.* New York: Routledge.

King, J. E. (1991). Dysconscious racism: Ideology, identity and the miseducation of teachers. *Journal of Negro Education, 60*(2), 133–146.

King, J., & Ladson-Billings, G. (1990). The teacher education challenge in elite university settings: Developing critical perspectives for teaching in a democratic and multicultural society. *The European Journal of Intercultural Studies, 1*(2), 15–30.

Ladson-Billings, G. (1996a, Spring). Silences as weapons: Challenges of a Black professor teaching White students. *Theory into practice, 35*(2), 79–85.

Ladson-Billings, G. (1996b, Autumn). "Your blues ain't like mine": Keeping issues of race and racism on the multicultural agenda. *Theory into Practice, 35*(4), 248–255.

Ladson-Billings, G. (1998). Just what is critical race theory and what's it doing in a nice field like education? *Qualitative Studies in Education, 11*(1), 7–24.

Ladson-Billings, G., & Tate, W. (1995). Toward a critical race theory of education. *Teachers College Record, 97*(1), 47–68.

Lynn, M. (2004). Inserting the 'race' into critical pedagogy: An analysis of 'race-based epistemologies.'*Educational Philosophy and Theory, 36*(2), 153–165.

Macedo, D. (2000). The colonialism of the English only movement. *Educational Researcher, 29* (3), 15–24.

Mattai, P. R. (1992). Rethinking the nature of multicultural education: Has it lost its focus or is it being misused? *Journal of Negro Education, 61*(1), 65–77.

McLaren, P. (1991). Critical pedagogy, multiculturalism, and the politics of risk and resistance: A response to Kelly and Portelli. *Journal of Education, 173*(3), 29–31.

McLaren, P. (1994). *Life in schools: An introduction to critical pedagogy in the foundations of education* (2nd ed.). White Plains: Longman.

Milner, H. R. (2003). Reflection, racial competence, and critical pedagogy: How do we prepare pre-service teachers to pose tough questions? *Race, Ethnicity and Education, 6*(2), 193–208.

Obidah, J. B. (2000). Mediating boundaries of race, class and professorial authority as a critical multiculturalist. *Teachers College Record, 102*(6), 1035–1060.

Ogbu, J. U. (1990). Minority education in comparative perspective. *Journal of Negro Education, 59*(1), 45–57.

Omi, M., & Winant, H. (1994). *Racial formation in the United States*. New York: Routledge.

Sleeter, C., & McLaren, P. L. (1995). *Multicultural education, critical pedagogy, and the politics of difference*. Albany: State University of New York Press.

Swartz, E. (2003). Teaching White pre-service teachers: Pedagogy for change. *Urban Education, 38*(3),                    255–278.

Titscher, S., Meyer, M., Wodak, R., & Vetter, E. (2003). *Methods of text and discourse analysis*. London: Sage.

Valencia, R. R. (Ed.). (1997). *The evolution of deficit thinking: Educational thought and practice*. London: Falmer.

Watkins, W. H. (1994). Multicultural education: Toward a historical and political inquiry. *Educational Theory, 44*(1), 99–117.

Young, P. (2001). What's race got to do with it?: The dynamics of race relations in the Oakland teachers" strike. *Race, Ethnicity and Education, 4*(2), 125–143.

# Chapter 8

# Critical Pedagogy
# and Authoritarian Culture:
# Challenges of Jamaican
# Migrant Teachers
# in American Urban Schools

Carol Hordatt Gentles
*University of the West Indies, Mona*

The recent recruitment of some 600 Jamaican teachers to fill teaching vacancies in American urban schools adds new dimensions to discussions about preparing teachers for work in diverse settings. The fact that these are teachers who have been trained for work in Jamaican schools but who often have no prior knowledge of the sociocultural realities of life and schooling in the United States raises important questions. How well are these teachers prepared to teach in urban American schools? What programs or strategies can we put in place to prepare Jamaican migrant teachers to deal with the challenges they may have to face?

The impetus to recruit Jamaican teachers comes from the growing problem of teacher shortages in North American schools. It has been estimated that due to growing enrollments, decreased class sizes, and high rates of retirement, the United States will need over 2.5 million teachers over the next 10 years (Butty, 2003; National Center for Educational Statistics, 2000). The problem is exacerbated in poor urban communities, where problematic social and economic conditions make it difficult to attract certified teachers even if financial incentives are offered (National

**129**

Commission on Teaching and America's Future, 1996). To address this growing problem, teachers have been recruited from Canada, Europe, Asia, Africa, and since 2000, from the Caribbean. The most recent statistics suggest that between 2000–2003, Jamaica lost over 2,000 teachers to migration; over 600 of them are currently employed in New York and other American cities (Wyss, 2004).

Discussions about these issues have focused on the need to help Jamaican migrant teachers cope with problems such as poor and dangerous working conditions, inadequate orientation procedures, flawed relocation procedures, the stresses of culture shock, and biased immigration policies (Butty, 2003; Wyss, 2004). Efforts have also been made to recoup the social and economic costs of teacher migration for Jamaica.[1] However, there has been little discussion about the impact of Jamaican teacher migration on the students whom they have been hired to teach. Little has been said about the importance of helping Jamaican migrant teachers to become culturally responsive to the sociocultural realities and needs of their American students. This silence is a serious omission that is addressed in this chapter by critically examining the issues involved in preparing Jamaican teachers for work with urban students.

If we consider this silence from a policy perspective, we can appreciate how unfair it is to expect Jamaica's overextended, underfunded teacher education programs to concern themselves with training teachers for work in a wealthy first-world nation. But for the students it affects, this silence bears disturbing implications. The problems affecting students in urban American schools such as low achievement levels (Duarte & Reed, 2004), low self-esteem (hooks, 2003), and inadequate and decaying facilities (Butty, 2003; hooks, 2003), are not that different from the problems that plague inner-city urban schools in Jamaica (King, 2001). Students who attend inner-city schools in both societies live in communities marginalized by factors such as race, ethnicity, low socioeconomic status, "poverty, homelessness, joblessness, crime, violence, single-parent households, and drugs" (Haymes, 2003, p. 230). As marginalized individuals, their experience of schooling is one that renders them voiceless and challenged in their ability to bid "for social respect, personal dignity and autonomy from both parasitic State power and culturally dismissive society" (Gray, 2004. p.19).

This failure of schools in both societies to meet the intellectual and sociocultural needs of urban inner-city students is, in part, a reflection of the traditional and "technicist" rationalities[2] that dominate schooling in both Jamaica and North America. These are conservative approaches to teaching and teacher education that seem more concerned with issues of conformity, behavior management, standardization, and "credentialism" than with nurturing the intellectual development and human spirit of the child. They have produced institutional school cultures characterized by traditional and technicist type ideologies[3] that "subvert the development of democratic forms of education," (Solomon & Allen, 2001, p. 220) by limiting "opportunities for teachers to integrate into their curriculum and pedagogy their own insights, perspectives, and lived experiences" of the sociocultural, historical, and political issues that impact their students' lives.

Identifying the major challenge for reforming urban education as an ideological issue that is common to both societies leads me to reformulate the task of this discussion. I suggest that instead of identifying specific ways to prepare Jamaican migrant teachers for work in American urban schools, it is more important to examine the challenges involved in preparing Jamaican teachers to move beyond the ideological boundaries that limit their abilities to construct pedagogies that can be relevant and meaningful in any urban context. Thus, I suggest, the preparation of Jamaican teachers for the challenges of teaching in poor, urban schools should focus on facilitating movement away from traditional and technicist conceptions of teaching, toward the use of critically conscious thinking and pedagogy instead. This would mean engaging them to commit themselves to "the development of a culture of schooling that supports the empowerment of culturally marginalized and economically disenfranchised students" by transforming "those classroom structures and practices that perpetuate undemocratic life" (Darder, Baltodano, & Torres, 2003, p. 11).

The problem with this suggestion is that there are few, if any models of critical pedagogical practice in Jamaican teacher education programs (Hordatt Gentles, 2003). Thus, before we even think about inviting student teachers to become critical educators, we must focus our attentions on encouraging Jamaican teacher educators to develop the critical consciousness that will motivate them to practice critical pedagogy. It is even more important that we devise strategies to ensure that they become models of critically conscious practice–"living examples of the very kind of critically oriented pedagogical practices that they seek to have their students adopt" (Liston & Zeichner, 1987, p. 133).

I suggest this because in Jamaica, in spite of various curriculum reforms to encourage movement from authoritarian and traditional to more progressive types of student-centered teaching, we have had limited success with helping our teachers make the necessary paradigm shift. We are not doing enough at the pre-service level of teacher education to interrupt the traditional and authoritarian conservatism that colors the "institutional biographies" (Tabulawa, 1997, p. 191) of our student teachers. Through my own research (Hordatt Gentles, 2003) and professional work in Jamaican teachers colleges, I have come to realize that even though teacher educators say they support the use of nontraditional methods and actively encourage their student teachers to use these, they themselves continue to rely on traditional teaching techniques. Thus, their students have few opportunities to experience nontraditional teaching. Without models of student-centered practice, they have only their own lived experiences of traditional teaching to use as guides for their subsequent practice.

The purpose of this chapter is to propose a strategy for engendering critical pedagogy with two main objectives. First, it is designed to provide opportunities for Jamaican teacher educators to experience "transformative moments" (Shor & Freire, 1987, p. 34) that will motivate them to develop and practice critical and culturally responsive pedagogy. This will mean asking them to participate in workshop sessions that give them time and space to focus on thinking and theorizing about their own teaching and learning experiences using critical concepts as intellectual tools for analysis and reflection. Second, these sessions will be facilitated by an educator whose guidance models critically conscious practice as a means of demonstrating the intrinsic value of modeling as a teaching tool, and the importance of modeling critical consciousness and sensitivity as a means of encouraging the use of critical pedagogy.

However, before outlining this strategy and discussing the rationale that supports it, it is instructive to clarify my understanding of what it actually means to practice pedagogy that is critical.

## CRITICAL AND CULTURALLY RESPONSIVE PEDAGOGY

Much of the research on teaching for urban schools is grounded in cultural difference theory. This blames teaching methods that are incongruent with students' cultural backgrounds for the academic difficulties faced by urban inner-city students in diverse communities. Efforts to overcome such inconsistencies focus on developing culturally responsive teaching and teaching methods (Bartolome, 2003) and/or classroom management strategies (Weinstein, Tomlinson-Clarke, & Curran, 2004) that are supposed to help teachers connect the curriculum with their students' everyday lives. Duarte and Reed (2004) describe *culturally responsive teachers* as those who try to make learning more effective by using their students' cultures and background experiences as instructional vehicles. In response to these concerns, many teacher education programs are trying to improve the multicultural competence of teachers by offering courses to improve their awareness of cultural diversity, and equip them with dispositions and teaching skills that can be used to raise achievement levels of students in poor, urban communities.

I have some difficulties with this approach because its focus on identifying teaching methods that will work best with underachieving students reflects a technical rationality. This search for "generic" teaching methods (Bartolome, 2003, p. 409), that can resolve the academic issues of all poor students constructs the problem "in primarily methodological and mechanistic terms dislodged from the socio cultural reality that shapes it" (Bartolome, 2003, p. 408). It produces a sort of "myopic focus" on methods (Bartolome, 2003) that leads teachers to ignore the ideological and political dimensions of their students' cultural differences.

To become culturally responsive, teachers need first to recognize and validate the myriad of individual differences and sociopolitical and/or historical factors that constitute their students' cultural diversity. More importantly, teachers need to understand that it is not these differences—race, color, ethnicity, religion, sexual orientation, nationality, political affiliation, or social class—that cause students to underachieve. It is rather their individual and collective locations as members of culturally subordinated groups, and the oppression and dehumanization they suffer as a consequence, that compromise their potential to do well in school.

I suggest that the real challenge in preparing teachers to work in urban inner-city schools is to devise ways to help them understand and problematize their student's social and political status as subordinated individuals who exist in subordinated cultures. Understanding how students in urban classrooms become subordinated involves recognizing that knowledge is socially constructed and "deeply rooted in a nexus of power relations" (McLaren, 1994, p. 178). In our socially constructed reality, the knowledge of dominant cultures usually has "more power and legitimacy than others" (McLaren, 1994, p. 178). This is because dominant cultures exercise domination over subordinate groups through *hegemony* (Gramsci, 1971), a process in which both dominant and subordinate cultures learn to support the ideologies of the dominant culture through consensual participation in "social practices, social forms, and social structures produced in specific sites such as the church, the state, the school, the mass media, the political system, and the family" (McLaren, 1994, p. 182). In all these activities and experiences, the ideologies of the dominant culture are privileged over those of subordinate groups. Both dominant and subordinate cultures therefore come to accept the dominant knowledge and ideologies that shape their lives as natural and inevitable.

The key to helping teachers become capable of constructing pedagogies to challenge hegemony and subordination is to teach them how to humanize the educational experiences of their students. The theoretical basis of a critical humanizing pedagogy is Freire's (1972) belief that humans have an "ontological vocation," (pp. 20–21), an existential right, to become fully human. Freire recognized that in traditional and technical schooling, the privileging of the dominant culture's knowledge produces asymmetrical power relations, and the misuse of authority that serves to subordinate silence and thus dehumanize students. Schooling thus becomes an experience of social injustice and oppression that makes the oppressed Objects rather than Subjects of their own experience.

Freire believed that overcoming subordination by the process of humanization involved affirming and developing certain key elements of the distinctiveness of being human such as a critical consciousness of one's Self, one's historicity, and the world. The role of a critical, culturally responsive educator, therefore, would be to find ways to interrupt hegemony and subordination in the classroom by facilitating the emergence of critical consciousness and critical literacy, or the ability to "read the world" (Freire & Macedo, 1987). To do this the teacher would have to work continuously to renegotiate relations of power with his or her students by enabling students to find their voice.

In schools where power relations are asymmetrical, the voice of students, the way they are able "to use language to paint a picture of" their "own reality" (Wink, 1997, p. 58) and experience, is silenced by the dominant voice of the teacher. The critical teacher works to stop privileging his or her voice over that of his or her students so that they will develop the confidence to engage in dialogue. This is a process of sharing lived experiences in order to promote "social praxis that entails both reflection and political action…with the objective of dismantling oppressive structures and mechanisms" (Freire, 1998, p. xiv).

This rebalancing of power in the classroom through the expression of voice and dialogue facilitates the production and celebration of students' subjugated knowledge. By encouraging this, teachers work to make their classrooms democratic public spheres in which "students learn the knowledge and skills necessary to live in a critical democracy" (Giroux & McLaren, 1986, p. 224). Students get to practice challenging the status quo and their subordinated status, and are encouraged to undermine their own oppression and dehumanization by affirming themselves as the Subject of their own experiences. The confidence to do this is facilitated by the teacher, who demonstrates critical and cultural responsiveness by treating students with respect and dignity.

Thus, critical and culturally responsive pedagogy involves critically understanding, recognizing, validating, and respecting students' individuality, as well as trying to understand the political and ideological dimensions of their cultural location as subordinate groups in society. It entails recognizing that classrooms with asymmetrical power relations silence and subordinate students, thereby reflecting the oppression and social injustice of the wider society. Critical and culturally responsive pedagogy allows students to challenge the status quo through democratic activities in the classroom in the hope that they will apply the critical democratic practices they learn to their life in society beyond the classroom walls.

There are difficulties, however, with bringing visions of critical pedagogy into practice, particularly so in traditional, authoritarian educational cultures like those in Jamaica. These are ideological and theoretical challenges that we should take into account when developing strategies for critical change. These are discussed in the following section.

## IDEOLOGICAL CHALLENGES

Engendering critical pedagogy is not a simple matter of replacing one ideology with another. In proposing strategies for promoting ideological change, we need first to construct an understanding of the idiosyncrasies of the cultural contexts in which they operate—"why certain ideologies prevail at certain times and whose interests they serve" (Giroux, 2001, p. 161). This was demonstrated to me while doing research at a Jamaican teachers' college (Hordatt Gentles, 2003), in which I set out to critically examine its pedagogical culture. My objective was to use the cultural insights gleaned from this study to explore the possibilities for critical reform in Jamaican teacher education. I went into the study with the erroneous conception that if I found evidence of authoritarianism, it would be due to some commonly held authoritarian ideology that could be described, deconstructed, and then changed.

What I found instead was a pedagogical culture that was strongly traditional and authoritarian insofar as it was conservative, used a banking style of education (Freire, 1972), and was informed by a traditional view of authority (Giroux, 1997). It was also characterized by a strong tendency toward teacher centeredness in the choice of teaching methods, in its social and pedagogical relations, and in the cultural life of both teacher educators and student teachers. Yet, in spite of their heavy reliance on authoritarian pedagogy, many of the teacher educators voiced their support for the use of more progressive, student-centered teaching methods, claimed they used these themselves, and even insisted their students use them when they went out to schools for teaching practice. Some of the teacher educators admitted that they relied on traditional teaching methods but were forced to do so because time constraints, high student–teacher ratios, excessive bureaucratic demands, and poor physical resources made it very difficult to implement student centered lessons.

In trying to understand the inconsistencies between what the teacher educators practiced and what they preached, I recognized the powerful influence of a complex and dynamic set of collegial and personal ideologies that informed the authoritarian pedagogical culture of the college. These were bureaucratic and/or technocratic, religious, authoritarian, benevolent utilitarianism, and pragmatic ideologies. These played out on an individual and collective level to inform each teacher educator's practice in different permutations and to varying degrees.[4]

This dynamic ideological complex was more supportive of teacher centeredness than of student-centered teaching. Thus in spite of their better intentions to use more progressive student- centered methods, teacher educators continued to teach in teacher-centered ways. This unique sociocultural reality supported the resilience of authoritarianism in the college's pedagogical culture. It suggested that critical ideological change would involve a long and complex process of finding ways to give teachers the opportunity and intellectual tools to reflect critically about their own practices, and then to develop new, critical ideological assumptions about the roles they want to play as critical educators.

My research also pointed to the importance of recognizing and understanding "deep-seated interferences to transformative education" that may confound "the transformation of teachers and students from authoritarian to democratic habits" (Shor, 1996, pp. 28–29). For example, encouraging teacher educators in Jamaica to practice critical pedagogy will mean asking them to "teach against the grain" (Simon, 1992) in a traditional system. This can be lonely, and as Kohli (2000) says, "risky business." (p. 31). Teachers who locate themselves as radical practioners in traditional, authoritarian institutions may be seen as troublemakers. They may risk marginalization and other serious repercussions by their peers, their students and their employers. These are serious issues that may discourage teachers from choosing the critical approach. After all, the act of accepting and practicing critical and democratic values does not vanquish personal and economic needs for success within the bureaucracy in which one is employed.

In making the paradigm shift required to change from an authoritarian to a critical pedagogy, the teacher educators will also have to deal with their own fears, insecurities, and psychological discomforts about the process. The act of trying to use critical pedagogy in classrooms with students accustomed to traditional teaching may produce fears by teachers about losing control of their students or losing the respect of their students (hooks, 1994). My study showed that the fear of losing control was an issue for teacher educators when they tried to use student-centered methods. Being assured of their students' respect and deference was extremely important to them.

Developing a critical ideology means making a commitment to engage in a continual struggle for *praxis*, that dynamic space where theory and practice are united dialectically (Freire, 1972). This involves developing critical consciousness, a process of confronting one's historicity. Aronowitz's (1998) explanation of this process shows how difficult it is:

> The accomplishment of critical consciousness consists in the first place in the learner's capacity to situate herself in her own historicity, for example, to grasp the class, race and sexual aspects of education and social formation and to understand the complexity of the relations that have produced

this situation. Such an accomplishment entails a critical examination of received wisdom, not as a storehouse of eternal truths but as itself situated in its own historicity. Implicit in this process is the concept that each of us embodies universality but that it does not necessarily dominate us. Thus, the active knower, not the mind as a repository of "information," is the goal of education. (p. 14)

The critically conscious teacher is thus called upon to generate practice from his or her own critical consciousness. This is difficult and emotionally draining work because it requires the teacher to become critical of long-held and deeply engrained assumptions and ideologies about the nature and purpose of his or her teaching. It means letting go of beliefs about the best way to get the job of teaching done, and building new repertoires of untried methodologies. It means moving to a place of emerging "dangerous memories" (Welch, 1985, p. 39), ongoing theoretical and methodological tensions and uncertainties, a place to which many teachers are unwilling to go.

## THEORETICAL CHALLENGES

There are also theoretical considerations in strategizing to promote critical educational change. The difficulty with helping educators to practice critical principles is that the very essence of critical pedagogy is dialectical, and therefore should not be prescriptive. Although certain principles, such as commitment to the struggle for social justice and democracy, are outlined in critical theoretical discourse as essential in developing a pedagogy that is critical, these are not specific guidelines but stand rather as a set of theoretical parameters within which to construct and develop a critical pedagogical practice.

For critical educators like myself, who enjoy struggling against the currents of traditional and technicist views of schooling, the nonprescriptiveness of critical pedagogy is wonderfully appealing. But when trying to concretize possibilities for incorporating critical pedagogy into teacher education this nonprescriptiveness is also frustrating. How do we encourage others who work in traditional and/or technicist school cultures to practice pedagogy that, in order to preserve the ideological integrity of its theoretical foundation, resists providing the packages of curriculum objectives, strategies, and directives for assessment that teachers have come to expect? How do we justify the addition of yet one more curriculum innovation in programs like Jamaica's teacher education, where time and resource constraints are the bane of every attempt at curriculum reform?

The answer to this question lies in understanding that a teacher should not be asked to do critical pedagogy because it is part of a curriculum innovation or because it is a new trend. The real challenge is to encourage teachers to become critical, with the belief that teachers who engage in an ongoing process of developing their critical consciousness will become committed and self- motivated to practice pedagogies that are critical. In theory, the aims of a plan to encourage critical pedagogy would be to help educators cultivate what Wink (1997) calls a caring heart and critical eye that motivates them to:

- Value and nurture an ethos of critical caring, love, and respect toward their students;
- Become critically aware that oppression exists through silencing and marginalization in traditional, authoritarian classrooms, and that it is complicit in the objectification (subordination) of students and teachers, which denies them the opportunity to become Subjects of their own knowledge;
- Become committed to developing their critical consciousness of how this objectification (subordination) happens in the real world of their own classrooms;
- Recognize and practice the dynamic potential of critical pedagogical practices that encourage voice and dialogue as a means of overcoming oppression and social injustice.

In practice, as we have recognized already, such a process brings with it various daunting ideological and theoretical challenges. But these are not insurmountable. It is by increasing our critical and cultural awareness of the factors that may hinder attempts at critical reform, that we set the stage for developing enabling strategies, as now demonstrated.

## STRATEGIES FOR ENGENDERING CRITICAL CONSCIOUSNESS—PROBLEM-POSING AND MODELING

The preceding discussion suggests that serious attempts to engender critical consciousness among Jamaican teacher educators will have to work around and through the "real" challenges involved in trying to introduce critical pedagogy to educators who teach and learn in traditional, authoritarian school cultures. Many attempts at reform fail because they try to implement changes in spite of contextual factors. Thus, in the Jamaican setting, strategies for critical change will need to recognize first that this will have to be a slow, patient process reflecting cultural sensitivity to the difficulties educators may face as a result of their involvement. It will have to anticipate and work to overcome resistance to change by finding ways to make the development of critical consciousness an indigenous, self-motivated process.

The strategy I suggest is to devise and structure pedagogical situations in which teacher educators can experience critical pedagogy in action as modeled by a critically conscious educator and/or facilitator. The guidelines for planning such situations will be to provide opportunities that:

- Facilitate expression of voice and dialogue among small groups of teacher educators by ensuring that topics for dialogue and critical analysis are directly related to their lived experiences and concerns. This approach reflects Freire's (1972) "problem-posing education" in which teachers' relations with the world are made problematic. Participants will be increasingly challenged through the posing of various problems that relate to themselves in their world and with the world;
- Introduce teacher educators to critical concepts such as *voice, silencing, power, authority, privilege*, and *dominant* and *subordinate cultures* in order to provide participants with conceptual tools that can be used for critical analysis;
- Facilitate and celebrate the practice of democratic relations between and among the facilitator and teacher educators.

The format for these pedagogical situations might be workshops with small groups (no more than 12 to 14 teacher educators). In order to diffuse the tensions that may arise if the participants think the session is about criticizing their own practice of teaching, the focus for discussion can be a topic that pertains to their students' development as teachers, but at the same time pertains to them. This may increase opportunities for stimulating critical consciousness because the caring and concern the teacher educators have for their students in the situation ensures heightened positive emotional responsiveness.

Thus, for example, the topic for discussion can be the tendency for student teachers to use traditional teaching techniques, even though they are taught to do otherwise. Initial questions raised may include: What is teacher centeredness? Is it really important for us to be concerned with moving away from teacher centeredness? What will moving away from teacher centeredness really do for our students? As the dialogue gets going, the facilitator can guide the discussion to questions about the teacher educators' practices: Am I doing enough to help my students move toward learner-centered teaching? Are my own teaching practices teacher-centered? If they are, how are they so?

The challenge for the facilitator of the workshop will be to keep the proceedings as democratic as possible. This may not be an easy task because, as Matthews (1996) points out, although critical pedagogical concepts such as *voice* and *dialogue* are appealing, they are "thinly theorized" (p. 40) in relation to real educational settings. In theory, these concepts are presented idealistically as the given outcome of being invited to express our "dangerous memories." "Critical pedagogies rely heavily on dialogue and the presumption that if we all talk enough together, we will be able to come to understand each other" (Kohli, 2000, p. 38). But in real practice, this does not always happen (hooks, 1994). In many classrooms with people from different backgrounds, "multiple identities or subjectivities dramatically complicate the process of dialogue" (Kohli, 2000, p. 38).

It is possible that some of the teacher educators will simply not want to share. Or they may not be able to be rational when expressing their feelings or sharing their pain. The "myth of the rational individual in dialogue" (Kohli, 2000, p. 38) makes it hard for us to see that fear or reluctance to express hurts may hinder the creation of democratic spaces in the classroom. It will be important therefore for the facilitator to demonstrate sensitivity to these difficulties. One strategy may be to lay the issue on the table and ask the teacher educators for ideas on how to deal with them. This could become a full-blown discussion that examines questions such as: How do we ensure that everyone gets a fair chance to talk? How do we tell someone they are dominating the conversation? Should we do this? Should everyone be expected to talk? Is it fair to force someone to share? How do we encourage those who feel uncomfortable with disclosure to share? Possible strategies can be for the whole group to suggest and agree on rules for participation, for building confidence in expression of voice. The benefit of this approach is that by placing so much importance on nurturing and safeguarding voice and dialogue, the facilitator is modeling critical and culturally responsive practice.

Another challenge will be to keep relations in the workshop as democratic as possible. This will mean working to de-center the authority and power of the facilitator. Small gestures of physical posturing such as arranging seating equitably in a circle are useful strategies. It will be important to ensure that each participant's contribution is publicly appreciated by the whole group and valued as a source of knowledge by emphasizing the value of participants' experiential knowledge and refraining from privileging the facilitator's academic knowledge.

Finally, it will be vitally important to help the teacher educators construct self-confidence in their ability to use their stories to generate theory and plans of action to counter teacher centeredness. This will introduce them to the concept of *praxis* (Freire, 1972), "the intentional capacity to identify and implement alternatives" (Miron & Lauria, 1998, p. 189) that is essential in the process of bringing critical consciousness to critical practice. The teacher educators can be asked to devise some strategies for helping student teachers to de-center their practice, and then to share their ideas with the group. If the group has moved the focus of the dialogue onto their own practice, they can be asked to think of strategies for de-centering their own teaching practices. They can also be asked to identify any difficulties that they or their students may encounter in the process of trying to teach in less teacher-centered ways.

By the end of the workshop the teacher educators' engagement with critical ideas and concepts through the critical examination of questions that relate to the realities of their students, themselves, and the experience of being guided by a critically conscious facilitator in a democratic pedagogical environment will give them a foundational exposure to critical pedagogy. The workshop can end with the gifts of books that celebrate the practice of critical pedagogy. To encourage further critical reflection and praxis, the teacher educators can be encouraged to try out the practical strategies for student-centered teaching that they suggested. The facilitator can invite them to stay in touch with him or her and each other, via telephone, Internet, or personal visits. If they express a desire to participate in another similar workshop, the facilitator can agree to organize another such opportunity to engage in critical pedagogy.

## SEEING THE SELF IN THE OTHER— THE HEURISTIC VALUE OF TRANSFORMATIVE MOMENTS

A primary objective of these pedagogical situations will be to create possibilities for the teacher educators to experience personal "transformative moments"—moments of "transition from passivity or naiveté to some animation and critical awareness" (Shor & Freire, 1987, p. 34) about their own lived experiences. The rationale for working toward personal transformative moments comes from my strong conviction that all individuals who have been to school have experienced conditions of voicelessness, marginalization, and oppression. These are inherent to the asymmetrical and undemocratic power relations that characterize traditional and technicist schooling, regardless of socioeconomic location. (Students who are poor and disenfranchised are more likely to experience such conditions in an ongoing and more intense basis.) Thus, engaging individuals—in this case the teacher educators—in a process of critical analysis of their own lived experiences of schooling, and exposing them (through modeling) to alternative, critically sensitive ways of dealing with learners may trigger what Greenman and Dieckmann (2004) call "awakenings" and "first steps" toward critical consciousness.

This approach of awakening critical consciousness through invoking personal memories of oppression in the classroom sets the stage for teachers to become culturally sensitive and responsive to the needs of their students. Teacher education for cultural awareness typically relies on the premise that the act of making teachers cognizant of issues pertaining to cultural differences and diversity improves their chances to understand their students whose backgrounds are culturally different from their own. What this really does is to invoke a unintentioned "exoticising" sympathy for individuals from culturally different backgrounds that actually does little to diffuse the teachers' habitual objectification of their students. True cultural understanding means the ability to connect with—to see and read the world, through the eyes of cultural insiders. Outsiders of cultural groups that are perceived to be subordinate tend to engage in *othering*, a process of "objectifying people who are different than the...self in a manner that renders them inferior" (Villenas, 1996, p. 713). Overcoming the disposition to "other" requires the outsider, through a long process of cultural immersion and interaction, to move to a location of cultural insider. I do not think that giving teachers one or more courses on cultural differences and diversity is adequate time or opportunity to interrupt the habits of Othering and objectifying students.

This makes the challenge of preparing teachers for work in urban settings even more difficult. It makes the possibilities for preparing migrant teachers (whose period of tenure may be short-term) for work with urban students even more problematic. The key I suggest to overcoming this difficulty is to establish points of connection between students and teachers that stem from similarities of experience through the common condition of being human. By helping teachers to recognize commonalities between their own experiences of voicelessness and oppression in classrooms and those of their students, we are helping them to see points of human connection that can become a foundation for the development of a critical ethos of empathy and caring. In effect, teachers will be motivated through praxis to do critical pedagogy in spite of the ideological, theoretical, or situational challenges because in the oppression of their students—the Other—they recognize themselves.

If we can prepare Jamaican teachers to espouse and embody such a critical ethos, we can be sure they are prepared to teach anywhere and in any cultural situation. The humanistic understanding they gain from developing critical consciousness will help them to see and read the worlds of their students with a heightened cultural and critical sensitivity. This does not mean, however, that teachers who practice critical pedagogy are prepared to save the world! It does not mean that Jamaican migrant teachers who have been educated to be critical practioners will carry with them magic solutions to the problems of urban children.

Indeed, no amount of critical caring and concern can change the social injustice of the realities of urban schooling. As Bartolome (2003) so aptly says, "a teacher's political clarity will not necessarily compensate for structural inequalities that students face outside the classroom" (p. 413). What preparing Jamaican teachers to engage with critical pedagogy can do is to empower them so they can "to the best of their ability, help their students deal with injustices encountered inside and outside the classroom" (Bartolome, 2003, p. 413). They will do this by creating democratic, loving, respect-filled learning environments where students come to see and believe in themselves as human beings who have the political and human skills and knowledge to change their own worlds.

## CONCLUSION

When considered in light of the predicted massive shortage of American teachers, the discussion here is both timely and relevant. As long as the demand for Jamaican teachers makes them players on the American educational scene, it is critical for the welfare of American students that we pay attention to the type of impact these teachers will make. But making a critical issue of the challenges involved in preparing Jamaican migrant teachers for work in American urban schools brings several other important issues into sharper focus.

Currently, the source of migrant teachers from developing countries like Jamaica remains certain. Economic pressures and the opportunity to earn American dollars continue to make it attractive for Jamaican teachers to leave their jobs, families, and homes for work abroad. Until now, their arrival on the North American scene has gone relatively unnoticed. But, political pressure by foreign governments for compensation for the loss of their teachers, growing academic interest in this new phenomenon of "global poaching" (Wyss, 2004), and discussed here, concerns about its impact on urban students, are adding economic, moral, and political dilemmas to what until now has been a relatively simple solution to a pressing social problem.

This means that American educators will also have to look to themselves for ways to meet the challenges of American urban education. They need to see with a critical eye how the failure of American teacher education programs to prepare their students for work in urban school settings has negatively impacted American society. The reality of American teachers fleeing urban classrooms and abandoning students who do not have the option to leave is a social injustice that cannot be overlooked. Ironically, therefore, the questions I raised at the beginning of this discussion about the preparedness of Jamaican migrant teachers for work in American urban schools pertain to American teachers as well. Is enough being done to help American teachers develop the political clarity, the critical cultural consciousness, the ethos of love and caring, the determination to act as agents of meaningful social change, so that they too can be ready to meet the challenges of teaching in American urban schools?

## ENDNOTES

[1] In 2003, the Jamaican government (along with other countries who are losing teachers to migration) lobbied the Commonwealth Ministers of Education Conference for a more structured and just approach to recruitment by foreign

interests. These include requiring foreign governments to assist in funding local teacher training, and/or to consider setting up offshore training institutions that can produce teachers for export.

[2] Traditional teachers are usually conservative, often authoritarian, and overly concerned with social reproduction of the status quo. They see students as passive recipients of time-tested cultural knowledge that should not be questioned or critiqued. Technicist teachers approach teaching as a politically neutral applied science in which their role becomes "operational or technical, devoid of social or political contexts" (Solomon & Allen, 2001, p. 220). The effect of this approach is to "trivialize the relationship between teacher and learner by assigning teachers to the role of technical, value-free behavior manager" (Liston & Zeichner, 1987, pp. 26–27).

[3] Ideologies are "frameworks of thought that are used in society to explain, figure out, make sense of, or give meaning to the social and political world" (Donald & Hall, 1986, pp. ix–x).

[4] Students and teacher educators had been socialized by their daily participation in bureaucratic activities to subscribe to certain bureaucratic myths, such as (a) the inevitability of social differences between students and teachers, (b) the overvaluing of efficient use of time, (c) the importance of placing bureaucratic interests above those of individuals, and (d) the improbability of implementing bureaucratic change. Together these reinforced a bureaucratic and/or technocratic consciousness or ideology. The pedagogy of the teacher educators was also guided by a historically grounded colonial authoritarian ideology, which espoused the view that it was the duty of teachers to guide and control their students in order to help them improve morally and socially. Because the college was a Christian institution, it also embodied a strong religious ideology, which placed religious devotion at the core of daily activities. The lecturers' choice of traditional methods over others was also informed by an ideology of pragmatism. Although they said they preferred using student-centered methods, they stuck with teacher-centered methods because they believed these were the most efficient way of helping students to pass their examinations. Although pedagogical relations were traditional and at times authoritarian, social relations were generally warm and well meaning. Some lecturers demonstrated an ethic of caring and commitment that went beyond the call of duty, through pedagogy that reflected an ideology of benevolent utilitarianism. This was grounded in a concept of *social justice* that linked the use of pedagogy at the college to the goal of helping disadvantaged students climb the ladder of economic and social opportunity.

## REFERENCES

Aronowitz, S. (1998). Introduction. In P. Freire (Ed.), Pedagogy *of freedom: Ethics, democracy, and civic courage* (pp. 1–19). Lanham, Oxford, England: Rowman & Littlefield Publishers, Inc.

Bartolome, L. I. (2003). Beyond the methods fetish. In A. Darder, M. Baltodano, & R. D.Torres (Eds.), *The critical pedagogy reader* (pp. 408–429) New York: Routledge.

Butty, J. L. M (2003). Caribbean teachers in U.S. urban schools. In T. Bastick, & A. Ezenne (Eds.), *Researching change in Caribbean education: Curriculum, teaching and administration* (pp. 165–193). Jamaica: Department of Educational Studies, University of the West Indies.

Darder, A., Baltodano, M., & Torres, R. D. (2003). Critical pedagogy: An introduction. In A. Darder, M. Baltodano, & R. D. Torres (Eds.), *The critical pedagogy reader* (pp. 1–21). New York: Routledge.

Donald, S., & Hall, S. (1986). Introduction. In S. Donald, & S. Hall (Eds.), *Politics and ideology* (pp. i-x). Philadelphia: The Open University Press.

Duarte, V., & Reed, T. (2004). Learning to teach in urban settings. *Childhood Education: Annual Theme 2004 Olney, 80*(5), 245–250.

Freire, P. (1972). *Pedagogy of the oppressed*. Harmondsworth, England: Penguin.

Freire, P. (1998). *Teachers as cultural workers: Letters to those who dare to teach*. Boulder, Colorado:Westview Press.

Freire, P., & Macedo, D. (1987). Literacy: Reading the word and the world. South Hadley, MA: Bergin & Garvey.

Giroux, H. A. (1997). *Pedagogy and the politics of hope: Theory, culture, and schooling. A critical reader*. Boulder, Colorado: Westview Press.

Giroux, H. A. (2001). *Theory and resistance in education: Towards a pedagogy for the opposition*. Westport, CT: Bergin & Garvey.

Giroux, H. A., & McLaren, P. (1986). Teacher education and the politics of engagement: The case for democratic schooling. *Harvard Educational Review, 56*(3), 213–238.

Gramsci, A. (1971). *Selections from the prison notebooks*. London: Lawrence & Wishart.

Gray, O., (2004). *Demeaned but empowered: The social power of the urban poor in Jamaica*. Kingston, Jamaica: University of the West Indies Press.

Greenman, N. P., & Dieckmann, J. A., (2004). Considering criticality and culture as pivotal in transformative education. *Journal of Teacher Education, 55*(3), 240–255.

Haymes, S. N. (2003). Toward a pedagogy of place for Black urban struggle. In A. Darder, M. Baltodano & R. D.Torres (Eds.), *The critical pedagogy reader* (211–237). New York: Routledge.

hooks, b. (1994). Teaching to transgress: Education as the practice of freedom. New York: Routledge.

hooks, b. (2003). Rock my soul: Black people and self-esteem. New York: Washington Square Press.

Hordatt Gentles, C. (2003). *The pedagogical culture of new college: A critical examination of pedagogy in a Jamaican teachers college*. Unpublished doctoral thesis, Ontario Institute for Studies in Education of the University of Toronto, Canada.

King, R., (2001). Historical and comparative perspectives: Education and society in Jamaica. challenges and solutions. *Caribbean Journal of Education, 23*(1 & 2), 99–112.

Kohli, W. (2000). Teaching in the danger zone: Democracy and difference. In D. W. Hursh & E. W. Ross (Eds.), *Democratic social education: Social studies for social change* (pp. 23–42). New York: Falmer Press.

Liston, D. P., & Zeichner, K. M. (1987). Critical pedagogy and teacher education. *Journal of Education, 169*(3), 117–137.

Matthews, J. (1996). Radical pedagogy discourse: A skeptical story. *Curriculum Perspectives, 16*(1), 39–45.

McLaren, P. (1994). *Life in schools: An introduction to critical pedagogy in the foundations of education* (2nd ed.). Toronto, Ontario: Irwin Publishing.

Miron, L. F., & Lauria, M. (1998). Student voice as agency: Resistance and accommodation in inner-city schools. *Anthropology and Education Quarterly, 29*(2), 89–213.

National Center for Education Statistics. (2000). Projections of education statistics to 2010. (Rep. No. NCES 2000071). Washington, DC: U.S. Government Printing Office.

National Commission on Teaching and America's Future, (1996). Report: *What matters most: Teaching for America's future.* Washington, DC: Author.

Shor, I. (1996). Education is politics: Paulo Freire's critical pedagogy. In P. McLaren & P. Leonard (Eds), *Paulo Freire: A critical encounter* (pp. 25–35). New York: Routledge.

Shor, I., & Freire, P. (1987). *A pedagogy for liberation: Dialogues on transforming education.* New York: Bergin & Garvey.

Simon, R. (1992). *Teaching against the grain: Texts for a pedagogy of possibility.* Toronto, Ontario: OISE Press.

Solomon, R. P., & Allen, A. M. A. (2001). The struggle for equity, diversity, and social justice in teacher education. In J. P. Portelli & R. P. Solomon (Eds.), *The erosion of democracy in education: From critique to possibilities* (pp. 217–244). Calgary, Alberta: Detselig Enterprises.

Tabulawa, R. (1997). Pedagogical classroom practice and the social context: The case of Botswana. *International Journal of Educational Development, 17*(2), 189–204.

Villenas, S. (1996). The colonizer/colonized Chicana ethnographer: Identity, marginalization, and co-optation in the field. *Harvard Educational Review, 66*(4), 711–731.

Weinstein, C. S., Tomlinson-Clarke, S., & Curran, M., (2004). Toward a conception of culturally responsive classroom management. *Journal of Teacher Education, 55*(1), 25–38.

Welch, S. D. (1985). *Communities of resistance and solidarity: A feminist theology of liberation.* Maryknoll, NY: Orbis Books.

Wink, J. (1997). *Critical pedagogy. Notes from the real world.* New York: Longman.

Wyss, B. (2004). Global poaching: Jamaica's brain drain. *Econ-Atrocity Bulletin.* Center for Popular Economics, Amherst, Massachussetts.

# Chapter 9

# Confronting Postcolonial Legacies Through Pre-Service Teacher Education: The Case of Jamaica

Hyacinth Evans
Joan Tucker
*University of the West Indies, Mona*

Any understanding of teaching and learning in urban Jamaican schools must be culturally and historically situated. This situating helps to understand the kind of teaching that occurs in most of these classrooms; it also provides signposts for the changes that are necessary and the ways in which these changes can be effected. This chapter consists of two parts. In the first part, we provide the social, cultural, and historical context of education in Jamaica and discuss the problems of race, color, class, and poverty as they are enacted in urban schools. The second addresses the challenges that this legacy poses for teacher education and describes a unique course that addresses some of the legacies of this social–historical context. Based on the experience of this course, the chapter proposes ways in which initial teacher education can prepare teachers who are capable of combating the legacies of colonialism and the inequities that it brought about, and who are able to adopt progressive pedagogies and engage in respectful relationships with diverse students.

## SOCIOCULTURAL AND HISTORICAL CONTEXTS
## OF EDUCATION AND TEACHING IN JAMAICA

Jamaica, the largest of the English-speaking Caribbean islands, was a colony of Great Britain from 1655 to the granting of its independence in 1962. Between British conquest and emancipation from slavery in 1838, the society was economically and socially structured and dominated by a White minority. This society was socially and racially stratified, and has been referred to as the "slave plantation society." Whites, Blacks, and later browns or "coloreds" formed differentiated parts of a single socioeconomic system.[1] It was during the period of slave plantation society that the paradigm of Caribbean social structures was first laid down. It was also during this period that the "absolute identification between race, color and 'caste status' was established" (Hall, 1977, p. 161). After emancipation from slavery was granted in 1838, the former slaves were for the most part dependent on the plantation system and most lived in poverty.

During and after slavery, a social group emerged—the coloreds or browns who were the offspring of White men and Black women. This social and racial and/or color stratification has remained a feature of Jamaican life from emancipation through independence to the present day. Although there has been some social mobility for a large number of individuals, especially since the 1970s, and although the vast majority of those with political power are Black, this ideological structure remains and exercises a great influence on social and institutional life as well as on individual behavior and social interactions. The indicators of status, however, have changed over the years to include non-ethnic elements such as education, lifestyle, manner, speech, dress, and so forth. And the gradations of color can also be tempered by considerations such as texture and length of hair. But color and/or race remain the overriding criterion that is often combined with others in making social determinations.

Formal education began shortly before emancipation in 1834, when schools were established for the Black masses. These were the elementary schools, later named "all-age schools," which spanned what is now the primary and the first years of secondary education. The wealthy White elite did not send their children to these schools; they were educated privately at home or sent away to metropolitan centers. Thus the early school was intended to continue the socialization that the plantation system had earlier enacted through the social structure and social practices. Social stability in the postemancipation period required indoctrination in values such as order and regularity of work as well as acceptance by the different social classes of their ascribed statuses and roles. Teacher preparation was instrumental in the maintenance and reproduction of the social order (Turner, 1987):

Teachers colleges were established for the preparation of teachers who could play their role in this socializing process. Teacher candidates were trained to be morally upright Christian citizens who knew their subordinate place in society and who could impart the same values to their students. Many were also trained to accept their lower social status in a society that was rigidly stratified. And so part of their preparation was the acceptance of English civilized values. This meant for the mass of Jamaicans an acceptance of the superiority of English culture. (p. 68)

Independence in 1962 and the rising aspirations of the populace led to changes in the primary and secondary curricula as well as an increase in the number of schools, thus widening access to education. However, in several areas of reform, the strategy was to retain the essence of the colonial system without a fundamental break with the past (Miller, 1999). The structure of the system and its implied goals also continued in teacher preparation, although some changes were made to the subjects offered and the level of academic attainment in these subjects. There were limited changes made to pedagogy and to the process of learning to teach. In 1981, there were more substantial curricular changes, especially in knowledge of subject matter. In 2003, this program was again revised in order to make the college program more in tune with the new programs introduced at the primary and secondary levels. One of the stated aims of this revised teacher education program is to prepare teachers who are more student-centered and more able to address the needs of diverse students.

This brief review shows that colonial education served to alienate Black Jamaicans (90% of the population) from their own heritage, and was not designed to make them accept or assert themselves with pride as Black people. Although many who received this education did not describe it as such, colonial education created an acceptance of a distorted representation of both Black and White achievements. Whiteness, the British culture (their values, their entire way of life), whether in Britain or in Jamaica, were represented as more desirable, socially acceptable, and proper; what was African was denigrated. The discourse of race and color in Jamaica before independence marked Blackness and all its associations—kinky hair, broad nose and hips, Black skin, poverty and its associated lifestyle—with distaste. At the same time, the discourse created admiration and desire for everything with which Whiteness and brownness are associated.

Because colonial education was expected to socialize young people to this way of thinking, education in many ways reinforced the messages of the wider society; it alienated young people from their own history, culture, and ancestors. The psychological difficulty that results in denial and displacement, and the complexity of identification with the "other" have been described by Fanon (1967), Hall (1996), and Lamming (1983, cited in Lewis, 1988, p.

239). In writing of this dilemma experienced by Black Caribbean persons, Lamming made reference to a "fractured consciousness, a deep split in its sensibility…the psychological injury inflicted by the sacred role that all forms of social status would be determined by the degrees of skin complexion; the ambiguities among Blacks themselves, about the credibility of their own spiritual history…" (Lamming, 1983, cited in Lewis, 1988, p. 239).

This "fractured consciousness" was a result of the internalization of negative attitudes and beliefs toward self on the part of Blacks and their idealization of the other (European), what Hall (1996) referred to as the "internalization of the self as other" (p. 445).

There have been some changes during the postcolonial period. During the 1970s, this attitude toward self and to Blackness changed somewhat as a result of external influences such as the Black power movement in the United States, internal influences such as Rastafarianism, and the efforts of a number of Caribbean politicians and activists who sought to redress the social and economic imbalances of colonialism. In this period, Blackness was affirmed rather than denied by many and became an important signifier in the Caribbean identity (Hall, 1990). However, since these radical changes of the 1970s, there has been a shift in practices, allegiances, and expressions of identities beginning in the 1980s. Thomas (2002) pointed out that the class and/or color and/or gender and culture nexus has become increasingly unstable as a result of the infusion of the cross-class appeal of popular cultural forms and the influence of American culture. Although there continues to be class and/or color stratification, there is increased cultural confidence among the urban poor who have taken more social power within Jamaican society. And so during this "so-called" postcolonialism period, colonialism, neocolonialism, and postcolonialism as ways of thinking and believing continue to coexist in Jamaica.

This brief historical sketch has shown that race, color, and class in Jamaican society are manifested in complex ways. They create a social complexity that is peculiar, perhaps unique to Jamaica and parts of the Caribbean. This social complexity and the social differences among people exercise a hold over the psyche and the imagination, and thereby influences behavior. Relations between social groups are determined—perhaps overdetermined— by these factors. These factors exercise a powerful influence in the arena of social interaction in schools as well as in the wider society,. Any attempt to "de-colonize," to disrupt preconceptions, and to educate for social justice and self-empowerment is very difficult and complex, stemming in part from the fact that these attitudes are rarely discussed and admitted. In the public discourse, there is a silence about the self and Blackness and the value placed on what is European as opposed to what is African. Such discussions in public may be embarrassing because they may reveal the deep ambivalence of identity and desire (Hall, 1996).

So historically, schools served to socialize students to an acceptance of White supremacy and the undervaluing of Blackness. Teachers were important "socializers," even after independence when the society was contesting race, color, class, and later, gender. Following independence, major efforts were made to address this through the inclusion of African and Caribbean themes in the curriculum. Despite these curricular changes, the institutional culture of teachers colleges had difficulty changing, particularly the acceptance of the class and/or color and/or race hierarchy. Changes in teacher education have traditionally focused on subject matter knowledge, and have ignored the curricular activities that would enable teacher candidates to confront their socialization with respect to color and class and the social complexities that result from our history as a people. Until a reform in 2003, the teacher education system did not focus on the teacher's own identity and views of self and students. Today, although teachers are more qualified in terms of subject matter knowledge, they have not undergone a professional program that allows them to examine their views of race, color, gender, and the social and cultural complexities.

Attitudes toward Blackness and toward self-identity have not radically changed since colonial times, and society continues to subscribe to the neocolonialist values inculcated over many years —values that privilege a certain color and class. Within the school, this is evidenced in some teachers' relationships with students from a poor background. It has been shown in previous research that Jamaican teachers, like teachers in other countries, have difficulty establishing caring relationships with students from this socioeconomic level. Evans (2001) showed the many ways in which an absence of mutuality and respect between teacher and students can lead to a breakdown in the teacher–student relationship. In a more recent study of an upgraded high school (high schools that were originally established as secondary and junior high schools), whose student body is mainly from the low socioeconomic groups, Evans (2001) found similar sentiments and actions on the part of teachers and students. Only a minority of teachers—approximately 20%—were able to develop a caring attitude toward students. The other teachers display teaching styles characterized by emotional distance, controlling behavior, punitiveness, and verbal and sometimes physical abuse.

Why do teachers alienate students from economically poor backgrounds? The research has shown that some teachers have difficulty developing a good relationship with students who are different from them—whether on the basis of class or race. Yet the teachers in these upgraded high schools are, for the most part, of the same class and racial origins as their students. In a hierarchical society such as Jamaica, one reason for this inability to establish a respectful teacher–student relationship could be that society does not accord social prestige to parents and students from a low socioeconomic background. Teachers as an occupational group are not immune from the assumptions and class prejudice of the wider society. Their students do not have the social status that is determined by skin color and/or complexion, and the other nonethnic factors such as parents' income, speech, and/or use of the Creole, lifestyle, and dress. Many teachers may find it difficult to establish a caring and warm relationship with students who lack this status and whose expressive behaviors do not make them model students.

## THE CHALLENGE FOR TEACHER EDUCATION

In this second section, we discuss the challenge that this educational legacy poses for teacher education. It is now increasingly recognized in multiracial societies in Canada, the United States, the United Kingdom, and Australia, that White teachers must confront their own racism and bias in order to interact effectively with their diverse students. They have to learn about their students' cultures and perceive the world through diverse lenses (McAllister & Irvine, 2000). The need to learn the students' culture assumes that the teachers come from a different social and racial background and are geographically separated with very little knowledge of their student body. In making the case for this intercultural knowledge and understanding, critics argue that one cannot teach by relying on teaching methods and subject matter knowledge alone (Bartolome, 1994). Teachers have to care for students, respect them as persons, and be able to connect with them on many levels.

In the case of Jamaica, the teachers and students are invariably from the same racial and social groups. However, as Delpit (1995) pointed out, middle-class teachers of the same racial background can and do hold damaging stereotypes of poor children of the same race as themselves. Foster (1995), in discussing the education of African American students in the United States, has also argued "similar background does not guarantee productive, fluid or uncomplicated relationships between teacher and student. Teachers of similar background will sometimes judge students more harshly because they remind them of their former selves" (p. 575). So although intercultural knowledge and awareness is not as crucial in Jamaica as it is in situations where the teachers are from different social or racial groups, nevertheless, there is a need for teachers to confront stereotypes and to learn about the students as persons. Above all, there is a need for teacher education in Jamaica to allow teacher candidates to confront their own "fractured consciousness" (Lamming, 1983, cited in Lewis, 1988), and to acknowledge their own racial and ethnic identity. This is necessary in order for them to be able to able to establish good respectful relations with all their students, including those from an economically poor background. At the same time, there is the need for teachers to use a progressive pedagogy that acknowledges and builds on own students' experiences.

We now report on one effort to address these two critical needs—to develop a sociocultural consciousness and a cultural solidarity with their students, and to embrace new more progressive approaches to teaching. We describe the development, design, and implementation of a course that was part of the reform of teacher education carried out in 2003. This course was created as part of a larger reform of the curriculum, the main aim of which was to extend teacher candidates' knowledge of subject matter as well as to make them more prepared to engage in active participatory pedagogy. The course made the first step toward the development of sociocultural awareness—an understanding of self and one's biography that lays the foundation for the further development of cultural and racial awareness. First, we present some sociodemographic data on the communities served by the practicum schools in which candidates learn to teach.

## SOCIOECONOMIC DESCRIPTIONS OF COMMUNITIES

Jamaica, with its 2.6 million inhabitants, is a country of contrast—physically, socially, and culturally. The legacy of the colonial past is still evident in the sociocultural features of Jamaican life; communities are divided according to a marked disparity in income, wealth, and consumption. There are sections of the country, especially in the capital of Kingston, that compare with the wealthy sections of cities in developed countries, with large lavish houses and all the related accoutrements. And there are sections of extreme poverty where families of three, four, and five persons live in one or two rooms in buildings lacking basic amenities and that do not meet safety standards. Sections of Kingston that are referred to as inner-city communities are similar to inner-city communities in North America. Although the social divisions are not always along racial lines, over 90% of the population is of African lineage and the overwhelming majority of those living in poverty are Black. The national literacy rate was 79.9% in 2002.

The social and economic divide is part of the context in which Jamaican students live, a divide that can be explained in part by the structure of the economy that existed at emancipation, which relied heavily on agriculture. With only limited industrialization since then, there has always been a high level of unemployment. Many laborers migrated from the rural areas in search of work in Kingston, which now has more than one half the population of Jamaica. The poverty line set by governmental agencies in 2002 was $47,128.70 (roughly $800.00 in the United States) per person per annum. Based on these figures, the government estimates that 16.9% of Jamaicans live in poverty (Planning Institute of Jamaica, 2002). However, because this poverty level is set ridiculously low, the real incidence of poverty is much higher.

High schools in Kingston and other parts of the country reflect this social divide. There are 59 traditional high schools, many of which were established during colonial times and enjoy a high status among the Jamaican population. And there are 75 upgraded high schools originally established as secondary and junior high schools. For the most part, high schools reflect their history; their students are drawn mainly from the middle classes whereas children in the upgraded high schools are from the working-class and the urban poor. In most cases, upgraded high schools lack the physical and material resources of the traditional high school. The academic performance of these two types of schools has also differed, with more students in the high schools gaining passes in the regional Caribbean Examination Council (CXC) examination than those in the upgraded high schools.[2] In the urban areas such as Kingston, many upgraded high schools are in the cramped physical environment of the inner city. Some of these schools may coexist in close proximity with traditional high schools; in a few cases, they may even be located close to middle-class residential areas. Parents of students attending the upgraded high school would be employed in jobs that fall at the lower end of the occupational scale, such as dressmakers, attendants salespersons, small shop owners, cashiers, nurses aids, bartenders, drivers, security guards, janitors, or domestic helpers. Teachers who were born in areas such as these would not normally live in them. Many teacher candidates come from these communities.

## THE INTRODUCTION OF THE COURSE: THE EMERGENT TEACHER

In 2002, revisions to the teacher education curriculum became necessary as a result of curricular reforms introduced at the primary and secondary levels. These new curricula required radical changes in teaching methods. Teachers were now expected to be student-centered, to help pupils to use knowledge in new ways, and to construct their own understanding of their teacher education knowledge. Teacher candidates would use their experiences and "make connections between what they learn in all subjects, and between school and the world outside...and construct meaning for themselves" (Ministry of Education, Youth, and Culture, 2000). So the revised program had to prepare a new kind of teacher. It was expected that the Foundations of Education courses prepare teacher candidates with the appropriate dispositions and skills to be student-centered and help their students construct meaning, make connections, and solve problems.

This revision of the Education curriculum provided candidates with the opportunity to address other needs that teacher preparation had ignored in the past, such as a focus on the teacher as a person and their views of self and students. Some teacher educators agreed that it was time for candidates to examine their views of race, color, gender, and the social and cultural complexities of Jamaican society. Some teacher educators observed that teacher candidates exhibited the same lack of respect in their relations with low-income students as teachers had shown in previous research. Thus, the new course entitled The Emergent Teacher was designed to meet two critical needs—to help teacher candidates embrace new more progressive approaches to teaching as was required in the New National Curriculum, and to develop a sociocultural consciousness and a cultural solidarity with their students.

The development of the new curriculum was a collaborative effort. A steering committee composed of representatives of the teachers colleges, the Ministry of Education, and the Institute of Education (a department of the University of the West Indies in which we are both employed and that has responsibility for faculty and curriculum development) was formed to design the program and the content of each of the courses. Course developers were also members of the Ministry of Education, the teachers colleges, and the Institute of Education. The result of the deliberation of this team was that the new Education program would now comprise five courses, of which the course The Emergent Teacher would be the first in the sequence.

The 30- hour, 2-credit course had as its goals to help teacher candidates to:

- develop an awareness of the impact of personal biography on their attitudes and definitions of teaching and examine how their own biography influences their relationships with students;
- reflect on and critically examine their beliefs and assumptions about teaching and their roles as teachers;
- reflect on their learning experiences as students as well as current practices in order to understand how teachers' practices can have an impact on students;
- develop strategies for continued learning and to create learning communities as teachers; and
- understand their attitudes to gender and sexuality and the ways in which beliefs about these issues lead to stereotyping in the classroom.

The course was designed around three topics in three units—understanding self, understanding gender, and beliefs about teaching and the role of teachers. The method was primarily group discussions in class, with students given assignments to recall, reflect, discuss, and reformulate. In designing the course, members of the design team took into account research on teacher education, which shows that the student teacher's prior experiences with teaching, and the beliefs, assumptions, and definitions with which they enter college must be taken into account in teacher preparation (Lortie, 1975; Richardson, 1996). This research also suggests that when teacher candidates examine, scrutinize, and critique their initial beliefs and assumptions about teaching and learning, they are better able to reconcile conflicting beliefs and assumptions. Instead, when teacher education candidates do not engage in such self-examination and scrutiny, whatever is learned is modified to match initial beliefs (Richardson, 1996). Throughout the course, teacher candidates were able to reflect on both their experiences as students in Jamaican classrooms and their assumptions and expectations about teaching. The course also allowed them to examine their own personal biography and their beliefs about their own identity.

The evidence from the first presentation of this course suggests that it enabled teacher candidates to unearth memories—often disturbing and even dangerous—of their life as students, of childhood and adolescence, and of teaching and learning in Jamaican classrooms. College lecturers have reported that such issues were often emotional and heartrending. Perhaps because society encourages silence, many of these students had not had the opportunity to discuss these painful events nor the emotions associated with them, and some students required counseling in order to deal with these memories. Some college lecturers themselves were unsure of their competence in teaching this course because it required unusual sensitivity. Many college lecturers and students reported that this was a course such as they had never experienced before. The candidates found the exercise useful but troubling. Such reactions reflect the emotionally charged experiences of schooling and early experiences in Jamaica.

As outlined earlier, the course The Emergent Teacher focuses on the teacher candidates' reflection on their biography and their early experiences in schools. It also challenges them to examine their beliefs and assumptions about teaching—a challenge that lays the foundation for developing alternative ideas about teaching, learning, students, and the curriculum. But a course provides only a necessary first step in the effort to disrupt the preconceptions that teacher candidates have. Engaging in this initial course is useful in helping the teacher candidate to get in touch with the self, to recognize conflicts and contradictions, and to confront some influential social issues. It is necessary therefore that lecturers help teacher candidates make links between their experiences and the goal of self-awareness and sociocultural consciousness. This activity also helps to develop habits of reflectivity and self-scrutiny and to recognize the educational value of examining one's own experiences. Such a course is necessary in an education system that has never included such experiences in its curriculum.

The course The Emergent Teacher has given teacher candidates voice, and allows them to use their personal experiences as the mental and emotional frameworks through which they encounter new knowledge. It has made it evident to teacher educators and administrators that candidates' early experiences of school and home cannot be ignored in the teacher preparation process. However, if we want to address the issues of sociocultural identity and teacher candidates' ability to develop respectful relations with all students, it is necessary to go beyond the foundation that this course lays. Our proposal includes activities that aim at (a) the development of sociocultural consciousness, (b) of caring and affirming attitudes toward all students, and (c) the ability and commitment to work for their development. In this regard, we have been influenced by the work of Bartolome (1994), Foster (1995) Ladson Billings (1990), and Villegas and Lucas (2002a). The proposal below considers the role of the teacher in a post-colonial society, the critical need for a sociocultural consciousness, and the importance of having affirming views of caring and committed relationships with urban students from economically poor backgrounds. The proposal also includes a new approach to pedagogy and the link between such pedagogy and the overall aim of a progressive liberatory education. The goals include self-awareness and attitude changes with respect to class, color, and gender, and the learning of pedagogical strategies for teaching and creating caring and learning-oriented classrooms.

The seven-point proposal begins with:

- Create an awareness of oneself, one's beliefs, and values, and leads to following goals and activities described in the course, The Emergent Teacher.
- Create an awareness of one's sociocultural identity. This set of activities requires deeper "autobiographical exploration, reflection, and critical self-analysis" (Villegas & Lucas, 2002b, p. 22) with respect to the class, color, gender, and sociocultural group to which one belongs. Students are encouraged to examine experiences of inclusion, exclusion, rejection, attachment, envy, and desire that have accompanied these experiences. They examine their own and others silence over the use of terms such as *Black*. One aim of these explorations is to reveal the fractured consciousness—the internalization of attitudes and beliefs that privileges Europocentrism and that, if not recognized, will influence the behavior of the teacher toward Black lower class students. Teacher candidates' experiences, reactions, and sentiments are placed in a sociohistorical context. It is expected that at the end of this set of activities, the student will develop a cognitive awareness that power is differentially allocated in society and that there is a relationship between social location and power. They will also recognize that schools play an important part in creating this social differentiation and that the teacher's power and authority can be used and abused. Through these and similar activities, teacher candidates will recognize the political dimensions of education and begin to reflect on their political role as teachers.

• Develop and be able to demonstrate an affirming attitude toward students from urban poor. This set of activities is linked to the first set, in which teacher candidates recognize the political nature of teaching in a postcolonial society. To achieve this goal, teacher candidates confront and scrutinize their own beliefs about and attitudes toward students from poor backgrounds, who have a lifestyle that they as teacher candidates may want to forget, and their attitudes to language such as Creole (a denigrated language) and those who speak it. The method for developing and demonstrating an affirming attitude and/or stance toward students from poor backgrounds includes observation (e.g., videotapes) as well as case studies of such affirming behavior. To develop and demonstrate affirming attitudes toward poor children requires that teacher candidates learn about students from poverty- stricken backgrounds. Although some if not most of the teacher candidates are from social backgrounds similar to their future students, it is necessary that they learn about (a) students as persons, (b) the issues and problems with which they come to school, and (c) the perspectives they have on teachers and schooling. Solomon, Khattar Manoukian, and Clarke (chap. 5, this volume) describe different methods in which teacher candidates can engage in sustained meaningful activity with urban, inner-city communities as a dimension of their professional learning. These meaningful activities include observational learning in the community and various types of service learning activities in community-based projects.

In cases where teacher educators are unable to provide the sustained activities in the urban communities, an alternative approach that approximates this is to have the field experiences associated with college courses carried out in these communities. This has been done in Jamaica with one college course on Health and Family Life, in which teacher candidates are required to learn about the communities and the homes in which children live. Such field experiences are intended to increase teacher candidates' sensitivity to the conditions under which children live so that they become more emotionally connected to them.

Activities such as those described by Solomon et al. and the field experiences associated with this Health and Family Life course provide the basis for the experiential knowledge of their students that is necessary for making connections with their students. Teachers need to know their students well if they want to teach in a constructivist manner (Villegas & Lucas, 2002a).

• Develop an understanding that there are different ways of seeing the world—what Villegas and Lucas refer to as *sociocultural consciousness*. These ways of seeing are dependent on one's race and/or color, class, and gender. This consciousness will be a foundation for creating positive relations with students and for teachers' use of constructivist approaches in the classroom.

• Develop constructivist views of learning that recognize the value of building on students' ideas and experiences. This view of learning is in line with an affirming attitude to students and that acknowledges the value of accommodating students' experiences and ways of thinking. Such constructivist approaches to pedagogy give students voice and respect as well as responsibility. As Villegas and Lucas (2002a) pointed out, constructivism is more consistent with principles of social justice than the transmission model of teaching. To develop these views of pedagogy requires a radical alteration in teacher candidates' notions of teaching. They often experienced an "apprentice of observation" (Lortie, 1975) in which they have seen teaching as telling, controlling, and punishing. Changing attitudes to teaching will require a critical teacher education pedagogy including the use of case studies, modeling, observation, and much practice and discussion. Videotapes of constructivist teaching are useful here because the teacher candidates have not yet conceptualized these models (see Villegas & Lucas, 2002a). To teach in a constructivist manner requires that teacher candidates are able to create caring-constructivist, learning-oriented classrooms. Although this is an extension of their ability to engage in constructivist teaching, this ability highlights the importance of the relationship between teacher and students, as well as the climate established in the classroom and the respect and support provided to students. This relationship and classroom environment becomes the context in which students learn and the setting in which they spend the greater part of the day.

• Use the many opportunities that the arts present for teacher educators and students to bond through their common folk culture. Jamaican folk culture, which has a prominent place in many schools, provides a vehicle for expression and validates the origins and history of poor Black Jamaicans. In music, dance, and dramatic gestures (commonly called choral theatre), African-derived expressions are learned and valued. It has been shown that where the arts gain prominence in a school, community teachers and students have often been seen to bond, to learn together exchanging knowledge of a shared culture, thus breaking down some of the hierarchies that exist between teachers and students. This breaking down of barriers can also occur at the teacher education level.

• Teacher candidates have to begin to see the curriculum as flexible so that they can address students' concerns and are able to include topics with which the students identify (e.g., drug abuse, teenage pregnancy, relationships with parents, relations between the sexes, popular culture, and other matters that are of interest to students). As Ladson-Billings (2001) argued, effective teachers of urban students "are compelled to integrate their social commitment into the academic skills and knowledge of the curriculum" (p. 121).

## THE CHALLENGE OF IMPLEMENTATION

This six-step proposal for an innovative approach to the education of teachers for inner-city schools in Jamaica incorporates a new vision of teaching and learning that is placed alongside a new vision of the teacher. For these outcomes to be achieved, there will also have to be a transformation in the pedagogy of teacher education. Because teacher education is a powerful model for future practitioners, only with transformative pedagogy in the teacher preparation classroom environment can the teacher envisioned in this proposal be prepared. The kind of pedagogy that we expect teacher candidates to create when they get their own students and classrooms should also exist in the preparation process.

We are cognizant of the fact that the culture of teacher education is highly resistant to new ways of conceiving and transmitting knowledge. To counteract this resistance and the many challenges to be faced, there should be a strong investment in ongoing faculty development, as Villegas and Lucas (2002b) recommended. Such faculty development has been shown to be critical to the success of any reform or innovation. But it must be recognized that faculty development activities aimed at fostering racial and class identity and awareness will not be comfortable. It is also suggested that teacher education institutions establish structures and processes that foster collaboration among all those involved in the enterprise, those in the foundations of education, in field experiences, and those in the subject curriculum areas. Because in our context candidates are also taught by noneducational faculty, it is critical that the program be coherent and that teacher candidates not receive contradictory messages. Although initial and continuing faculty development is critical in order to introduce new conceptions of pedagogy and knowledge, equally important will be continued discussions and critique about interdisciplinarity. Such interdisciplinarity is necessary to allow the teacher educators to maintain the new vision of the teacher, innovative notions pedagogy, and to anticipate and avoid contradictions in the way in which knowledge is presented and teaching is practiced. Only with such continuing focus on faculty development and collaboration can the vision of teaching and learning presented in this chapter be maintained and continue to influence practice.

Another challenge of the proposal is the silence that exists around questions of class, race, and identity in Jamaica. Teachers have not experienced a professional preparation program or operated in an institutional culture that allows them to examine the social, political, and cultural complexities of Jamaican society. Tertiary institutions in Jamaica, unlike those in many metropolitan cities, do not facilitate or foster protest. In Jamaican teacher education institutions, matters pertaining to color, class, and gender are not integral to its scholarship and discourse, although discussions may take place within certain subjects like social studies and history. This silence makes it easy for teacher candidates who are poor to feel that poverty is somehow their problem rather than a societal one. Through this silence, the teacher education reproduces the status quo even as it represents an opportunity for socioeconomic mobility for Jamaican students from a poor background. Without changes in institutional culture, it will be difficult for candidates to liberate themselves from the view that poverty and Blackness are matters beyond discussion and are symptomatic of disability and inadequacy. Related to the reticence to address issues of color and class clearly and with specific definitions, there has been no substantive discussion on the stratification of the education system. The absence of a forthright acknowledgment of us as Black people who have inherited a stratified society, and the culture of silence that exists in institutions on personal and emotional matters, constitute major challenges to transformative teacher education.

## ENDNOTES

[1]The use of the term *Black* does not reflect an essentialist position. For as Hall (1996) pointed out, "Black is essentially a politically and culturally constructed category, which cannot be fixed in a...racial category" (p. 443).

[2]Although schools within each of these categories vary in quality and in the academic achievement of their students, the results of the regional CXC examinations in 2002 showed that on average, 49% of students in traditional high schools passed the mathematics examination compared with 16% of those in the upgraded high schools. In the case of English language, the pass rates were 54% for the traditional high school compared with 37% for the upgraded high schools.

## REFERENCES

Bartolome, L. (1994). Beyond the methods fetish: Toward a humanizing pedagogy. *Harvard Educational Review, 64*(2), 173–194.

Delpit, L. (1995). *Other people's children: Cultural conflict in the classroom.* New York: The New Press.

Evans, H. (2001). *Inside Jamaican schools.* Kingston, Jamaica: University of the West Indies Press.

Fanon, F. (1967). *Black skin, White masks.* New York: Grove Press.

Foster, M. (1995) African American teachers and culturally relevant pedagogy. In J. Banks & C. Banks (Eds.), *Handbook of Research on multicultural education* (pp. 570–581). New York: MacMillan.

Hall, S. (1977). Pluralism, race and class in Caribbean society. In *UNESCO, Race and class in post-colonial society*. Paris:UNESCO Publications.

Hall, S. (1990). Cultural identity and diaspora. In J. Rutherford (Ed.), *Identity: Community, culture, difference* (pp. 222–237). London: Lawrence & Wishart.

Hall, S. (1996). New ethnicities. In D. Morley & K.-H. Chen, *Stuart Hall: Critical dialogues in cultural studies* (pp. 441–449) London: Routledge.

Ladson-Billings, G. (1990). Culturally relevant teaching. *Teachers College Record, 155,* 20–25.

Ladson-Billings, G. (2001). *Crossing over to Canaan: The journey of new teachers in diverse classrooms.* San Francisco: Jossey-Bass.

Lewis, R. (1988). *Garvey: His work and impact.* Kingston, Jamaica: Institute of Social and Economic Research Publications.

Lortie, D. (1975). *School teacher: A sociological study.* Chicago: University of Chicago Press.

McAllister, G., & Irvine, J. (2000). Cross cultural competency and multi-cultural teacher education. *Review of Educational Research, 70*(1), 3–24.

Miller, E. (1999). Educational reform in independent Jamaica. In E. Miller (Ed), *Educational reform in the Caribbean.* Washington DC: OAS Publications.

Ministry of Education, Youth, and Culture. (2000). *The National Curriculum.* Kingston: Ministry of Education, Youth, and Culture Publications.

Planning Institute of Jamaica. (2002). *Survey of living conditions*, Kingston: Planning Institute of Jamaica Publications.

Richardson, V. (1996). The role of attitudes and beliefs in learning to teach. In J. Sikula, T. Buttery, & E. Guyton (Eds.), *Handbook of research on teacher education* (2nd ed.). New York: MacMillan.

Thomas, D. (2002). Modern Blackness: What we are and what we hope to be. *Small Axe, 12,* 25–48.

Turner, T (1987). The socialization intent in colonial Jamaican education 1867–1911. *Caribbean Journal of Education, 14*(1&2), 54–87.

Villegas, A. & Lucas, T. (2002a). *Educating culturally responsive teachers: A coherent approach.* Albany: State University of New York Press.

Villegas, A., & Lucas, T. (2002b). Preparing culturally responsive teachers: Rethinking the curriculum. *Journal of Teacher Education, 53*(1), 20–32.

# Part III

# CULTURALLY RELEVANT PEDAGOGY AND ADVOCACY IN URBAN SETTINGS

The third and final part of this volume demonstrates that culturally relevant pedagogy and advocacy work is two dimensional. Chapters 10, 11, and
12 are anchored in the specifics of curriculum work, and are based on the
belief that subject matter and pedagogical skills are important dimensions
of teacher competence for urban schools. Chapters 13 and 14 move from
classroom pedagogy to teachers' political activism. In chapter 10, Sekayi
provides insights into student resistance to an alternative school curriculum
and pedagogy that they perceived to be culturally irrelevant and counter-
productive to their educational progress. Her ethnography unearthed
some root causes of students' intellectual indignation and its degeneration
into despair, apathy, and irresponsible behavior. She identified two projects in this alternative school with the potential for democratic empowerment and cultural relevance. In chapter 11, Minott-Bent explores the
challenges of integrating computer-facilitated learning in urban schools
through the lenses of her pre-service teacher. Writing from a social-justice
perspective, she raises issues of access for students marginalized due to
their identities, but more so by institutional structures and teacher attributes that signal the students' lack of preparedness for technology in the
classroom. Pre-service teachers' resolve to "push back the margins" signals
the readiness of the next generation of teachers for computer-facilitated
learning in urban classrooms. In chapter 12, Brooks continues the exploration of culturally relevant pedagogy and uses a teacher's cultural knowledge
to deepen and expand her urban adolescent students' interpretations of
ethnically diverse novels. Her analysis suggests that students rely on ethical
beliefs, family narratives, community life, and popular culture as sources of

**163**

cultural knowledge in textual interpretations. Teachers engaged in the literacy development of ethnically diverse learners should therefore develop the competence to understand how literacy interpretations are influenced by the cultural "fabric" permeating students' lives.

In chapters 13 and 14, teachers engage in political activism that moves beyond classroom pedagogy, exploring forms of activism in bringing about equity, diversity, and social justice in urban schools and communities. In chapter 13, Solomon, Allen, and Campbell investigate the political strategies utilized by a unique group of teacher graduates to achieve the pedagogical goals of curriculum diversity and social justice. The chapter also reveals the challenges of advocacy and its potential debilitating impact on the personal and professional lives of advocates. In the 14th and final chapter, Reid continues the exploration of teacher activism in urban schooling and presents a brand of activism that emerges from a unique alternative teacher preparation program located in the inner city. A unique feature of this initiative is its provision of access to inner-city residents (e.g., racial minorities, the economically deprived, immigrants, Aboriginal and/or First Nation's Peoples) who are denied postsecondary education due to various forms of discrimination and social disenfranchisement. Using narrative inquiry, Reid presents the life story of a graduate activist, the legitimization of her activism, and her transformational work in inner-city communities.

# Chapter 10

# Student Resistance to Culturally Irrelevant Curriculum and Pedagogy: The Role of Critical Consciousness

Dia N. R. Sekayi
*Walden University*

Contrary to popular belief, culturally relevant pedagogy is not about "making students feel good" without regard for challenging academic content. Rather, academic competence is a common thread in most responsible models of culturally relevant pedagogy (Bennett, 2003; Ladson-Billings, 1998). Furthermore, fostering critical consciousness, or encouraging students to think beyond their immediate context, is also an important element of culturally relevant pedagogy. This chapter presents a case of resistance to academic content lacking rigor from an unexpected group—students in an alternative school program. It further addresses the unintended outcome of the development of critical consciousness among students as a result of their resistance to an unchallenging curriculum.

Both Ladson-Billings (1998) and Bennett (2003) present models of culturally relevant pedagogy that are multifaceted. The former lists cultural competence, academic competence, and critical consciousness as key elements. The latter outlines four categories as central aspects: curriculum reform, teaching toward social justice, equity pedagogy, and multicultural competence.

The focus of this chapter is an alternative school, an environment in which the standard of providing challenging curriculum to the students was not met. Ironically, the students' resistance to the curriculum was the impetus for the development of another aspect of culturally relevant pedagogy: critical consciousness, in Ladson-Billings' model, and teaching toward social justice, in Bennett's model. As a result of their intellectual indignation regarding the curriculum (Sekayi, 2001), the students began to develop a critical consciousness and awareness of the impact of inequity on their respective futures. In this study, I examine the first year in the life of an alternative education program that served students with a myriad of problems that impacted their academic performance. This intellectual resistance was so unexpected because of the frequent academic failure prior to this alternative placement.

Branton Institute is a small, full-day, 1-year, alternative program associated with the Baldwin Public School district located in a suburb of a Midwestern city. Although Baldwin High School is approximately 50% African American and 50% European American, Branton Institute is overwhelmingly African American and male.

Underachieving but capable students were invited to Branton Institute primarily from three sources: the 8th grade class of the high school's feeder elementary program, the 9th grade of the Baldwin High School, and occasionally the 10th grade of Baldwin High School. Of the four categories of programs for "at risk" students outlined by Duke and Canady (1991), Branton would be considered a remediation program. "The purpose of a remedial/compensatory program is to intervene in the regular educational program of at-risk students in order to correct learning deficiencies and increase the odds that students will improve their performance in conventional classroom settings" (p. 58). The mantra of the Branton Institute community is "a second chance," providing a second chance to experience academic success at Baldwin High.

Although students are invited, the decision to attend is left to the students and their families. The capacity is set at 75 students; although 64 students accepted the challenge, the first school year ended with 57 students.

When studying an alternative school, one of the first questions that comes to mind is what might be different about it. Sanoff (1994) suggests that alternative schools "must involve choice and they must be different from the standard school in the community" (p. 98). I would find over the course of the year that what was different related primarily to class size, teachers' attitudes, and the physical space. The curriculum and approach to testing could be categorized as *very traditional*, with a few notable exceptions explored in later discussion. Although there is a great deal of debate in the literature on the education of African American children (see Bennett, 2003; Delpit, 1988; Kunjufu, 1985; Ladson-Billings; 1998; Shujaa, 1996), from my observations and the data collected, Branton Institute adopted no model that specifically addressed the vast majority of their population—African Americans. In general, the pedagogy was not culturally relevant. The students resisted this traditional approach to their education, and had different expectations for this school. The chapter is not meant to prescribe a particular pedagogy, but to demonstrate the potential for using student resistance to inform any pedagogy and advance it toward cultural relevance.

## METHODOLOGY

I was brought into the Branton Institute project to provide a qualitative evaluation of the first year of the program. I met with the faculty prior to the opening of the school to discuss my planned approach to the collection of the data that would be used in the evaluation. I took a phenomenological approach to this single site case study (Bogdan & Biklen, 2003). If we are committed to alternative education that works for children, I believed it would be important to seek an understanding of the perspectives of the stakeholders directly involved—teachers, students, and administrators.

I visited the school on approximately 25 occasions. To enhance validity, a combination of methods was used to collect data from teachers, students, and the administrator (Glesne, 1999). Each of the five teachers was interviewed, once formally and once informally, and interviews took place on the occasion of each visit.

All of the teachers allowed me to observe their classes on each visit. On some days, I followed a class of students to observe their experiences with each teacher and in each classroom. On other days, I would stay with the same teacher for the entire visit to observe the interaction between that teacher and a variety of students.

Students were observed and interviewed, and six students participated in individual interviews. This number, approximately 10% of the total student body, reflects the number of students who returned signed informed consent forms. Forty-five students participated in focus groups, facilitated by me at the end of the school year in the absence of any school personnel. The administrator was interviewed both formally and informally on multiple occasions throughout the school year. Furthermore, school documents such as attendance and grade statistics, student work, and district newsletters, were gathered and analyzed.

Data from interviews and observation began to suggest differences between student and teacher perceptions about the program, which would become the basis for the intellectual indignation expressed by the students. This chapter focuses on the narrated perceptions of the students and teachers regarding the value of the program and the specific themes that emerged.

## INITIAL IMPRESSIONS

I knew from previous visits and meetings at the schools that the students would be attending Branton Institute by their own "choice." I assumed that their parents' choice was probably more accurate for many of the children. Over the course of the day, I would discover just how many of the children did not want to be there. If I had to choose one word to describe the atmosphere, it would be "resistance." This resistance and the adult response to it would threaten the creation of a strong positive ethos, which Grant (1988) argues can be the difference between a school that works and one that does not.

I saw frustration in the eyes of the teachers, which indicated to me that they were not prepared for the magnitude of resistance, nor did they recognize positive possibilities of this resistance. Categorization of *resistance as deviance* was evident in the informal pathological labeling of resistant children as "probably ADHD or bipolar." I locate this study, however, within the conceptual framework of *student resistance*.

## CONCEPTUAL FRAMEWORK

There is significant literature that deals with student resistance to subject matter (e.g., Keeley & Shemberg, 1995; Moore, 1997; Wolff, 1994). Although Branton students did resist the content, this resistance was more symbolic than literal. It was not that the content itself was offensive. Rather, they found the level of the curriculum unchallenging. The presentation of unchallenging curriculum led them to frustration surrounding their level of readiness to reenter the mainstream high school setting, which in turn led them to resistance in the form of intellectual indignation. Both Ladson-Billings (1998) and Bennett (2003) include student achievement in their models of culturally relevant pedagogy. The students at Branton quickly realized that even though most of them had better grades than ever before, they said that these higher grades only provided "a false sense of hope." In five separate focus groups, students agreed regarding the academic content, commenting that "the work is too easy," "there's too much slack and the standards are low," "the work is the same as last year," "we're not prepared for the math proficiency."

Miron and Lauria (1995) write about identity politics and student resistance and discuss students' engagement in political and collective forms of resistance. This phenomenon frames my discussion of the students and Branton Institute. Although the students were not "organized" resistors whose actions would be considered "collective" by casual observers, there were ways of thinking about and analyzing their experiences that were shared by large numbers of students. A great deal of this thought and analysis was related to students' identity and the politics of shaping and reshaping those multifaceted identities. Miron and Lauria (1995) argue,

> for middle-class African Americans, their personal and collective identities redraw cultural and social boundaries, new boundaries which distance them from their African American *underclass* counterparts. In either case, both social groups resist the identity labeling of the abstract racial category of *Black*. (pp. 34–35)

Although these researchers compare two schools that serve different kinds of African American populations, I use this framework to discuss one group of students in an alternative school and how they struggle with the labels earned from their participation in this particular alternative program.

Resistance within this framework is not viewed as an innately negative phenomenon. Similarly, MacLeod's (1995) ethnography looks at resistance as rooted in "political and moral indignation" rather than "psychological dysfunction" (p. 21). MacLeod draws from Giroux's (1983) work on this alternative view of resistance, which critiques any overreliance on reproduction theory with its corollary absence of discussions of human agency. Although I agree with him to an extent, the real issue is what students in schools believe. If they believe they have no control over their own destinies, they cannot exert that perceived nonexistent control. Resistance within that set of beliefs is futile. What I describe is what occurred at Branton Institute when students began to resist. These data reveal what I conceptualize as "intellectual indignation."

## RESISTANCE AND RATIONALE

It would be impossible to tell the story of student perceptions without discussing the concept of *resistance*, as it was a major theme that emerged from the analysis of my observations at Branton Institute. Henry Giroux (1983) argued that most educational studies assume that students are nonresistant recipients of instruction, and that the school can easily manage the students. In *Ain't No Makin' It*, MacLeod (1995) writes "resistance theory examines the ongoing, active experiences of individuals while simultaneously perceiving in oppositional attitudes and practices a response to structures of constraints and domination" (p. 19).

Aronowitz and Giroux (1985) argue, "conservative educators analyzed oppositional behavior primarily through psychological categories that served to define such behavior not only as deviant, but more importantly, as disruptive and inferior—a failing on the part of the individuals and the social groups that exhibit it" (p. 72). Patrick Solomon's (1992) research on Black resistance in the Canadian high school context and his discussion of the school as an arena of conflict is relevant to the Branton case. Admissions of resistance surfaced continually throughout structured and informal discussions with the students, and in some instances, students went so far as to use the term explicitly.

According to teacher feedback, there are at least three categories for the resistance at Branton Institute: *verbal expression, passive–aggressive behavior*, and *aggressive behavior*. These terms suggest a level of pathology, in keeping with the way resistance was typically viewed. The verbal expression began on the first day of school. Many students blatantly expressed dissatisfaction with the school, the teachers, and the overall situation. They complained of teachers' attitudes, the size of the school, the length of the classes, and the number of students.

The behavior categorized as passive aggressive included incidents of ignoring direct instructions from teachers, disposing of school work, walking out of classrooms, and leaving school grounds without permission. The aggressive behavior included talking or shouting over teachers in and out of the classroom, mumbling threats to teachers or other students, throwing objects, and standing on desks behind the backs of teachers. One of the teachers describes resistance this way:

> When I first got here, it was like they didn't want to be here. Almost all of them feel as though they had been dumped here. And peers were looking at them as if they were underachievers. Students were talking and cursing, so they brought all that with them when they got here the first week or two.

This teacher categorizes the reaction from the students as frustrating, but is able to contextualize it within the real experiences of the students. Another teacher feels that the goals of the school are not being met: "I think the first quarter, we were fighting so much resistance. I feel better now, and can see a little bit of progress. But it seems that no matter what you do, it's a battle."

Much of this resistance is manifested in student–teacher relationships. I observed a variety of behavior, from blatant disrespect to indifference, depending largely upon the activity or moods of students and teachers. One teacher spoke extensively about the issue of respect, and in response to a question about how this experience at Branton Institute compares to previous experiences, she laughs and states:

> The biggest difference is the respect. I think I was prepared for everything else, but not the lack of respect, for the children, for the teachers.... I guess when you just say please sit down and you get this whole lecture on your tone of voice and quit looking at me and who do you think you are.

Delpit's (1988) discussion of power and pedagogy in the education of children from cultures different from one's own can be used to interpret this response. She writes about the difference in perspective on authority, and contends:

> Many people of color expect authority to be earned by personal efforts and exhibited by personal characteristics. In other words, the authoritative person gets to be the teacher because she is authoritative. Some members of middle-class cultures, by contrast, expect one to achieve authority by the acquisition of an authoritative role. That is, the teacher is the authority because she is the teacher. (p. 288)

Based on this and other discussions, this teacher's beliefs are more in line with those of the middle-class cultures of which Delpit speaks, whereas conversations with the students at Branton Institute suggest that their beliefs are similar to the people of color in Delpit's discussion. Therein lies the conflict, and the basis of the main roots of resistance; intellectual indignation. The next section addresses the issue.

## ACADEMIC AND SOCIAL PREPAREDNESS AS A RATIONALE FOR RESISTANCE

Many students talked about the second chance they were being given through their participation in the Branton Institute program. One comments:

> Well, I think I'm lucky to have this opportunity because I know I really screwed up last year. And I'm just happy that I could come back here and make up for it, because it's easy to make up for it because they doing the same things as last year, except I know it all now.

Although the students as a whole appreciated the purpose of the school, there was another strong theme that dealt with the level of the work. The overall sentiment was that they were not being challenged, and many feared that they would not be prepared to reenter the high school at the appropriate grade level. One might therefore ask if this is really a second chance. Ogbu's (1978) discussion of institutional deficiency can be used to interpret the students' fears. He wrote of lower class Blacks' concern that schools were not preparing their children with the specific skills needed for economic success. Unlike the students in Kaplan's (1999) study, who felt that they were learning more in their alternative program than they would have in the regular program, the students at Branton were concerned that they were not learning anything new. Several of Kaplan's students acknowledged that their grades in the alternative program were lower than they had been in the regular program because the standards were higher. The Branton students also stated that their high grades did not indicate that they were learning more. They admitted that they were in the program because they did not perform well elsewhere. However, they still learned enough of the material for it to seem like "baby work" when exposed to it again at Branton.

This fear of being unprepared or underprepared is not simply in the minds of the students. Except for mathematics, where two levels are offered, the remainder of the curriculum was the same for all students. A large proportion of the students spent their freshman year at Branton Institute, while another large group spent its sophomore year there. The Branton curriculum was essentially ninth grade, and although the students generally believed that ninth graders would be fine, the tenth graders were concerned they would be in serious academic trouble. Alternative programs have been criticized for this kind of mediocrity (Gold & Mann, 1982). Many of the students in the focus group expressed a desire to stay at Branton for the remainder of their high school years. One student summed it up by saying: "What's the use of going to the high school? We won't know anything."

In many ways, social preparedness is closely related to academic performance. The academic performance of many of the Branton students has been hindered by social and behavioral problems. Many of the students acknowledge that social immaturity has been their downfall. If Branton does not deal effectively with these social concerns, the academic successes students experienced in their controlled environment are at risk of being neutralized when they return to a mainstream high school setting, where there is temptation for "backsliding" into the immaturity that first led them to an alternative setting.

Regarding social preparedness, the feedback is mixed. In my interviews with the adults in the building, I inquired about what was being done to prepare students for their social transition to Baldwin High, and if there was an explicit attempt to prepare the students for the social differences between Branton Institute and Baldwin High. The answer was that the closest preparation most adults felt the students were receiving was their occasional trips to the high school for physical education classes. Branton students were given the opportunity to participate in assemblies and extracurricular activities at Baldwin High, the response to which was that many students expressed feelings of embarrassment in socializing with Baldwin High students while enrolled at Branton. There was a similar response regarding the boarding of the buses for Branton in the morning.

There was also some concern on the part of the adults involved with the school regarding the readiness of Branton students to enter the high school. Readiness was discussed in terms of two categories—social and academic. One teacher is hopeful about the improvement of social skills: "Some students are actually making it. I can see some progress in some of their academic work and also their social skills." He spoke specifically about a young man who took a strong leadership role for a fund-raiser, which the teacher observed "gave him some responsibility, and I felt very good that he could do that." However, this same teacher had a serious concern for the overall academic preparedness of the students, especially regarding the proficiency exams. The teacher implied that even though students may experience success at Branton, that success may be misleading based on the level and nature of work completed. "So you say, 'you got an A here,' but when it comes time for the real thing [proficiency exams], if you don't know it, how are you going to do it?" One teacher expressed intellectual indignation when verbalizing concern with the level of academics.

Thus, although some teachers simplistically assumed that resistance in the form of negative behavior was solely a result of psychological or behavioral disorders, the students' fear of, and frustration with, academic content that was not challenging could actually explain a significant proportion of their resistance to schooling at Branton.

## DEMOCRATIC EMPOWERMENT AS A RESPONSE TO RESISTANCE

Wood (1998) writes, "attitudinally, vast numbers of citizens refuse to participate politically due to despair, apathy, or refusal to take responsibility." I believe that this antidemocratic notion can be applied to the present case study. What began for many students as intellectual indignation could easily degenerate into despair, apathy, and refusal to take responsibility for their behavior. This may very well be manifested as resistance, particularly the passive–aggressive and aggressive types already described. For many students, this degeneration did begin to take place. Wood offers four cognitive, personal, and communal skills necessary for democratic empowerment: (a) the individual's right and responsibility to participate publicly; (b) the intellectual skill and belief that this participation is important and does make a difference; (c) valuing equality, community, and liberty; and (d) knowing that alternatives to the status quo exist and are worthwhile. These aspects of democratic empowerment are very similar to the elements of culturally relevant pedagogy, the goal of which is to engage students in a way that will allow them to become productive members of society. There were two events I observed that were steps in the direction of democratic empowerment, and by extension, cultural relevance.

## THE LANDSCAPING PROJECT

My introduction to this project was at a teachers' meeting about 1 week before school began. The plan was a beautification of the Branton grounds, involving integrating academic subject matter. Students would take part in all aspects of the project, from the planning to the planting. Most students initially expressed very negative attitudes about physical labor, and compared what they were doing to being on a chain gang in prison. Even so, the vast majority participated.

Academic goals were being met and social lessons learned. Elements of mathematics, science, social studies, and family and consumer sciences were integrated into this project. The students had to work efficiently within a budget to purchase supplies, use science to choose appropriate flowers and soil, and mathematics to arrive at precise measurements.

They were experiencing the practical application of their in-class planning work, and were witnesses to the change that could take place through collective effort.

## SCIENCE IN THE SUNSHINE

Twenty-five Branton students voluntarily participated in this program, the purpose of which was to expose the second graders to several miniscience lessons in the outdoors. When the second graders descended upon them, and once they realized that the children were looking to them for guidance, there was excitement in the air. From my discussions with the students, I believe that they were beginning to understand the challenges their own teachers face each day, and gained a new appreciation for what it takes to teach.

There were several students who volunteered to participate, but were not allowed to come due to behavioral issues. This may have been a missed opportunity to engage students who do not connect with a traditional approach. All students will be given the opportunity to volunteer for the next installment of this project.

## CONCLUSION

It seems that the source of student resistance was about much more than students simply rejecting the value of education. Although their resistance was often reduced to this by many of the adults involved, their resistance was in fact far more complex. Initially, many students resented being pulled out of the "regular" environment. Over time, many students felt deceived and came to resent the unchallenging curriculum, calling it "babyish." This program was advertised to use the unique approach of alternative education. According to the description of several staff members, and consistent with my own observations, the structure of the program was very traditional. In fact, successful alternative approaches, like Science in the Sunshine, were off-limits to the students who may have benefited from this unique project.

Furthermore, the content was seen as unchallenging and even insulting by many students. As the curriculum was at a ninth-grade level, for many of the students this was the second time learning this material. From an educator's perspective, it makes some sense that if students do not successfully complete a grade that they did not learn the material from that grade. From my discussions with students, I learned that sometimes failure simply meant that homework was not completed or that nonacademic activities took precedence over academic ones. Apple (1990) writes about viewing conflict more constructively. In keeping with this notion, I assert that the leading cause of conflict at Branton is misperception, based on lack of effective communication between adults and children. Much of this conflict revolved around academics; the students enter the school knowing that they are capable, but also know that for a variety of reasons, they have not demonstrated this capability. The teachers enter the school with general information about the students' performance, but are not always aware of the reasons for the poor performance. This gap is fertile ground for misinterpretation and misperception on the part of both parties.

Although it probably happens in some cases, the narrated experiences about resistance at Branton do not imply resistance for the sake of resistance. Students were able to articulate their rationale for resistance to me in a way that was quite logical. Teachers' responses reflected the teachers' truth. The source of the conflict was the gulf between self and other, or in this case teacher–student. The organizational structure of the school is constantly being refined. The school was managed reflectively, due largely to the strong onsite leadership (Stringfield & Herman, 1997). When policies or ideas did not work, there was reflection and revision. Each time I visited, the atmosphere was slightly different because of some change that had been instituted. Many of these changes were motivated by students' feedback. This willingness to consider students' input in the change process should have been a lesson for students, and could have potentially demonstrated the positive outcomes of respectful resistance, and thus constituted a testament to the power of human agency. Critical consciousness is also a component of a culturally relevant educational experience. Realizing the power of one's individual and collective voice is an important element of critical consciousness. At times, the staff "worked the hyphen" between teachers and students well (Fine, 1994); when communication was most effective, pedagogy was most innovative, democratic empowerment was fostered, and students learned.

But an educational experience that lacks a challenging academic content cannot be fully culturally relevant. How will the Branton students become their best without the confidence that academic preparation provides? Ironically, the lack of one element of culturally relevant pedagogy became fertile ground for the development of another. Compelled by their struggle with a curriculum that students perceived as repetitive, by their fear of reentering the mainstream high school program, and by their frustration with the teachers and administration behind the curriculum, the students began to vocalize their concerns. They were not just bored with it, but saw the connection between their current academic experience and their future. They spoke in terms of readiness, success, fairness, teacher quality, misrepresentation, and justice; this from students who were simply seen as academic underachievers.

Most of the adult staff listened with open minds, and changes were often made. The best lesson in this case might be that students think critically, express their concerns, and see change as a result. That is the beginning of a critical consciousness, the sense of empowerment that comes with knowing that one's voice is heard. The lesson to be learned for teachers is that student resistance can be a source of information for the reflective practitioner. Good teachers already know that student feedback can inform teacher practice. Good teachers do not plow through academic content without regard for how their instruction is being received. This is a lesson that can be applied beyond the alternative education context.

## REFERENCES

Apple, M. (1990). *Ideology and curriculum*. New York: Routledge.

Aronowitz, S., & Giroux, H. (1985). *Education under siege: The conservative, liberal and radical debate over schooling*. South Hadley, MA: Bergin & Garvey.

Bennett, C. (2003). *Comprehensive multicultural education: Theory and practice*. Boston: Allyn & Bacon.

Bogdan, R., & Biklen, S. (2003). *Qualitative research for education: An introduction to theory and methods*. Boston: Allyn & Bacon.

Delpit, L. (1988). The silenced dialogue: Power and pedagogy in educating other people's children. *Harvard Educational Review. 58*(3), 280–298.

Duke, D., & Canady, R. (1991). *School policy*. New York: McGraw-Hill.

Fine, M. (1994). Working the hyphen: Reinventing self and other in qualitative research. In N. Denzin & Y. Lincoln (Eds.), *Handbook of qualitative research* (pp.70–82). Thousand Oaks, CA: Sage.

Giroux, H. (1983). *Theory and resistance in education: A pedagogy for the opposition*. South Hadley, MA: Bergin & Gravey.

Glesne, C. (1999) *Becoming qualitative researchers: An introduction*. New York: Longman.

Gold, M., & Mann, D. W. (1982). Alternative schools for troublesome secondary students. *The Urban Review, 14*, 305–316.

Grant, G. (1988). *The world we created at Hamilton High*. Cambridge, MA: Harvard University Press.

Kaplan, E .B. (1999). It's going good: Inner city Black and Latino adolescents' perceptions about achieving an education. *Urban Education, 34*, 181–213.

Keeley, S. M., & Shemberg, K. M. (1995). Coping with student resistance to critical thinking: What the psychotherapy literature can tell us. *College Teaching, 43*, 140–145.

Kunjufu, J. (1985). *Countering the conspiracy to destroy Black boys*. Chicago: African American Images.

Ladson-Billings, G. (1998). Toward a theory of culturally relevant pedagogy. In L. Beyer & M. Apple (Eds.), *The curriculum: Problems, politics and possibilities* (pp. 201–229). Albany: State University of New York Press.

MacLeod, J. (1995). *Ain't no makin' it: Aspirations and attainment in a low-income neighborhood.* Boulder, CO: Westview Press.

Miron, L., & Lauria, M. (1995). Identity politics and student resistance to inner-city public schooling. *Youth and Society, 27,* 29–54.

Moore, M. (1997). Student resistance to course content: Reactions to the gender of the messenger. *Teaching Sociology, 25,* 128–133.

Ogbu, J. (1978). *Minority education and caste: The American system in cross-cultural perspective.* New York: Academic Press.

Sanoff, H. (1994). *School design.* New York: Van Nostrand Reinhold.

Sekayi, D. (2001). Intellectual indignation: Getting at the roots of student resistance in an alternative high school program. *Education, 122*(2), 414–422.

Shujaa, M. (Ed.). (1996). *Beyond desegregation: The politics of quality in African American schooling.* Thousand Oaks, CA: Corwin Press.

Solomon, R. P. (1992). *Black resistance in high school: Forging a separatist culture.* Albany: State University of New York Press.

Stringfield, S., & Herman, R. (1997). Research on effective instruction for at-risk students: Implications for the St. Louis public schools. *Journal of Negro Education, 66,* 258–288.

Wolff, J. (1994). Writing passionately: Student resistance to feminist readings. *Composition and Communication, 42,* 219–229.

Wood, G. (1998). Democracy and the curriculum. In L. Beyer & M. Apple (Eds.), *The curriculum: Problems, politics and possibilities* (pp. 201–229). Albany: State University of New York Press.

# Chapter 11

# Integrating Computer-Facilitated Learning in Urban Schools: Challenges to the Pre-Service Teacher

Rupertia Minott-Bent
*Peel District Board of Education*

One of the main goals for education today is to equip children with skills that will prepare them to enter the information-driven workforce. Students are expected to be able to problem solve, analyze, evaluate, communicate, and create, essential skills that require the ability to question and discuss. However, subtle everyday classroom practices prevent many students from experiencing and accessing those skills needed to eventually enter the workforce. These exclusions are organized around such social differences as race, gender, class, ability, and access. A review of the literature on computer equity indicates that advances in technology have not promoted equal access for all. Many females and poor minority students continue to have less access to computers both at home and at school (Novak & Hoffman, 1998).

The current shift calls for teachers to arrange for access to appropriate resources, create organizational structures, and develop a supportive environment so that students in urban schools can succeed. The preparation of new teachers to integrate computers into urban classrooms has been an area of limited yet necessary research. The role of technology in school reform is to provide students with tools and information to support communication, problem solving, and knowledge creation. These

**179**

practices are crucial, as they will have a major effect in defining who is included in and who is excluded from the new social space. Further to the lack of preparation in the integration of information technology, Minott-Bent (2003) notes that some pre-service teachers feel apprehensive about being placed in urban practicum placements. The lack of pre-service teacher computer education and pre-service teacher apprehension about being placed in urban schools has implications for those concerned with pre-service teacher education.

This chapter examines the learning needs of a pre-service teacher as she attempted to integrate information technology into her urban-setting classroom. It draws on my dissertation research to explore computer integration in inner-city classrooms by examining the experiences of a pre-service teacher named Flora (pseudonym). This study examined how to best assist pre-service teachers in integrating computers into curricula and explored the needs and concerns of pre-service teachers in implementing computer-facilitated learning. These needs and concerns were explored in an online computer conference with pre-service teachers by studying the interaction between pre-service teachers as they attempted to break from tradition in their mode of teaching and learning. This research explored five case studies to seek understanding of the experiences and contexts within which pre-service teachers were working. What were the experiences and dynamics of the learning community in an online setting? And what kind of support did pre-service teachers say they needed when integrating computers into the curriculum? This study also explored the relationship between reflection and practice in computer-mediated communication. The computer-mediated approach is new to action research, and therefore the attention to the layers in this process allowed for the generation of recommendations and key principles to guide further work in computer-mediated action research.

This study was focused on the reflective practice of pre-service teachers as they implemented computers into their classrooms. Online action research was used as a key instrument to guide teachers' reflection on their implementation process. It was important to conduct my research in a way that would capture the experiences and reflections of teachers. To do so, I used a qualitative approach, which incorporated two face-to-face meetings, two online surveys, and observations of online communication. The methodology used to collect data was a qualitative and narrative inquiry case study through the use of an online action research conference.

The rationale for the case study approach emerged from the action research examination of specific situations (computer-facilitated learning) in a specific setting (a computer-mediated environment) with a particular group of pre-service teachers. Pre-service teachers in this study identified their research questions, areas of interest, timelines, established projects, implemented computer-facilitated learning projects, and reflected on their participation. This allowed me to capture the unique experiences of the teachers in the group and to evaluate my own role as an online facilitator.

The online action research group consisted of five teacher candidates in their second and third year of a concurrent or consecutive education program, and myself as the Researcher and/or Facilitator. The pre-service teachers had a variety of teaching and computer experiences, a range of classroom practicum experiences, and differing practicum locations. The number of participants needed to be small enough to reasonably collect sufficient data to highlight the experiences I required, but a large enough number to capture the diversity within the group. Five candidates were chosen from what Hammersley and Atkinson (1983) called a purposive sample base. One criterion for selecting pre-service teachers was that they could not be in their first year of study in the concurrent education program, because I was a course director of first-year concurrent students. The second criterion was teacher willingness to explore computer-facilitated learning in their teaching practice. Seven participants responded to the request for volunteers; two of the seven participants respondents were first-year students and were not selected to participate in the study.

The goodwill of classroom teachers and the time that pre-service teachers spend in schools are seen as vital to pre-service teacher development (Dunne, 1992). Teachers are likely to face difficult situations in inner-city schools (Banks & Banks, 2001). They note that some teachers may react to the overwhelming situation of their students in inner city schools, and the lack of support their school district provides them by, exhibiting anger and frustration. These feelings may surface in classrooms as unsympathetic attitudes, the callous treatment of students, and the planning of unchallenging "busy work." Banks and Banks state, "Too many urban schools thus become chaotic, angry places, where students roam the halls and teachers scream at them to get in class, sit down, and be quiet" (p. 90). Not only do teachers have attitudinal concerns about working in urban schools, but there is also a disparity of resources between dominant and marginalized classes.

At the time of this study, Flora's practicum placement was in a Grade 8 classroom at Scradon Elementary School, a kindergarten to Grade 8 school with a culturally diverse student population. Scradon had approximately 800 students and was over 25 years old, and is located among a variety of dwellings ranging from large detached houses to smaller subsidized apartments. On the southern perimeter of the school, there is a homeless shelter, various restaurants, and a bank. The school is situated east of the city's manufacturing district where the residents work in textiles, restaurants, and importing and financial industries. Many of the families live and work in the area. The socioeconomic backgrounds of families in this area range from low to high income, although the majority were low-income families from newly immigrated populations. The primary languages spoken in the community were Cantonese and Mandarin, with a smaller African and South Asian population. Approximately 45% of the student population spoke Cantonese and Mandarin, and approximately 25% of students spoke English; approximately 25% of the student population was South Asian, and approximately 5% were of African descent.

## FLORA'S COMPUTER EDUCATION CHALLENGES

The significance of Flora's case study is that she grapples with many issues surrounding computer-facilitated learning in an urban school setting. Equity issues, structural barriers, and curricula implications are explored in her experience of integrating computer-facilitated learning. Raising both personal and curricula concerns, she examined how the prevalent use of computers in schools affects those students who have limited access to the technology they are expected to use. Throughout her narrative, issues of equity and mentoring support were common themes:

> Lately I've noticed how dependent teachers and students have become on computers and how often it is assumed that we have access to computers. I've always wondered about the impact computers have had on school life. How it is used as a tool to make life easier and learning more varied, but also the negative impacts of computers on society.

Flora elaborated on the kinds of negative impacts she believed computers had on society:

> I worry about not getting my assignment in on time because I don't have a computer that currently works. I also worry when teachers suggest that a student has more pride in their work, or are more capable students simply because their homework is printed from a computer rather than handwritten or hand drawn. What will happen if teachers are too afraid to use or too disdainful of computers, and don't help their students develop the skills and tools to utilize technology and critically view information presented through that technology?

Flora was very adamant that teachers needed to consider the social effects of computer access in the classroom:

> As a teacher, it is important to take into consideration the various circumstances of my students before I assign them a task that might cause them anxiety because of difficulties with accessing computers. The ques-

tion of how computers are used in teaching and learning are very important, but teachers and researchers cannot operate only from middle to upper class assumptions.

Flora believed that not enough effort was made by teachers to be more inclusive of those students who did not have access to computers. She also addressed language and gender differences that might affect various cultural groups:

> Computers can exclude students based on ability as well as access. English as a second language learners, and computer programs that do not appeal to girls, are important concerns. Stereotypes can be further reinforced and the disadvantaged further oppressed. I do not think that teachers take time to think about the powerful impact their role has on determining the relationship between computers and learning.

Flora did not feel that her mentor teacher would be a computer resource for her:

> My host teacher doesn't know about the students' computer access at home or their comfort level with computers. She is looking to me to provide some classroom leadership in this area. After speaking with her about the kinds of topics I wanted to look at for my project, she was very supportive and felt that she would learn with me along the way.

Numerous researchers investigating equity and access to computers have failed to establish clear definitions of *equity* and *equality*, an ambiguity that leads to an often-inaccurate understanding of equity. This inaccuracy of equating equity and equality creates negative implications for students in lower socioeconomic areas and locations with large minority populations. Goslee's (1998) study on low-income communities in the information age reported a growing inequity in access to technologies ranging from telephones to the Internet. Coley, Cradler, and Engel's (1997) study tracked the student-to-computer ratio in the United States, and found that access to and use of computers depended on several factors: race, gender, and socioeconomic status. Schools with large proportions of poor and minority students were much less likely to have access to technology than those with higher income White students. Secada (1989) argues that equity is a qualitative property, and refers to judgments concerning social justice and equality as a qualitative property that describes parity among groups along some index (e.g., access to computers, attitudes toward computers).

Decisions and instructional practices leading toward social justice can only be achieved through a reallocation of institutional power and resources, thereby creating equality among students. Schools often engage in a redistribution of resources, making them more available to certain students based on academic need. Jerold and Orlofski's (1999) study found that computer equity is becoming more complicated. Although the number of students per computer is about equal in poor schools and affluent schools, inequities reappear regarding Internet connectedness. Jerold and Orlofski (1999) report that poorer schools have an average Internet connected computer-to-school ratio of approximately 17 to 1, whereas the wealthiest schools have a 10-to-1 ratio. The researchers also report that the digital divide is most evident between the rich and the poor. Only 20% of students from households earning less than $30,000 per year have a home computer, compared with 80% of students in households with incomes of $75,000 or more. Thus, school boards seeking greater access to computers for students of lower socioeconomic status (SES) should favor lower SES schools with equitable equipment and support.

The lack of mentoring was seen as another challenge for Flora. Many of her cohorts in this study felt isolated from others in their learning community who shared common interests in computer-facilitated learning, and found themselves in traditional host classrooms that offered little support for computer integration. Such lack of support is reported in the research literature. For example, a study from the University of Sussex that examined the relationship between mentor teachers and pre-service teachers found that more than two thirds of the pre-service teachers considered their mentor teachers not very able or unwilling to relate classroom practices to wider educational principles (Kunje, Lewin, & Stuart, 2002). Many of the participants shared feelings of isolation and frustration from host-school experiences. To treat all students equally and not recognize their individual needs is an inherently inequitable practice.

## NARROWING THE FOCUS

Flora's aim in this project was to first investigate the computer access of students in the four Grade 8 classrooms at the school. Her goal was to track and offer additional support to students who did not have access to computers at home and who were required to complete assignments using computers. She worked closely with the Grade 8 teachers to find out students' computer access and needs, and her aim was to establish a new structure for computer-facilitated learning experiences and develop a support system in her practicum school to increase computer access for these students. Flora describes her experience:

> I've been through many plans in the last few weeks, trying to hone my project so it is manageable but still relevant to the issue I want to explore. I handed out a Computer Access Survey to all of the Grade 8 teachers at the

school to share with their students. From this information, I will be able to track those students as they work on an assignment that has to be completed on the computer to see what supports can be set up at the school.

Flora didn't feel that her peers saw issues of access to computers at home as an area of concern:

I shared the intent of my topic with other student teachers at my practicum school. I was shocked at the response that I got. My classmates thought that it would be more important to learn how to use a new computer program. Comments were made to me that, in this day and age, everyone should have a computer. I am questioning the importance of my project and am prepared to change my topic if there isn't a need in my school community.

Flora had a strong belief that teachers needed to be advocates for students' equitable access to computers. She believed that the curriculum should be based on improving social conditions, and could not be neutral.

Students should be made aware of issues that affect their lives, and encouraged to think critically about the world around them. Computer-facilitated learning is a powerful tool to make the world smaller. Information about different societies can be discovered as well as information about current events. Teaching children how to be socially conscious and critical of the media is a responsibility that teachers should be taking on.

Seeking to understand the motivation of pre-service teachers for computer-mediated activities is important in order to gain insights into how and why pre-service teachers want to implement computers into the curricula. Understanding the stages that pre-service teachers go through as learners will create a positive context for teacher educators.

In my study, the cycle of pre-service teachers' motivations as related to computer-facilitated learning was a stage I termed *critical dependence*. At this stage, pre-service teachers are deeply critical of their mentor schools and host classrooms, and teachers do not see their host teachers as valuable sources of information in their learning process. The desire to form partnerships is limited, and at times, pre-service teachers will remain on the periphery of the classroom, interacting very little with students or the mentor teacher. This stage is very complex, as pre-service teachers are at a critical moment in their development of confidence and competence. Motivation toward professional growth is restricted because the sense of connection to the classroom is limited. Many external challenges are named as reasons why change cannot take place.

During the next motivational stage, which I named the *dependence stage*, pre-service teachers begin to find ways to connect their personal experiences to the classroom. They recognize a need for input from their host teachers and begin observing practices in the classroom as opportunities to learn and grow. The desire to find their voice as a teacher begins to emerge, and initial creative pedagogical ideas begin taking shape. Involvement in routines in the classroom emerges, but the confidence to make changes to these routines does not yet occur.

The later stage of pre-service teacher development is the *collaborative autonomy stage*. Confidence of pre-service teachers grows and they enter into a partnership with their mentors. They have a desire to share and contribute to the classroom in meaningful ways and to explore ways to implement new ideas and discover techniques to express their uniqueness as a teacher. Pre-service teachers at this stage see their host teachers as partners in the classroom and desire to enter into professional dialogue about teaching and learning. Inward-bound reflective questioning of what can be done to create meaningful learning experiences in the classroom occurs, as opposed to only naming challenges that prevent action from taking place.

A beneficial issue in teacher education is the realization that pre-service teachers feel that knowing more computer programs will lead to better instructional practices. A shared vision of computer literacy creates a common foundation for the learning community. An understanding of the importance of computer-facilitated learning and the commitment to forward momentum is a necessary foundation for this type of research. The general message for teacher educators is that exploring participants' understanding and perceptions of computer literacy helps guide their individual computer instructional goals.

An important precondition for teacher educators in preparing teachers for urban schools is to assist them in problem solving. By shifting one's role from expert to participant, pre-service teachers are forced to develop strategies and networks to solve their own problems. The space to allow for professional growth toward collaborative autonomy needs to be created by positioning oneself as a participant and/or facilitator. The mere presence of an expert creates a hierarchy that silences participants from exploring their own ways of knowing and doing. Opposing stagnant or top–down models of knowledge construction, assisting pre-service teachers to solve their own problems actively constructs knowledge. As a catalyst of computer facilitated learning, one must invest time understanding the pre-service teacher's motivations, concerns, histories, biographies, social milieus, and past and present computer experiences, as these will all affect curriculum planning. Teachers play a vital role in the kind of educational opportunities inner-city school students receive. It is essential for teachers to strive toward self-knowledge, and become conscious of how their own cultural values and beliefs affect their attitudes and expectations toward students from different social groups and their achievement.

Understanding the stages of support that pre-service teachers may experience, as well as the preconditions for successful computer facilitated learning, is critical. Inequitable opportunities for students to learn will result in inequitable learning outcomes. The literature on teacher education (Banks & Banks, 2001) notes that affluent suburban students are provided the "wherewithal to achieve and to learn high status knowledge, what some people call social capital " (p. 92). Inner-city youth are typically denied those opportunities. Teachers are ideally positioned to develop students who are socially different and insightful, and critically understand computer knowledge for an emerging technological society and their place within it.

## FLORA'S COMPUTER-FACILITATED LEARNING PROJECT

Flora worked collaboratively with grade-level teachers to uncover students' needs and access to computers:

> The first step to my project was to meet with grade 8 teachers to share the project and the survey results with them. My mentor teacher was instrumental in gaining support from the grade 8 teachers. They were all on board before the meeting. Through the surveys, I found out that many students spend most of their computer time either surfing the Net, playing games, or using MSN Messenger to chat with their friends.... The students that I am working with for this project have had little exposure to various computer applications and have limited knowledge of the Internet.

She strongly believed that teachers needed to work together planning effective experiences for students. Flora worked with her colleagues who taught at the same grade level to create a computer-facilitated project that linked to the curriculum and had a socially conscious focus.

> I think it is important that teachers work together to plan learning experiences. I think it would a shame if other grade 8 classes don't have an opportunity to participate in this project. The grade 8 teachers have been very open to working together, and have given me things to think about that I would have never thought of on my own. I will be inviting the Special Education and ESL teacher to our next meeting.

Research skills, presentation skills and the examination of a current event were facilitated through Flora's project.

> I think that creating an assignment for students to use the skills that I will be teaching will help to motivate them. Creating a platform for them to

share their findings and analyze different Web sites that were effective empowers those students who usually aren't empowered. When the classes presented their projects, I noticed that there was a high participation rate. All the ESL-identified, Special Education students and those with no outside computer access had completed the project, which I believe is due to the provisions I made for them.

Flora used a variety of groupings within the larger computer study group to work on the project.

Today was the first day that the support group met. The Special Education teacher and the ESL teacher joined the class. I welcomed the group and shared with them the project on which we would be working over the next few weeks. There were 19 students present. I introduced the activity and students were asked to choose a partner with whom to work over the next 7 weeks. The title of the project that we decided as a grade level was Not Just Cloning Around: A Critical Study of the Issues and Views Involved in Cloning. We brainstormed as a group what they knew about cloning.

Flora saw a need to provide support for students as a grade-level initiative. A new way of approaching instructional time was needed to support students' access to computer-facilitated learning.

I wanted students to have as much support as possible to be successful on the research project. They were asked to find a Web site about human, animal, or plant cloning. I told them that they could use Web sites in languages other than English, but the presentation must be in English.... The grade 8 teachers were able to free up a 45-minute period for these select students to work with me in the computer lab, while their classes worked on the project with the classroom teacher.

Flora explained the benefits of building on students' existing knowledge by asking for student input.

I then asked the class how they would go about finding the information they needed to complete the project. I was surprised to see how limited their knowledge of search techniques was.... I allowed the class time after reviewing the Internet policy to conduct searches based on what they knew already.

Flora noted the increase in confidence that she observed in students in her host class and the similar response from the other Grade 8 classes.

At our grade-level meeting, the teachers revealed that the students involved in the computer study group (CSG) were very excited when it was time to go to the computer lab. They enjoyed working with other students from different classes. These students are also having opportunities to go to the lab during the scheduled lab time to work on their projects. At the lab during regular class time, I noticed that the computer study groups do better at problem solving. Prior to this project, many of these students got into trouble frequently during lessons. During lab time, it was really obvious that they were not exhibiting any negative behavior.

The individual learning styles and motivation of pre-service teachers must be considered in computer education. Some will ask for the instructor to demonstrate the tasks or skill, whereas others will prefer trial and error. Although Owston (1998) sees planning as the key ingredient for successful use of the Internet for professional development, I would argue that knowing what the concerns are or challenges that pre-service teachers are faced with should be the starting point. Pre-service teachers need the freedom to discover, through exploration and reflection, different ways to build, construct, and facilitate knowledge. They need to spend time working with problems and searching for solutions in ways that they intend to teach.

The issue of successful computer facilitated learning is intimately connected with those who teach it. The attitudes teachers possess toward a specific classroom practice are reflective of their belief systems and experiences. Novak and Hoffman's (1998) research in the area of equity and computers indicates that in all schools, the most innovative computer opportunities were disproportionately available to high-achieving and well-behaved children, whereas at-risk and low-achieving students were less likely to be involved in such enterprises. Banks and Banks (2001) also note that inadequately trained teachers assign rote drill and practice games that do little to enhance information processing. In affluent areas, students are learning Logo™, Pascal™, or BASIC™. They report that basic skills are typically presented to students in workbooks and on dittos in inner-city classrooms, whereas affluent suburban districts are using inquiry-based learning. Subsequently, the limited availability of software and hardware in low SES schools makes the goal of equity difficult. When educators combine such realities with limited expectations for certain groups of students, equity becomes an unattainable ideal.

## MAJOR STUMBLING BLOCKS

Flora perceived her major stumbling block to be time. She specifically focused on how long it took to organize and schedule computer time with supervision that met the needs of the entire grade level.

As a pre-service teacher, I have more flexibility in my timetable. I am not the only one responsible for a class. I am grateful that I have this flexibility

to go from class to class to talk to other teachers as well as come to the
school on days that I'm not at the university to gather resources or plan
lessons. A classroom teacher would have to use volunteers and others on
staff to create a more equitable computer environment.

Another issue of time that Flora perceived as a stumbling block was the
time involved in planning experiences that met students' needs.

A few students asked me today to show them how to produce a Web site. I
decided to hold a Web page workshop for the senior grades during lunch-
time for anyone interested. I had never produced a Web page before and
had to learn quickly. I asked the librarian if the school had any software
that could create Web pages. I didn't want too much time to pass from the
time the request was made of me. The librarian shared that the school had
Claris Home Page 3.0, which was Ministry [of Education] licensed software, and lent me a copy to take home and experiment with.

Flora mentioned several times that commitment and support from the
school team was important.

I can't overemphasize how important it has been for all the grade-level
teachers and support teachers to support this project. If there isn't support from the teachers and the principal, then creating equity across a
grade level, division, or school would be difficult. Those who don't see the
value or the need for equity-based access and support for students might
not want to assist in scheduling, and the flexibility that is needed to ensure
that students' needs are met outside of the classroom.

In the online conference, Flora stated some internal conflict with allowing
ESL students' opportunities to research information in their native language:

I find it difficult to make sense of some of the messages that I have received about students doing research in their original language. In the
Language course at the university, I am learning that children should
spend as much time immersed in English. I think that it would be more equitable if students could research information in their original language,
and later articulate it in English. I asked some teachers at the school what
they thought, and the response I received was around [concerned with]
Internet safety: If I couldn't read the information, how would I know if it
was appropriate or not. I think that the argument makes sense but it still
makes me uncomfortable.

Flora identified an internal dilemma of inequality that exists for minority students in the kind of educational processes available to them. When
minority students and students from European descent receive similar edu-

cational resources, the effects are not identical. Most graduates of teacher education programs know little about cultural behaviors, values, and attitudes that different children of color bring to the classroom. Most teachers' cultural backgrounds and value orientations are compatible with European middle-class culture, and they use these to establish routines for students, thereby placing them at a learning disadvantage.

## DILEMMAS

Flora's experiences revealed a number of dilemmas, ranging from feelings of isolation, lack of mentorship, and internal conflicts about culture. In the research literature (Kunje et al., 2002; Minott-Bent, 2003), pre-service teachers felt isolated from others in their learning community who shared common interests in computer-facilitated learning, and found themselves in traditional practicum classrooms that offered little support for computer integration.

Both studies also reveal frustration about the organization of the teaching day. Pre-service teachers were confined to a prescriptive timetable in order to teach, and a disproportionate time was spent negotiating additional time to support computer-facilitated learning experiences. Kunje et. al.(2002) revealed that the day-to-day practices of student teachers tended to be ad hoc: "A little bit here and there and no time to do it properly" (p. 46). It was felt that pre-service teachers needed additional release time to read around a particular topic, and our experiences revealed that the participants expressed the wish that more time had been devoted to team teaching and to teaching individual pupils.

The advancements of technology have tremendous benefits on the daily lives of all citizens. However, the fact that our society is economically and racially stratified has implications on the use of technology in schools. Although there are tremendous benefits of computer-facilitated learning, many poor minority students and females continue to have less access to computers both at home and at school (Novak & Hoffman, 1998). Sutton (1991) provided evidence that suggested that high school students whose parents had graduated from college were three times more likely to own computers than students whose parents were high school dropouts. A national survey in the United States investigating how computers were used revealed that children in high SES groups performed more higher order cognitive tasks (31%), whereas low SES students spent more time on drill-and-practice type programs and activities (Banks & Banks, 2001). Novak and Hoffman's (1998) work revealed that White students who owned computers at home came to school with mastery of the basic computer skills that assisted them in performing high order activities like programming. Poor minority students, due to limited computer resources at home and school, lacked such basic skills and computer access. Through Flora's case study, where she attempted to integrate computer-facilitated learning investigation, the issue of teacher attitude is intimately connected to the implementation of computer innovation. When educators combine such realities as low SES and low expectations for some socially different groups of students, equity is not realized.

## DISCUSSION AND IMPLICATIONS

Flora's success in integrating computer-facilitated learning began with her belief that schools must take responsibility for ensuring equitable access to computers. She contended that students who did not have access to computers at home might be perceived negatively if their projects and assignments were not completed on a computer. Her use of computer-facilitated learning examined the structures in school that would lend better support to those students with computer needs. She met regularly with the grade-level team, attended staff meetings, shared ideas from the online conference group, and spent time reflecting on her practices. Open communication, flexibility in scheduling, and a willingness to try new ideas were important to ensure an equitable computer-based learning environment. Flora also found that in addition to asking students what they knew about computers, talking to ESL and Special Education teachers offered insights into how to best meet students' needs.

## BEST PRACTICES FOR COMPUTER-FACILITATED LEARNING

Computer reform should begin with a redefinition of computer equity as inclusive of access to a variety of instructional processes informed by and responsive to students' cultural orientation and learning styles (Banks & Banks, 2001). The premise behind this definition is that structural barriers exist by way of insensitive, unequal, and hegemonic practices, rather than the inabilities of students. Expanding this view of equity requires educational reform, beginning with teacher preparation.

Some conditions are needed to support the implementation of computer-facilitated learning in urban schools. The first comes from awareness at a conscious level of the connection between computer concerns, beliefs, and their actions. The next requires opportunities for teacher reflection, through which teachers need to see for themselves the benefits and limitations of different instructional approaches for inner-city students. Sandholtz, Ringstaff, and Dwyer (1996) explain that teachers need opportunities to see others teaching effectively in order to confront their own actions and examine their motives. Sandholtz et al. (1996) also explain that teachers in training must reflect critically on the consequences of their choices and actions. Thus, pre-service teachers need to see exemplary practices "in the flesh."

My study revealed the tensions that pre-service teachers felt as they attempted to integrate computer-facilitated learning in urban schools where the curriculum is compartmentalized and knowledge negotiated in isolated pockets. There was an ongoing struggle for pre-service teachers to integrate computer-facilitated learning. The primary use of computers has been reported as "a supplementary activity after more necessary work is done or in computer lab settings where students perform a uniform task, learning the mechanics of using software, or gaining practice in computational or grammatical skills" (Becker & Ravitz, 1999, p. 358). Becker and Ravitz (1999) argue for a shift in the role of technology from a mere tool to a "mind tool," that "requires learners to think harder about the subject matter domain being studied while generating thoughts that would be impossible without the tool (p. 359). This they describe as occurring with groups of teachers who exhibit constructivist practices, including project-based work, collaboration, and hands-on activities (Becker & Ravitz, 1999).

The Office of Technology Assessment (OTA; 1996) argues that teachers are not great models of lifelong learners, and that the reason for this is structural rather than personal. The OTA (1996) argues that the major barriers to professional development for teachers are time, place, money, and academic discipline. The lack of administrative support is also a barrier to the implementation of new technologies (Rudden & Mallery, 1996). If placement schools are structured in ways that are not conducive for innovative practices, student teachers and classroom teachers cannot be mentored to implement technology in their teaching practices.

Innovative practices using technologies are likely to be part of an environment in which the school management is in favor of integrating technology into the curriculum (Connelly & Clandinin, 1999). Progressive school administrators faced with new curriculum materials will be encouraged by their teachers to try out the materials in field tests, and probe the new technologies as researchers. Pre-service teachers placed in these environments will then be supported in their academic growth toward integrating technology into the curricula.

In addition to teacher reflection in order to decode personal attitudes and behaviors, how values actively unfold in the assessment of various instructional strategies with students from low SES and multiracial groups is equally important. Ensuring that students have multiple points of computer and Internet access at home, school, and in the community is also important in decreasing the digital divide. Translating the concept of *educational equity* into practice requires reform in teacher preparation, curriculum design, classroom instruction, and access to hardware and software.

## REFERENCES

Banks, J. A., & Banks, C.A. (2001). *Multicultural education, issues and perspectives*, Toronto: Wiley.

Becker, H., & Ravitz, J. (1999). The influence of computer and Internet use on teachers' pedagogical practices and perceptions. *Journal of Research on Computing in Education, 31*(4), 356–383.

Connelly, F. M.., & Clandinin, J. D. (Eds.). (1999). *Shaping a professional identity: Stories of educational practice.* New York: Teachers College Press.

Cooley, R., Cradler J., & Engel, P. (1997). *Computers and classrooms: The status of technology in U.S. Schools.* Princeton, NJ: Educational Testing Service. Retrieved July 10, 2004, from http://www.ets.org/research/pic/compclass.html

Dunne, R. (1992). Competence as the meaningful acquisition of professional activity in teaching. *Aspects of Educational and Training Technology Series,* (25), 241–245.

Goslee, S. (1998). *Losing ground bit by bit: Low-income communities in the information age.* Washington, DC: The Benton Foundation and the National Urban League. Retrieved on July 10, 2004, from www.benton.org/Library/Low-Income/home.html

Hammersley, M., & Atkinson, P. (1983) *Ethnography: Principles in practice.* London: Routledge.

Jerold C., & Orlofski, G. (1999). Raising the bar on school technology. *Education Week's Technology Counts, 19*(4), 58–69.

Kunje, D., Lewin K, & Stuart, J. (2002). *Primary teacher education in Malawi: Insights into practice and policy.* University of Sussex Institute of Education [Country Rep. No. 3], Centre for International Education. Retrieved October 27, 2005 from http://www.sussex.ac.uk/usie/muster/pdf/cr_3_11_02.pdf

Minott-Bent, R. (2003). *Action research in computer-facilitated learning and the implications for pre-service teacher development: A computer-mediated approach.* Unpublished doctoral dissertation, University of Toronto.

Novak, T., & Hoffman, D. (1998). *The growing digital divide: Implications for an open research agenda.* Report Sponsored by the Markle Foundation. Nashville, TN: Vanderbilt University, Owen Graduate School of Management. Retrieved July 10, 2004, from www.markle.org/news/proj_index.html

Office of Technology Assessment. (1996). *Power on! New tools for teaching and learning.* Washington, DC: U.S. Government Printing Office.

Owston, R. (1998) *Making the link: Teacher professional development on the Internet.* Portsmouth, NH: Heinemann.

Rudden, M., & Mallery, S. (1996). *Systematic change in education.* Boston, MA: Beacon Press.

Sandholtz, J. H., Ringstaff, C., & Dwyer, D. C. (1996). *Teaching with technology: Creating student-centered classrooms.* New York: Teachers College Press.

Secada, W. G. (1989). *Equity in education.* New York: The Falmer Press.

Sutton, R. (1991). Equity and computers in the schools: A decade of research. *Review of Educational Research, 61*(4), 475–503.

# Chapter 12

# The Literary Voices of Urban Adolescents: Multifactor Influences on Textual Interpretations

Wanda Brooks
*Temple University*

Researchers, teacher educators, and school administers generally agree that pre-service teachers in the 21st century, who aspire to be responsive to an increasing number of children of color, must recognize, value, and capitalize on cultural backgrounds within the classroom setting. Today, many educators would likely agree that children can not help but bring parts of their cultural backgrounds into the various communities in which they belong. And as one of the primary communities inhabited by youth, schools are certainly not to be excluded.

With respect to literacy and, in particular, reading, a number of theorists contend that students rely on culturally influenced prior knowledge and experiences when interpreting literature (Bell & Clark, 1998; Harris, 1995; Hull & Rose, 1989; Lee, 1993; Moller & Allen 1988; Rickford, 1999). Thus, reading is a multifaced process, both constrained and enhanced by individuals who inhabit their own unique as well as culturally based knowledge structures (Holland & Quinn, 1987). No longer is textual interpretation viewed apart from the reader, the context in which the reading occurs, or the demands and expectations of the literacy task. Although this theoretical construct is certainly not a new one, practical examples depicting a variety of racial and ethnic groups drawing from distinct cultures, while constructing meaning from literature, are still needed.

Like reading, research that uncovers culture's unavoidable permeation into schools emerged within the past several decades concerning the ways students talk and write. Cazden (1988), Heath (1983), and Labov (1972) were three of the first researchers to bring to the fore how children from African American backgrounds rely on familial practices, knowledge, and language vernaculars when communicating. In particular, Cazden's (1988) research revealed how storytelling patterns (initially learned at home) eventually manifested and evoked particular kinds of responses from teachers. More recently, Dyson (1997) made one type of cultural experience apparent through an investigation of how young children from racially and ethnically diverse backgrounds incorporated and appropriated cartoon superhero references into a variety of written artifacts. Mahiri's (2004) edited volume presents several explorations of how a range of language and literacy practices learned outside of schools, (i.e., rapping, spoken word poetry, and online discussions) can be identified and used in students' classroom writings.

In keeping with this strand of language and literacy studies, this chapter offers a discussion of how one reading teacher in a low-income urban school recognized, valued, and capitalized on students' cultural backgrounds as they engaged in discussions of multicultural literature. The out of school–in school dichotomy (Hull & Schultz, 2002) was successfully bridged as cultural events taking place outside of a formal educational context translated into literacy events within school.

Data were collected throughout an academic year in Rhonda Hick's eighth-grade reading classroom and analyzed inductively (Patton, 1990). Categories of response encapsulate the analysis. The case study class consisted of 28 participants: 26 African American, 1 Puerto Rican, and 1 Dominican. (Names given for the participants described are pseudonyms.) I collected the following data: (a) observational field notes taken during reading instruction, (b) audiotape recordings of participants discussing several novels in large groups, and (c) the participants' written responses to the novels.

My discussion is twofold. First, while describing the students' responses to the literature, I illustrate how culturally influenced prior knowledge and experiences permeated the meaning-making processes of the study participants. My analysis identifies cultural sources relied on by the study participants when responding to three well-known and highly acclaimed culturally conscious novels (Sims, 1982): *Scorpions* (Myers, 1988), *Roll of Thunder Hear My Cry* (Taylor, 1976), and *The House of Dies Drear* (Hamilton, 1968). (See the appendix for a brief description of these novels.) Definitions of each cultural source category, followed by examples that demonstrate how students implicitly referenced culture in response to the stories read are given. Following this discussion, the various instructional decisions and pedagogical strategies the participants' teacher chose while viewing the culture of her students as a powerful influence on teaching and learning is explored.

## THE CASE STUDY CHILDREN: HOW CULTURE PERMEATES COMPREHENSION AND INTERPRETATION

The cultural knowledge and experiences relied on by study participants when responding to the multicultural novels derived from three sources: family members, community life, and popular media. I am not arguing here that these three are the only possible sources of cultural knowledge and experiences. Rather, perhaps due to the genres, topics, and analytic demands of the books, as well as the distinct make-up of respondents in the case-study class, these three source categories clearly stood out in the data. Descriptions offered throughout this chapter are drawn from the least ambiguous examples, as this exploratory analysis is a subset of data taken from a larger study of urban adolescents' responses to literature by and about African Americans.[1]

### Family Members

Family members constitute the first identifiable cultural source. Although some might consider the definition of family members quite straightforward, African American notions of family sometimes extend beyond the assumed, biological interpretation. Notwithstanding the referencing of specific family members by the participants, I did not conclude that these references referred to biologically related family members. Rather, fictive kin and extended intergenerational relationships may account for an individual being identified as a sister or grandmother in this research.

Family members as a source of cultural knowledge initially surfaced in the data when the students began discussing family responsibilities apparent in the story, *Scorpions* (Myers, 1988). Although this book depicts a single-headed female household, three different configurations of African American families are portrayed in the novels read by the participants, including single, two-parent, and extended. However, as now revealed, the adolescents' most significant reactions to the depictions emerged not because of family configurations but rather the family behaviors:

(1) Rhonda: Do you think a lot of Black families are like the Hicks family, or just some you know?
(2) Mark: Yeah and no.
(3) Rhonda: Why?

(4) Mark:      Because every Black family ain't like that.

(5) Rhonda:    Ok, so they are not typical?

(6) Mark:      Yeah, it's not typical.

(7) Rhonda:    Well, what makes them not typical or different from other Black families?

(8) Mark:      Mostly because it ain't too many Black families that's out there hustling and everything. Like my family, we got two or three people in my entire family who hustle and everything. But that's not most of us and not how most families are. Like the boy is only 12 years old or something. That 's really not true because you can't be 12 years old in a gang and hustling and just killing somebody like that.

In order to question the author's depiction, Mark relied on beliefs he held about African American families rooted in the experiences of his own family. He said, "Like my family, we got two or three people in my entire family who hustle [sell illegal drugs]" (line 8). On one hand, Mark's reasoning appears justifiable within a very personalized context, but if social statistics are accurate, there are indeed occurrences of 12-year-olds of all ethnic backgrounds belonging to gangs. Mark was possibly aware of this larger reality and, at the same time, seemed reluctant to reexamine his belief. His response of "yeah and no" (line 2) perhaps indicated the ambiguity he felt. Although he knew adolescent gang members existed (even in his class), Mark chose not to view African American youth in this way.

When considering the author's portrait of characters and their relationships, Mark's disbelief has implications for the interpretive processes he enacted while reading the story. Although outwardly quite interested in reading *Scorpions* (Myers, 1988), refuting an author's depiction suggests that Mark's interpretative practices allowed him to move beyond an uncritical acceptance of words on a page as well as the authority of the author. In the discussion, textual information from the novel is juxtaposed against Mark's previously held belief system. He chose to challenge the book's depiction instead of fully dismissing his lived cultural experiences about African American families.

The next example also displays the interpretive practices revealed by Mark. It occurred one afternoon when Rhonda allowed the children to infuse personal narratives into a discussion of *The House of Dies Drear* (Hamilton, 1968). Because the book's author focused on the possible existence of ghosts as part of an evolving mystery, Rhonda began this particular discussion with a question about how many students believed in the supernatural. Instantly, a number of students raised their hands, and various children talked over one another as they shared their thoughts. While they engaged in this lively exchange, a loud voice in the back of the classroom quieted everyone abruptly when she shared the following about her belief in spirits: "I think they are real because my cousin said she saw my Grandma, that she came back." After this candid confession, several of the students looked around surprised and others seemed to stare either in agreement or in disbelief. Next, a few participants eagerly began to tell supernatural (ghosts or spirit) stories to one another. Many tales centered on family members who had shared their sightings of the deceased. Because the study participants became so captivated by these family tales, Rhonda concluded her discussion of *The House of Dies Drear* (Hamilton, 1968) and encouraged the children to share family stories in small groups.

As a validation of their cultural knowledge and experiences, participants shared stories about themselves or others in their families. In doing so, they forged significant life-text connections as well as used comparison and contrast to construct meaning from the novel. As the children jointly talked and soon began creating their own tales, an understanding about the topic of the supernatural as presented in *The House of Dies Drear* (Hamilton, 1968) deepened. Thus, constructions of meaning regarding the novel evolved through the storytelling session and incorporation of their cultural knowledge and experience into a classroom literacy event.

As evidenced in these two examples, the students' beliefs were rooted in family member experiences and the stories they conveyed. These beliefs constitute knowledge obtained from their own lived experiences, and it would be extremely difficult to pinpoint when or where the children initially established and then developed these beliefs. Certainly, these interpretations are rooted in valid cultural interactions between family members and participants; these types of associations should be expected by teachers as well as considered reasonable influences on acts of literary interpretation.

## Community Life

Community life emerged as the second cultural source relied on by the study participants. *Community life* is defined throughout as a geographical boundary surrounding the participants' school, including particular institutions, events, and groups of people. Unfortunately, although the study participants' community life included positive role models such as entrepreneurs and coaches along with institutions such as churches, mosques, and youth centers that set out to uplift its members, other aspects of community life were less positive.

One instance illustrating the participants' incorporation of community life into their textual interpretations occurred while reading *Roll of Thunder Hear My Cry* (Taylor, 1976). In this historical fiction story, the Logan family decides to boycott the local mercantile because the store's owners play a role in lynching a neighbor. With a bit of probing, participants arrived at a deeper understanding of the Logans' boycott, due to an experience with a boycott recently orchestrated by their own teacher:

(1) Rhonda:    The Logans are staging a boycott. What is that?
(2) Devon:     When you stop buying something.
(3) Rhonda:    Yes. Didn't we just talk about this earlier this week…and you said you were not going to that place?
(4) Bennie:    Yeah, KFC! [Kentucky Fried Chicken]
(5) Rhonda:    And why aren't we going to eat there anymore?
(6) Lisa:      Because they sell messed up chicken.
(7) Rhonda:    They sell mutated chicken, so we are boycotting KFC. When you eat the chicken and their chicken is coming out with fingers and toes missing, well…?
(8) Bennie:    They are actually selling that? We can sue them, can't we?
(9) Rhonda:    Well, if the chickens have missing parts…
(10) Tevin:    So [laughing].
(11) Rhonda:   If it [the feed] will do that to the chicken, then what will it do to the inside of your body?
(12) Bennie:   That ain't funny, we eat it.

The Kentucky Fried Chicken fast food restaurant, or "KFC" as the children referred to it, was located in the school's immediate community. Participants often talked about buying meals from KFC after leaving school, and the fast-food restaurant employed a few of the students' older siblings. Earlier in the week, before facilitating the aforementioned discussion, Rhonda told the students about a newspaper article she read related to the poor quality of food at certain KFCs located in predominately African American communities, and the class then vowed to no longer purchase food from any KFCs. To boycott something as a political act of resistance is a well-known tactic carried out in African American communities throughout the past 200 years. I suspect the students' historical understandings of a boycott, as well as their own lived experiences with KFC, influenced their reading of the Logans' behavior in *Roll of Thunder Hear My Cry* (Taylor, 1976). Due to the participants' involvement in this type of community action, organized partly by Rhonda, in subsequent discussions about the depiction of the book's boycott, the participants' collective understanding appeared aware and detailed.

**Popular Media**

*Popular media*, the final cultural source, is defined here to include animated cartoons and movies, traditionally viewed on televisions and/or movie screens. Increasingly, computers are mediums that also carry these art forms. During the next discussion, several participants responded to an incident in *The House of Dies Drear* (Hamilton, 1966). While talking, the students attempted to figure out which characters in the story are ghosts. Their discussion was halted by a comical remark given by Cedric:

(1) Rhonda:  Why are the Smalls going to move?
(2) Tariq:  Well if the devil is there, I don't really think they are gonna stay there.
(3) Rhonda:  Who's the devil?
(4) Tariq:  Mr. Pluto.
(5) Rhonda:  That's Pluto with a mask on.
(6) Kevin:  They are gonna chase him and he's gonna pass out. Then they are gonna take the mask off and find out who he is.
(7) Cedric:  Like Scooby Doo in the cave [laughing].

This final comment about *Scooby Doo* (line 7) is seemingly intended for laughs but is perhaps Cedric's own attempt to compare the character's actions in the novel to a character from a different context. Reader-response theorists identify this type of connection as "intertextual" (Sipe, 2000). According to Sipe, an *intertextual connection* occurs when students, "relate the text being read aloud to other cultural texts and products such as other books, the work of other artists and illustrators, movies, video advertisements, TV programs or the writing or art of classmates" (p. 266).

A similar intertextual connection occurred with a movie appropriate for an older audience, unlike the presumed audience of *Scooby Doo*. Interestingly, as a former middle-grades educator, I quickly learned that adolescents consume a wide range of media, from cartoons to adult dramas. While still facilitating a discussion about the ghost in *The House of Dies Drear* (Hamilton, 1968), Rhonda asked:

(1) Rhonda:  Who are the two little children?
(2) Viviana:  Do you mean the twins?
(3) Rhonda:  No, not the brothers.
(4) Viviana:  The girl and the guy that were dead?
(5) Rhonda:  Did it say they were dead?
(6) Tramira:  No.
(7) Rhonda:  That was a question we had right? Were they dead? Well, who saw the two little kids?
(8) Cedric:  Just Thomas.
(9) Ronald:  This is like the *Sixth Sense*.

Ronald's instantaneous connection to the movie, the *Sixth Sense*, is intertextual and similar in nature to the reference to the *Scooby Doo* cartoon. There is an explicit link between Cedric's response in the conversation and Ronald's insight. When Rhonda asked, "Who saw the two little kids?" (line 7), Cedric responded, "Just Thomas." (line 8). Although this personalized sighting of a ghost occurs in the book, it also represents a significant portion of the storyline in the *Sixth Sense*. In the movie, only certain characters are able to see the ghosts. Ronald believes that Thomas is the only character in the story who witnesses the ghosts, and this enables him to forge an association between the book and the movie (line 9). Thus, cultural knowledge gained from popular media did influence his interpretation of the mystery embedded in the book; Ronald realized the ways in which the two art forms, the book and the movie, were both crafted to evoke the mystery genre. The just-cited examples of popular media references as a type of cultural source underscore how children make associations that often emerge from contexts situated in their immediate lives, although constructed geographically outside of the urban community resided in by the participants.

## THE TEACHER:
## PEDAGOGICAL PRACTICES AND THEIR IMPLICATION

Throughout the examples given, pedagogical decisions taking place before, during, and after the literature discussions enabled Rhonda to use cultural knowledge and experiences successfully in her classroom.

First, the multicultural selection of literature (although not the only type read by the participants) suggests that Rhonda is aware of ways to motivate adolescents through connecting to similar topics, interests, and understandings they may have. Research has shown that African American children's novels, as one form of multicultural or ethnically diverse literature, can appeal to African American readers because the images, language, topics and themes are either somewhat familiar or particularly compelling (Brooks, 2003; Harris, 1995; Sims, 1983; Spears-Bunton, 1990; Walker-Dalhouse, 1992). Selecting these types of books also contributes to the process children undergo as they read and concurrently shape their own identities, values, and belief systems (Ferdman, 1990; Fox & Short, 2003). These books can support students' reading engagement and comprehension, disseminate information about a wide variety of racial and/or ethnic groups, and allow adolescents to discover more about themselves.

Incorporating multicultural stories into one's curriculum is a first step toward creating a classroom supportive to racially and ethnically diverse children. Becoming aware of culturally inspired curriculum materials is difficult but necessary, especially in today's current focus on adopting commercially prepared reading and language arts programs. But when educators begin to more deeply understand how literacy instruction and the reading development of students of color can be enhanced through the types of books read during this research, we will increasingly pay more attention to the textual material we select and support. Selecting literature to appeal to some interests of the students, without perpetuating stereotypes through the three different representations of the African American families in the books read, was a decision jointly made by Rhonda and myself.

Teachers hoping to academically develop children, as described by Ladson-Billings (1994) and others (e.g., Foster, 1994), argue that successful teachers of African American children must move beyond add-ons into the curriculum. For example, extended benefits of reading multicultural literature may have gone unrealized without the book discussions and ongoing teacher scaffolding of familiar cultural knowledge and experiences, including the probing of students' curious interpretations. Rhonda's ability to probe without immediately silencing a student who has given a perhaps unexpected or controversial remark demonstrates the nonjudgmental and keenness in which she realized how varying interpretations of culture as actually lived invade the classroom on a daily basis.

And, unbeknown to Rhonda at the time, her willing participation in the children's community life allowed her to know and reference a boycott while reading a similar event in the story. Through a socially acceptable act of resistance, by encouraging students to boycott the Kentucky Fried Chicken, she sought to empower the participants in ways familiar to some African Americans and often depicted in African American literature (Harris, 1990).

## CONCLUSION

The findings presented throughout this chapter are categories that represent cultural sources of knowledge and experiences of predominately middle school, African American children from an urban environment. The three sources (family members, community life, and popular media) attempt to explicate the extremely complicated concepts of *knowledge* and *experiences* as they relate to culture. As suggested by these findings, the cultural knowledge and experiences of students of color influences their literacy practices in general and, in particular, while constructing meaning with texts. Finally, classroom teachers like Rhonda can incorporate pedagogical strategies—from a careful selection of diverse curriculum materials to considering the impact of cultural nuances on meaning construction—to increase academic achievement and foster a deeply felt interest in learning.

## ENDNOTE

[1] See, for example, Dyson (2003) for an elaborated discussion on additional sources of culture during contemporary childhood.

## APPENDIX

*The House of Dies Drear* by Virginia Hamilton (1968) is about a middle-class African American family, the Smalls, who has just moved from North Carolina to Ohio during the late 1960s. The Smalls are not sure if they will like their Ohio home because a strange mystery surrounds it. For years, the townspeople have been reluctant for anyone to move into the house on the Dies Drear property because they fear that ghosts who were once runaway slaves haunt it. The house is located on a former stop for the Underground Railroad.

*Scorpions* by Walter Dean Myers (1988) is a coming-of-age novel about a poor, African-American adolescent named Jamal Hicks. Throughout the book, he is confronted with a powerful temptation to join a gang, the Scorpions. Jamal's older brother was the leader of the gang before becoming incarcerated.

*Roll of Thunder Hear My Cry,* by Mildred Taylor (1976), is one within a series of books about the Logans, an extended, southern, African American family living during the Great Depression. The primary struggle for the Logan family and the origin of conflict in the book centers on their desire to maintain and preserve 400 acres of land that symbolizes the struggle for African American freedom in the face of overt discrimination and racism.

## REFERENCES

Bell, Y., & Clark, T. (1998). Culturally relevant reading material as related to comprehension and recall in African American children. *Journal of Black Psychology, 24,* 455–475.

Brooks, W. (2003). Accentuating, preserving, and unpacking: Exploring interpretations of family relationships with African-American adolescents. *Journal of Children's Literature, 29*(2), 78–84.

Cazden, C. (1988). *Classroom discourse: The language of teaching and learning.* Portsmouth, NH: Heinemann.

Dyson, A. H. (1997). *Writing superheroes.* New York: Teachers College Press.

Dyson, A. H. (2003). *The brothers and sisters learn to write: Popular literacies in childhood and school culture.* New York: Teachers College Press.

Ferdman, B. (1990). Literacy and cultural identity. *Harvard Educational Review, 60,* 181–203.

Foster, M. (1994, Spring). The role of community and culture in school reform efforts: Examining the views of African American teachers. *Educational Foundations,* 5–27.

Fox, D. & Short, K. (2003). *Stories matter: The complexity of cultural authenticity in children's literature*. Urbana, IL: National Council of Teachers of English.

Hamilton, V. (1968). *The House of Dies Drear.* New York: Simon & Schuster.

Harris, V. (1990). African American children's literature: The first one hundred years. *Journal of Negro Education, 59,* 540–554.

Harris, V. (1995). Using African-American literature in the classroom. In V. L. Gadsden & D. A. Wagner (Eds.), *Literacy among African American youth: Issues in learning, teaching, and schooling* (pp. 229–259). Cresskill, NJ: Hampton Press.

Heath, S. (1983). *Ways with words: Language, life, and work in communities and classrooms*. Cambridge, England: Cambridge University Press.

Holland, D., & Quinn, N. (Eds.). (1987). *Cultural models in language and thought*. New York: Cambridge University Press.

Hull, G., & Rose, M. (1989). "This wooden shack place": The logic of an unconventional reading. *College Composition and Communication, 41,* 287–298.

Hull, G., & Schultz, K. (Eds.). (2002). *Schools out: Bridging out of school literacies with classroom practice*. New York: Teachers College Press.

Labov, W. (1972). *Language in the inner city: Studies in the Black English vernacular.* Philadelphia: University of Pennsylvania Press.

Ladson-Billings, G. (1994). *The Dreamkeepers: Successful teachers of African American children*. San Francisco: Jossey-Bass.

Lee, C. (1993). *Signifying as a scaffold for literary interpretation: The Pedagogic implications of an African American discourse genre*. Urbana, IL: National Council of Teachers of English.

Mahiri, J. (Ed.) (2004). *What they don't learn in school: Literacies in the lives of urban youth*. New York: Peter Lang.

Moller, K. J., & Allen, J. (1998, December). *Connecting, resisting, and creating safe places. Students respond to Mildred Taylor's The Friendship*. Paper presented at the National Reading Conference, Austin, TX.

Myers, W. (1988). *Scorpions*. New York: Scholastic.

Patton, M. (1990). *Qualitative evaluation and research methods* (2nd ed.). Newbury Park, CA: Sage.

Rickford, A. M. (1999). *I can fly: Teaching narratives and reading comprehension to African American and other ethnic minority students*. New York: University Press of America.

Sims, R. (1982). *Shadow and substance*. Urbana, IL: National Council of Teachers of English.

Sims, R. (1983). Strong Black girls: A ten-year-old responds to fiction about Afro Americans. *Journal of Research and Development in Education, 16,* 21–28.

Sipe, L. (2000). The construction of literary understanding by first and second graders in oral responses to storybooks read aloud. *Reading Research Quarterly, 35,* 252–276.

Spears-Bunton, L. (1990). Welcome to my house: African American and European American students' responses to Virginia Hamilton's *House of Dies Drear. Journal of Negro Education, 59,* 560–575.

Taylor, M. (1976). *Roll of thunder hear my cry*. New York: Puffin Books.

Walker-Dalhouse, D. (1992). Using African American literature to increase ethnic understanding. *The Reading Teacher, 45*(6) 416–422.

# Chapter 13

# The Politics of Advocacy, Strategies for Change: Diversity and Social Justice Pedagogy in Urban Schools

R. Patrick Solomon
*York University*

Andrew M. A. Allen
*University of Windsor*

Arlene Campbell
*York University*

The efforts of progressive teacher educators to prepare teachers for diversity and social justice pedagogy have gained some momentum over the past decade. The once dominant assimilationist and other homogenized notions of education are gradually giving way to multicultural curriculum in teacher education scholarship and practice. Notions of equity and social justice in teacher education have also captured the imagination of enlightened educators committed to building a more just and democratic society.

But, as many will argue, efforts to prepare teachers to offer a more inclusive and socially just pedagogy in urban schools are being undermined by a number of complex and intersecting factors. Historically, urban, inner-city schools with economically poor and racialized minority students have been framed by a deficit-driven, ideological perspective by those who have the power and responsibility to determine the schooling process. As a result, the curriculum and pedagogy in these institutions are characterized by rigidity and social control. More recently, contemporary school reform movements that favor a standardized, outcome-based curriculum further distanced the schooling process from its urban community. Such a reform fits cogently with the new global marketplace and free-market economic arrangements. Tremendous pressure is therefore placed on schools to respond to the demands of such an economic system at the expense of preparing students for democratic citizenship in a heterogeneous society.

Schools that have standardized their curricula leave little space for diversity; hence, the voices, perspectives, and cultural capital of the socially different become marginalized. As Hyland and Meacham (2004) conclude,

> None of these practices build upon, or even acknowledge, the social, intellectual, cultural or political capital of students and their families.... The results of these institutional arrangements include a reification of deficit ideology about students of color and economically poor students, as well as an adversarial relationship between teachers and parents. (pp.114–115)

How do we then prepare teachers to transform rather than reproduce the negative educational culture that is so pervasive in urban school environments? Can teacher preparation deliberately resocialize and professionalize new teachers to transform the deficit ideology that is embedded in urban pedagogical practices? In this chapter, we document the professional lives of graduates of an urban diversity teacher education program designed to prepare teachers to integrate issues of equity, diversity, and social justice into all aspects of their curriculum and pedagogy. Their preparation focused on offering a culturally relevant pedagogy to children, a pedagogy that links school learning with students' experiences within their urban communities; "a curriculum of life" (Portelli & Vibert, 2002). But public schooling is contested terrain. Efforts to implement an inclusive social justice pedagogy in a traditional monocultural school culture will often be resisted and contested by stakeholders who have invested in "the way things are."

This chapter uncovers some of the challenges faced by teachers with a mission and the counterresistance strategies they employ. In conclusion, we offer suggestions that move beyond the standards–diversity debate and focus on ways to develop a more critical consciousness of teachers, one that interrogates the political embeddedness that tends to subvert diversity and social justice education.

## RESISTING DIVERSITY
## AND SOCIAL JUSTICE IN TEACHER EDUCATION

Pedagogies that seek to develop a critical perspective toward social difference, that is, critical multiculturalism, antiracism, feminism, antiableism, antihomophobia, anticlassism, and other forms of antioppressive education, have not been fully embraced by pre-service and in-service teachers. In fact, the research literature points to a vibrant continuum of resistance from teacher candidacy to certified practitioners in classrooms.

At the pre-service level, researchers document a number of reasons for resistance to diversity, equity and social justice education:

- exposure to "difficult knowledge"; knowledge that causes "cognitive dissonance"; knowledge that conflicts with one's belief system (Carson & Johnston, 2000);
- emotional turmoil such as guilt, shame, anger, despair caused by exposure to the inequities experienced by the socially different, such as racial minorities, and how the dominant (White) group is implicated in such inequities (Davidman & Davidman, 1994; Solomon & Levine-Rasky, 1996);
- the perspective that teacher education is primarily about the acquisition of subject area knowledge, learning to teach the basics, and less about preparing students to contribute to a socially just, democratic society (Kumashiro, 2003).

At the in-service level, teachers resist equity, diversity and social justice pedagogy for the same reasons just listed, along with the following:

- long-term investment in "the way things are" and a reluctance to change their pedagogy (Kumashiro, 2003; Sleeter, 1992);
- the belief that equity and diversity education will detract from the standardized curriculum and interfere with state-mandated learning outcomes (Solomon & Allen, 2001;
- the lack of scholastic preparation to understand and implement a critical multiculturalism and antiracism pedagogy (Howard, 1999; Solomon & Levine-Rasky, 2003); and
- dominant group negation of "Whiteness" and its power and privileges (Levine-Rasky, 2000; Schick, 2000; Solomon, Portelli, Daniel, & Campbell, 2005; Swartz, 2003).

Such a substantive list of reasons for rejecting equity and social justice pedagogy points to a deeper entrenchment in one's belief system and ideologies. As Kumashiro (2003) concludes, "students' identities, experiences, privileges, investments, and so forth always influence how they think and perceive, and what they know and choose to know" (p. 53). He argues that the constant repetition of certain inequitable practices and relations, if left unchallenged over time, will maintain and reproduce the oppressive status quo. He therefore advocates for a potent intervention "anti-oppressive teacher education which involves interrupting the repetition of common sense discourses of what it means to teach and to learn to teach" (p. 59).

How then do teachers committed to the principles and practices of equity, diversity, and social justice interrupt oppressive "commonsense" discourses that reside in urban schools and communities? In the next section, we introduce several graduates of an urban diversity teacher education program and their political strategies for subverting resistance.

## RESEARCH SETTING AND STUDY DESIGN

Data for this chapter are drawn from a larger 3-year follow-up study designed to determine the extent to which graduates of an urban teacher education program grounded in the democratic principles of equity, diversity, and social justice continue to integrate these principles into their workplace curriculum and pedagogy. The research had shown that school reform and restructuring for the global economic marketplace have dramatically impacted the political and pedagogical conditions of teachers' work and their social relations within and outside educational settings (Dehli, 1996; Dei & Karumanchery, 2001; McNeil 2000). For this chapter, we focus on the political strategies these teachers utilized and some challenges they faced when integrating antioppressive practices in their urban schools and communities.

Participants in this study are from two cohorts (graduates of 1995 and 1997) of the Urban Diversity (UD) Teacher Education Initiative at York University, Toronto, Canada. Elements of the program include: (a) a strong social and cultural foundations of education course that explores issues of social difference and schooling, (b) a self-study of identity formation and its impact on teaching and field-based practica in urban and inner-city schools, (c) dyad partnerships and practicum school cohort groupings based on social difference, and (d) inquiry-based, experiential community involvement. (See chap. 4, this volume, for a full description of this initiative.) Twenty graduates from each cohort (representing the racial, ethnic gender, and cultural diversity of the larger cohort and the metropolitan area) were selected from volunteers. At the time of the research, these graduates had been teaching in urban schools for 7 to 9 years.

We utilized qualitative research methods that combined data collection approaches such as in-depth, individual interviews, focus-group discussions, classroom and in-school observations, and analyses of participants' professional portfolios, teaching plans, and classroom resources. These approaches provided the opportunity for participants to reflect on their lived experiences and to give meaning to the complexities and contradictions to which they must respond in institutional settings (Gluck & Patai, 1991; Norquay, 1999).

A range of themes emerged from an analysis of the data collected. For this chapter, we focus on the political strategies graduates utilize to implement their diversity and social justice agenda in the schools they teach. The voices and experiences of graduates of color appear to be overrepresented in this chapter.

## Implementation Strategies

The findings of this study indicate that UD graduates developed a number of strategies to introduce diversity and social justice issues into the mainstream curriculum and pedagogy of the schools in which they were employed. Based on both lived and vicarious experiences, they developed and implemented political strategies to achieve their pedagogical goals. These include (a) understanding and navigating (negotiating) school culture, (b) assuming advocacy roles that promote diversity and social justice, (c) utilizing the power of collaboration, (d) seeking and utilizing administrative support, and (e) empowering marginalized and minoritized parent communities. Here we explore and theorize about these dominant themes, embedded in the narratives of the participants.

## Understanding and Navigating School Culture

In the excerpts that follow, the graduates were politically strategic in orienting themselves to the school culture before attempting to intervene for change. They made judgments about the established groups, and developed a plan of action for change:

> To achieve my objectives, I initially sat back and took in the full culture of the school because I felt I needed to understand what was already in place before I could initiate anything. I needed to know who the key players were. So I approached it from a very political standpoint. I observed because I don't believe that you can change the school culture unless you become part of it in an informed way. Then you need to set out a plan in order to change it. This really grounded me for the time that I was there. (Sandra)

> The school environment was not conducive to change. It was an "old boys' club," and people were set in their ways. They felt threatened, so we had to tread very carefully. (Jane)

From these excerpts, which represented the perspectives of participants in the study, it is evident that UD graduates are well aware of the procedural and political dimensions of transforming cultures. For example, the notion of identifying key players in institutional settings is supported by the research literature (Mundry & Hergert, n.d.; Rogers, 1971). Here Rogers identified the "adopter types" that change agents will likely encounter in school cultures. These range from innovators who are eager to try new ideas, leaders who are trusted by others, and resisters who generally contest and oppose new ideas. UD graduates were very strategic in studying and engaging these adopter types, and with their support, they deliberately developed a plan of action to transform some dimensions of school culture.

In his article, "Why Teachers Must Become Change Agents," Fullan (1993) argues "teachers must combine the mantle of moral purpose with the skill of change agentry" (p.12). He adds, "moral purpose without change agentry is martyrdom...change agentry without moral purpose is change for the sake of change" (p.14). The findings of this study indicate that participants are well grounded in their moral purpose, making schools more equitable, diverse, and socially just learning environments. But achieving such moral objectives is indeed an arduous task for newcomers to achieve. Change theorists such as Fullan alert us to the challenges of changing school cultures when insiders are heavily invested in "the way things are."

## Assuming Ownership and Responsibility

UD graduates became active "role players" in the diversity and social justice games their schools played. They assumed certain responsibilities because of their social identities as minority teachers or their moral commitment to antioppressive education. The following excerpts reflect their perspectives on how and why they became central to their school's initiatives:

> When anything that came up that was even remotely related to diversity or social justice, I was the one who was thrust forward; whether I did it on my own or people assumed that I would take that role. I guess I just didn't ask to because I felt that was part of who I was anyway. So if anything came up, whether it was organizing a committee, an assembly, or inviting someone to come in and do storytelling, I was the one. What happened after a couple of months was that people just assumed that I would take the role, and they came to me with questions such as, "Oh, I am having this difficulty with a particular student concerning race, what should I do, how do I handle it?" I became the expert, particularly with African Canadian students. I became the expert on *anything* to do with them. (Sharon)

> I actually volunteered to be the antiracist coordinator at the beginning of term because you usually get these sign-up sheets asking for volunteers for various things, and there is a big blank space next to "antiracist educator" and I stepped up to the role. I tried to find different ways to seek equity within the school and I communicated with teachers on that level right from the very start. (Angie)

> What I found within my particular environment was that there were no other teachers who were holding the same sort of belief systems, or wanted

to create anything, so it was me. Equity initiatives that I was trying to implement within the school became my responsibility. If there were posters
going up, it was me. If there were plays being planned, it was me. If there
were inspirational messages, if there was anything to do with religious
holidays or celebrations, it was me. I became the equity rep, not because I
volunteered for it, but it was me. If you are a person of color, sometimes
you just get it [the equity portfolio] automatically. You are going to be the
one who attends meetings, who informs others of what's going on. I was a
"one-person show" for many years. (Donnette)

These narratives capture the many ways UD graduates assumed responsibilities, or had it thrust upon them in their school communities. They
functioned in such capacities as curriculum resource leaders for equity,
knowledge brokers for cultural diversity, experts on racial minority issues,
staff development facilitators for learning opportunities relating to equity,
diversity, and social justice, and school representatives for matters related
to equity policy and practice.

It is important to note that UD graduates often assumed these roles and
responsibilities because they felt knowledgeable, competent, and professionally prepared. In addition, the graduates of color believed that their
own racial identity was synonymous to equity leadership in the school.
Their identity and their roles had become tightly wedded.

Assuming responsibilities in the schooling for equity and social justice is
well reported in the research literature. M. Foster's (1997) biographies of
Black teachers and their teaching, and Dixson's (2003) work on Black
women teacher's advocacy both parallel the experiences of the UD graduates. Although they felt empowered to assume such roles and responsibilities, the extent to which they could effect any real change in their
environment depended on the type of power that was built into the responsibility. We revisit this issue later.

## USING THE POWER OF COLLABORATION
## AND COMMUNITY BUILDING

Institutional capacity building for diversity and social justice required a
thoughtfully designed process of co-opting the like-minded, recognizing
people's levels of "equity consciousness," developing a framework from
which the committed can expand, and distributing ownership of the initiative among the interested:

Then I started looking for people who were like-minded that I could pull,
and got a group of about six teachers. I had the good fortune of being in a
portable classroom and we would just have meetings over lunch and discuss issues of diversity and equity. I had a number of teachers of Italian de-

scent, and few Black teachers who came on board. So they became the core
Diversity Committee. We started to strategize and came up with a plan.
My objective was to recognize that all teachers were at different points on
an equity continuum and to develop a strategy for moving them along. So
this group of six put together an action plan, took it to the principal for his
support, and invited the larger teaching staff to participate. Although it
was *our* original idea, in order to assume ownership, people needed to feel
a part of the development process. So we told them that what we did was
just the framework, so they should feel free to participate. We had about
20 teachers who became involved and were given an opportunity to be
part of the whole process. So that was very positive. (Sandra)

From their understanding of school culture, change agency, and
adopter types within institutions, UD graduates identified and worked strategically with a group of teachers they perceived as positively responsive to
an equity agenda in their school. Through such capacity building and the
provision of opportunity for all teachers to participate and assume ownership for this initiative, UD graduates laid a strong foundation for school
change. Institutional transformation "from the ground up" has a better
chance of survival than those from the "top down," those legislated, or those
initiated by a "marginal group."

It is interesting that these change agents perceived race and ethnicity as a
key factor in recruiting a critical mass for collaboration and community
building. This perception, supported by empirical research, shows that racial minority teachers are likely to be very supportive of equity-based
race-related policies and practices (e.g., antiracism pedagogy; Carr &
Klassen, 1997).

## UTILIZING ADMINISTRATIVE SUPPORT

Most participants in the study were knowledgeable about the power relations and hierarchies that exist within schools, and the school administrator's location within. They were also cognizant that the survival and success
of a diversity and social-justice agenda hinged on administrative support.
"The fact that the administrator supported the initiative that we were bringing forth made a lot of difference," said Jane.

In the following narratives, participants discuss school leaders' knowledge and awareness of school boards' equity policies and commitment to
their implementation.

> The principal of that particular school knew the Equitable Schools binder
> inside out. She ran her school according to the equitable schools policy
> and made sure that there was an inclusive curriculum. (Donnette)

We basically went to the principal and two vice principals with the equity goals we had developed. One of the vice principals, a woman of color, was on board with us 100 percent and supported everything we did around equity. She sat in on the meetings and we managed to get a two-part session where we could in-service the whole staff on the equity policy and had a discussion about it. (Angie)

What is evident in these excerpts is the graduates' admiration for school administrators with knowledge and awareness about policy and a commitment to the enactment of such policy. They displayed high regard for leaders who move beyond mechanistic and bureaucratic management that focused on the technical, procedural, rule-enforcing, and efficiency-maximizing approach to embrace a knowledge-based, committed, and authentic participation in equity initiatives within schools. Marshall, Patterson, Rogers, and Steale (1996) characterize this involvement as operating from an ethic of care that responds to contextual realities; a position that "enables schools to become caring communities that nurture all children, regardless of their race, class, or gender" (p. 276).

Also supporting the graduates' perspectives is W. Foster's (1989) notion of *educative leadership* that provides the environment for those within to interrogate taken-for-granted institutional arrangements and move toward a pedagogical model that promotes human agency. Corson's (2000) conception of *emancipatory leadership* fits well with these graduates' ideas for working equitably in diverse sociocultural environments and the importance of including marginalized groups in the decision-making circle.

But as these graduate teachers have alluded, transformational and emancipatory leadership is not always present in the schools where they worked. As revealed later, some leaders are often hampered by pedagogical shortcomings and political–ideological obstacles in their work environment.

## EMPOWERING MINORITY PARENTS AND THEIR COMMUNITIES

UD graduates were strategic in giving voice and representation to minority group parents and the inner-city, ethno-racial communities from which they come. Dissatisfaction with dominant group, middle-class "centricity" of their schools' learning materials and the underrepresentation or misrepresentation of the "other" has often driven parents into conflict and unproductive relationships with the school. Some lack the political skills to negotiate for positive change, so interactions with school personnel often disempowered and marginalized both them and their communities.

Participants in this study are instrumental in empowering parents to represent their children's interest in the schooling process.

One parent had refused to allow her daughter to go to the school library. She took a very political stance because there wasn't enough diversity represented in the learning materials there. So I coached her along without the school knowing. She responded well because she was the president of the school council, and I sat on the school council, which helped build our work relationship. She requested and received further coaching sessions, and developed the confidence to approach the principal to request a meeting with the entire teaching staff to discuss equity. (Donnette)

Here, the parent, already with political clout by virtue of her position in the school council (popularly labeled *Parent Council* by parents and teachers), was coached on ways to navigate the organizational and administrative structures of the school in order to bring about diversity in the learning materials. This is a significant accomplishment for teacher and parent to utilize the duly constituted school council to collaborate in a struggle to diversify curriculum materials in urban schools. Such a body has been critiqued for being a "rubber stamp" for administrative decision making that maintains the status quo (Delgado-Gaitin, 1991; Fine, 1993).

The notion of scaffolding of parents and teachers for political action is significant for this study. Dixson (2003), in her work, *'Let's Do This!' Black Women Teachers' Politics and Pedagogy*, makes explicit connection between the success of teacher advocacy work and support for their parents and students. She argues that teachers and parents sharing common ground (e.g., race, ethnicity) allows teachers to engage in a pedagogy that can be empathetic and politically potent.

Participants' advocacy work with parents and their communities is well rooted in their pre-service education that prepares them for a culturally relevant pedagogy, one that builds a symbiotic relationship between school knowledge and that of the community it serves (Solomon, Khattar Manoukian, & Clarke, chap. 5, this volume; Solomon & Lavine-Rasky, 2003). A participant talks about her involvement and advocacy, stating "One of the things I've always been committed to is community involvement: getting on the school council, advocating for kids and parents, and establishing a democratic classroom so that the kids should come to expect to have a voice in things."

## SUMMARY

The strategies employed by UD graduates reflect a group of change agents that are well grounded, knowledgeable, and morally committed to a pedagogy that is inclusive, equitable, and socially just. Their knowledge of power hierarchies that reside within schools and the ways these structures operate to maintain institutional culture provided them with productive transformational strategies. They utilized a sequence of approaches that worked complementarily in seeking the desired change. The process began with a reliable reading of school culture, and potential collaborators (teachers as well as administrators) who were instrumental in the change process. Even more political was collaborating with marginalized parents and their urban communities in challenging an inequitable and noninclusive school environment. Indeed, such involvement left UD graduates personally and professionally vulnerable in the contested terrain of schooling.

## The Challenges of Navigating
## the Contested Terrain of Urban Schooling

To engage in the politics of advocacy and the discourse of equity, diversity, and social justice is not without significant impact on the personal and professional lives of UD graduates in this study. For many, it was like navigating the minefield of oppression, bias, injustice, indifference, and "dysconsciousness" of the inequities of schooling. Here we examine two challenges that pervaded the narratives of UD graduates: responsibilities without power, and the burnout effects of engaging in multiple roles.

### Responsibilities Without Power

Many UD graduates were resource persons in their schools. They were given "expert" status and the task of dealing with the troublesome problems of social difference (e.g., resolving racial, ethnic, and/or immigrant issues), and engaging in organizational tasks that reflected the institution in "politically correct" postures of diversity and social justice. They became the "work horses" for implementing the schools' equity and diversity agenda.

On the other hand, they were labeled *militant and extreme* for advocating for the powerless, and vilified for developing the social justice consciousness of students, teachers, parents, and other members of the school community. The following excerpt reflects on these challenges and the potential impact on their personal and professional lives.

> If there was ever a problem that had to do with race I was the one that the administration slammed for it. I had an incident in my first year [of teaching] where one of my students and a student from another class were calling someone a "nigger lover." And because word of that incident reached the office, I was called down and the principal stated, "This is what happens when you do what you are doing in your class." So when trouble came concerning race, I was the one who took the fall for it. (Sharon)

Encoded in the principal's aforementioned statement is a damning critique of antiracism and other pedagogies that address social inequities in society. Indeed, any curriculum or pedagogy that interrogates, disrupts the taken-for-granted, or is perceived as confrontational or tension ridden, becomes problematic for school leaders whose priority is to maintain a stable, conflict-free school environment.

Consequently, the troublesome issues of race, racism, and antiracism are often perceived by school leaders as acrimonious, and therefore antithetical to the more harmonious and celebratory multiculturalism (Solomon, 2002). The enactment of antiracism policies therefore takes the form of "peace-making" and "conflict mediation" programs, as leaders manage their communities in ways that discourage and conceal potential conflict and disharmony. This is what Hargreaves (1991) conceptualizes as "contrived collegiality," a top–down management structure that forces collaboration and runs the risk of silencing dissenting voices. But silencing voices on race may only lead to the maintenance of a racially inequitable social system, and the continued oppression of racialized minorities.

Instead of blaming antiracist educators for exploring race in their curriculum, McLaren and Dantley (1990) insist that "those involved in educational leadership must engage in a discourse which systemically critiques the institutional, political, and social mechanics that perpetuate the asymmetrical power relations and other aberrations of democracy that currently dominate school curriculum and practice" (p. 38).

Building a more inclusive curriculum was equally contested by stakeholders involved in the schooling process. Such contestation was evident in such areas as religious and interfaith diversity. Despite provincial curriculum guidelines that permit the education about religion in its public schools,[1] conservatism among some faith communities made it challenging for UD graduates to introduce their students to the richness of Canada's religious heritage. Indeed, exclusivity in religious positioning has given rise to contentious, faith-based debates about such curricular issues as sex education, abortion, and homosexuality. Some groups became politically active in keeping such contemporary social issues out of school curricula, and have threatened legal action if their "religious rights" are violated.

In addition, critical liberatory pedagogies have also been contested. In the following excerpt, a UD graduate speaks about the tensions that developed when a parent resisted moving beyond the liberal approach to the exploration of Canadian heritage and the issue of race and racism within it:

> I had a big conflict of ideas with a parent aid. We were trying to plan a heritage day assembly, and I was approaching it from an antiracist perspective while she preferred to just gloss it over, and didn't like the "stop racism" posters. If you deal with conservative parents it's just as hard as a conservative administrator. Sometimes such parents get the administrator on their side. (Suzette)

In reflections on their status in their respective schools, both UD graduates mentioned realize the powerlessness in integrating an antiracism pedagogy into the curriculum. The conventional conservative culture of institutions and the administrators' apparent support appeared to disempower the teachers and restrict the work for equity and social justice in their schools. They reside in a contradictory world where they are given or have assumed certain responsibilities, but not the power to execute effectively.

## BURN-OUT EFFECT OF MULTIPLE ROLES

> I was getting burnt out and resenting the many hats that I had to put on, and the resistance that I was receiving from the rest of the staff. (Angie)

Throughout the study, UD graduates related the many roles and responsibilities they undertake to increase the possibility of a diverse and socially just schooling for urban students. Beyond their own formal classroom teaching, they assume (a) the informal task of curriculum diversification and resourcing, (b) the professional development of their colleagues, (c) serving on equity committees both inside and beyond the boundaries of their schools, and (d) advocating for urban groups often marginalized by the conservative culture and bureaucracy of the school. Research carried out on graduates of a teacher education program (Center X, California) whose core elements and principles include commitment to social justice, indicates that these graduate teachers engage in their professional work, especially in the areas of professional development and political activism, much more than colleagues from other programs (Goode, Hunter, Quartz, Barraza-Lyons, & Thomas, 2003). Their involvement was not restricted to pedagogical, cultural, and political activities, but rather they engaged intellectually with issues. So too are the graduates of the UD program, as this excerpt indicates:

> An easier way out is just sticking to the expectations of the Ontario Curriculum. But building on the issues of social justice sometimes requires that I go home at nights and just think. I have to think and write things out; not lesson plans, just my thoughts: how I am going to make equity and social justice connect with the curriculum. So at this point that's my intellectual work, and it takes time. I just need to learn to be patient. There's a whole bunch of other procedural, everyday classroom stuff that you need to take into account. But I guess I kind of want to do everything now, but it's not realistic. (Martin)

The role of teachers as intellectuals is supported by such schooling critics as Giroux and McLaren (1986) and Hartnett and Carr (1995), who insist that teachers' roles become more than merely operational and technical, unquestioning implementation of educational policies and programs that have emerged with state-mandated educational reform. Instead, Giroux and McLaren (1986) advocate for teachers who are "transformative intellectuals": those who can "adopt a more critical role of challenging the social order so as to develop and advocate its democratic imperatives" (p. 224).

But engaging fully in these professional tasks in a hotly contested area of schooling took a tremendous toll on the psyche of UD graduates. They experienced isolation, were often excluded from the mainstream because of their political activism, endured contradictory responses from their administrators and colleagues, and had to constantly defend their pedagogy against attacks from those protecting the status quo. These are some of the personal, professional, and psychological costs that must be explored by teacher educators for urban schools and communities.

## IMPLICATIONS FOR SOCIAL JUSTICE TEACHER PREPARATION FOR URBAN SETTINGS

This study of a group of graduates at an urban diversity teacher education program found that a solid grounding in the principles and practices of diversity and social justice has the potential to sustain professional practice over time. It also shows that UD graduates as change agents will develop pedagogical and political strategies to transform schools for the benefit of urban students and the communities from which they come. These findings are quite similar to those of the Center X teacher education research program in California (Goode et al., 2003; Hunter Quartz & The TEP Research Group, 2003). From these studies, we draw the conclusion that well-designed and executed teacher preparation programs that move beyond the traditional are potentially effective in transforming urban schools and communities.

But the study also uncovered some troubling issues of resistance to change in urban schools. UD graduates' advocacy was contested by various stakeholders in the educational enterprise; by dominant group parents and teachers who have invested in "the way things are," and administrators who would rather preside over a liberal, politically neutral, and harmonious work place than one that interrogates structural and pedagogical injustices. As a result, strategies for change were precariously hinged on shifting and unstable alliances with school culture, administration, colleagues, parents, and their communities. For example, a change in school administrative personnel could mean a complete withdrawal of support for a social justice agenda.

What are the implications for teacher educators? These issues have raised the need for a form of professional development that closes the ideological, knowledge, and commitment gap between new teachers who were prepared to work for social justice, and veteran colleagues who may not have received such preparation in their pre- and in-service teacher education. Such a "community of learners"[2] could be comprised of pre-service and in-service teachers, teacher educators, and resource persons from the communities in which the school is located, with each partner a potential contributor and beneficiary in this collaboration.

Arising from this study are significant issues with which such learning communities must grapple, three of which are (a) shared ownership of policies and practices of diversity and social justice, (b) centralizing the issue of race and racism in teacher education scholarship and practice, and (c) the inclusion of urban dwellers in the community of learners. There is an urgent need to redistribute the responsibility of diversity and social justice work among all teachers. This is not a task for only new or minority teachers, as is the current practice of delegation.[3] Antioppressive education will not be fully integrated into the school curriculum and pedagogy until dominant players with power and authority in institutional structures assume such responsibilities and leadership. As this research demonstrates, new teachers with moral consciousness, civic responsibility, and pedagogical skills have already sought leadership and collaboration for institutional change from their more experienced colleagues. In a "community of learners," there ought to be a level of interdependent learning among professionals. New teachers bring new scholarship and progressive pedagogy from their teacher education, while veteran practitioners bring their knowledge of community and experience of the school culture. Working together is potentially transformative.

The issue of race, racism, and antiracism education is pervasive throughout the UD graduates' narratives. It appeared to be engrained into the consciousness, behaviors, and experiences of those who self-identified as racial minorities.[4] They work in schools and communities where race is essentialized as a social marker in the habits, assumptions, and dispositions of people. Yet educators engage in the practice of "racelessness" and "colorblindness" in their pedagogy and social relationships in multiracial schools (see Cochran-Smith, 1995; Schofield, 1997, for an extended discussion of these perspectives). Educators must acknowledge the negative force of racism on a significant portion of its school population, and not simply normalize it as a prevailing societal norm and expectation. In a cross-racial learning community for teachers, it is critical that they embrace the opportunity to be sensitized by and learn from the knowledge and experiences of those marginalized by racial oppression. A progressive scholarship on race and education, combined with the realities of racism in institutional settings, makes for unsettling but critical learning for teachers.

Finally, teachers and teacher educators must come to see urban residents as important partners in the community of teachers and learners.

Their knowledge of the urban context and their experiences within it equip them to be powerful mentors of teachers and administrators.[5] They also provide strong links with residents and community resources as curriculum materials that were often overlooked or disregarded by schools. Their input will help teachers develop a more culturally relevant pedagogy. With this diversity of ideas, perspectives, and knowledge, along with the democratic involvement of community collaborators, emerges the potential to disrupt conventional pedagogy and lay the foundation for real change in urban schools.

## ACKNOWLEDGMENTS

We thank the Social Science and Humanities Research Council (SSHRC) of Canada for their financial support of this project. We also thank research assistants Marc Carver, Anna Chudnovsky, Randa Khattar Manoukian, and Laura Lindo.

## ENDNOTES

[1]In 1992, the Ontario Ministry of Education resource document, *Education About Religion in Ontario Public Elementary Schools,* made it clear that its goals are to educate and not indoctrinate: "to prepare students to participate effectively and harmoniously in our multicultural/multi-faith society. ...First in terms of the knowledge, skills, values and attitudes acquired by the student, and second, in terms of the different types of learning the student experiences" (p.16).

[2]Over the years such a learning community has become more formally constructed in the teacher education literature as Professional Development Schools (PDS). The Holmes Group (1990) conceptualize the PDS as a school–university partnership designed to provide progressive PD for all engaged in the schooling enterprise.

[3]It is common practice in schools to hire racial and ethnic minorities and invest in them the responsibilities for equity, diversity and social justice issues. But for these new professionals, these are responsibilities without power. Their success on the job is dependent on their senior colleagues, the administration, and parents in the community. Lack of support from these stakeholders generates negative emotional responses including frustration, anger, disappointment, and so forth.

[4]Most of the narratives in this chapter are from graduates who self-identify as people of color. In this study, they appear to be the group most likely to develop and execute concrete strategies for integrating social justice and directly confronting issues of racism and antiracism in their pedagogy. The research on teacher racial identity and urban schools appear to support these patterns (Carr

& Klassen, 1997; Haberman & Post, 1998; Hunter Quartz et al., 2003). We continue to analyze the data to ascertain the extent to which this pattern holds.

[5] It is a widely acknowledged fact that teachers in urban, inner-city schools are daily commuters and do not experience or relate to the community in any meaningful or intimate way. As a result, they are unaware of the richness of the emerging new immigrant population, which often includes educated professionals, who because of restrictive certification regulations are not given the opportunity to practice their craft, but none the less can contribute significantly to the schooling process.

## REFERENCES

Carr, P. R., & Klassen, T. R. (1997). Different perceptions of race in education: Racial minority and White teachers. *Canadian Journal of Education, 22*(1), 67–81.

Carson, T., & Johnson, I. (2000). The difficulty with difference in teacher education: Toward a pedagogy of compassion. *Alberta Journal of Educational Research, 46*(1), 75–83.

Cochran-Smith, M. (1995). Colorblindness and basket making are not the answers: Confronting the dilemmas of race, culture and language diversity in teacher education. *American Educational Research Journal, 312*(3), 493–522.

Corson, D. (2000). Emancipatory leadership. *International Journal of Leadership in Education, 3*(2), 93–120.

Davidman, L., & Davidman, P. T. (1994). *Teaching with a multicultural perspective: A practical guide.* New York: Longman.

Dei, G. J. S., & Karumanchery, L. L. (2001). School reforms in Ontario: The 'marketization of education' and the resulting silence on equity. In J. P. Portelli & R. P.Solomon (Eds.), *The erosion of democracy in education: From critique to possibilities* (pp.189–216). Calgary: Detselig Enterprises Ltd.

Dehli, K. (1996). Between "market" and "state"? Engendering education change in the 1990s. *Discourse: Studies in the Cultural Politics of Education, 17*(3), 363–376.

Delgado-Gaitin, C. (1991). Involving parents in the schools: A process of empowerment. *American Journal of Education, 100,* 20–46.

Dixson, A. (2003)). 'Let's do this!' Black women teachers' politics and pedagogy. *Urban Education, 38*(2), 217–235.

Fine, M. (1993). [Ap]parent involvement: Reflections on parents, power and urban public schools. *Teachers College Record, 94*(4), 682–710.

Foster, M. (1997). *Black teachers on teaching.* New York: New Press.

Foster, W. (1989). Toward a critical practice of leadership. In J. Smyth (Ed.), *Critical perspectives on educational leadership* (pp. 39–62). London: Falmer Press.

Fullan, M. (1993, March). Why teachers must become change agents. *Educational Leadership,* pp. 12–17.

Giroux, H., & McLaren, P. (1986). Teacher education and the politics of engagement: The case for democratic schooling. *Harvard Educational Review, 56*(3), 213–238.

Gluck, S. B., & Patai, D. (Eds.) (1991). *Women's words: The Feminist practice of oral history.* New York: Routledge.

Goode, J., Hunter Quartz, K., Barraz-Lyons, K., & Thomas, A. (2003). *Supporting urban educational leaders: An analysis of the multiple roles of social justice educators*. Institute of Democracy, Education & Access, University of California, Los Angeles.

Haberman, M., & Post, L. (1998). Teachers for multicultural schools: The power of selection. *Theory Into Practice, 37*(2), 96–104.

Hargreaves, A. (1991). Contrived collegiality: The micropolitics of teacher collaboration. In J. Blasé (Ed.), *The politics of life in schools: Power, conflict and cooperation* (pp. 46–72). London: Sage.

Hartnett, A., & Carr, W. (1995). Education, teacher development and the struggle for democracy. In J. Smyth (Ed.), *Critical discourses on teacher development* (pp. 39–53). Toronto: OISE Press.

Holmes Group. (1990). *Tomorrow's schools: Principles for the design of professional development schools*. East Lansing, MI: Author.

Howard, G. R. (1999). *We can't teach what we don't know: White teachers, multicultural schools*. New York: Teachers College Press.

Hunter Quartz, K. & The TEP Research Group (2003). "Too angry to leave": Supporting new teachers' commitment to transform urban schools. *Journal of Teacher Education, 54*(2), 99–111.

Hyland, N. E., & Meacham, S. (2004). Community knowledge-centered teacher education: A paradigm for socially just educational transformation. In J. L. Kincheloe, A. Burstyn, & S. R. Steinberg (Eds.), *Teaching teachers: Building a quality school of urban education* (pp. 113–134). New York: Peter Lang.

Kumashiro, K. K. (2003). Against repetition: Addressing resistance to anti-oppressive change in the practice of learning, teaching, supervising and researching. In A. Howell & F. Tuitt (Eds.), *Race and higher education: Rethinking pedagogy in diverse college classrooms* (pp. 45–67). Harvard Educational Review [Rep. Series No. 36]. Cambridge, MA: Harvard Educational Publishing.

Levine-Rasky, C. (2000) Framing Whiteness: Working through the tensions in introducing Whiteness to educators. *Race, Ethnicity and Education, 3*(3), 271–292.

Marshall, C., Patterson, J. A., Rogers, D. L., & Steale, J. R. (1996). Caring as career: An alternative perspective for educational administration. *Educational Administration Quarterly, 3*(2), 271–294.

McLaren, P., & Dantley, M. (1990). Leadership and a critical pedagogy of race: Cornel West, Stuart Hall, and the prophetic tradition. *Journal of Negro Education, 59*(1), 29–44.

McNeil, L. M. (2000). *Contradictions of school reform: Educational costs of standardized testing*. New York: Routledge.

Mundry, S. E., & Hergert, L. F. (n.d.). *Making change for school improvement: Leader's manual*. Andover, MA: The Network, Inc.

Norquay, N. (1999). Who rebels? Gender and class in stories of irrelevance and resistance. *British Journal of Sociology of Education, 10*(4), 459–473.

Ontario Ministry of Education. (1992). *Education about religion in Ontario public elementary schools* [Resource Document]. Queen's Park, Toronto: Author.

Portelli, J. P., & Vibert, A. (2002). A curriculum of life. *Education Canada, 42*(2), 36–39.

Rogers, E. (1971). *Diffusion of innovations*. New York: The Free Press.

Schick, C. (2000). By virtue of being White: Resistance in antiracist pedagogy. *Race, Ethnicity and Education, 3*(1), 83–102.

Schofield, J. W. (19997). Causes and consequences of the colorblind perspective. In J. Banks & C. Banks (Eds.), *Multicultural education: Issues and perspectives* (3rd ed., pp. 251–271). Boston: Allyn & Bacon.

Sleeter, C. E. (1992). *Keepers of the American dream: A study of staff development and multicultrural education*. London: Farmer.

Solomon, R. P. (2002). School leaders and antiracism: Overcoming pedagogical and political obstacles. *Journal of School Leadership, 12*(2), 174–197.

Solomon, R. P., & Allen, A. M. (2001). The struggle for equity, diversity and social justice in teacher education. In J. P. Portelli & R. P. Solomon (Eds.), *The erosion of democracy in education: From critique to possibilities*. Calgary: Detselig.

Solomon, R. P., & Levine-Rasky, C. (1996). Transforming teacher education for an antiracism pedagogy. *The Canadian Review of Sociology and Anthropology, 35*(1), 337–359.

Solomon, R. P., & Levine-Rasky, C. (2003). *Teaching for equity and diversity: Research to practice*. Toronto: Canadian Scholars' Press.

Solomon, R. P., Portelli, J. P., Daniel, B.-J., & Campbell, A. (2005). The discourse of denial: How White teacher candidates construct race, racism and "White privilege." *Race Ethnicity and Education, 8*(2), 147–169.

Swartz, E. (2003). Teaching White pre-service teachers: Pedagogy for change. *Urban Education, 38*(3), 255–278.

# Chapter 14

# The Confluence of Teacher Education and Inner-City Activism: A Reciprocal Possibility

Charlotte Reid
*University of Winnipeg*

## ALL THINGS INTERRELATED: TEACHER EDUCATION AND INNER-CITY ACTIVISM

Each year, an education conference is held in western Canada organized around the general theme of student teaching in relation to teacher education. This conference, entitled WESTCAST, serves as a type of barometer indicating developing trends and issues seen as current and relevant to the educational field. Recently, I saw a poster display advertising the following year's conference at the University of Alberta. The poster depicted a logo consisting of a row of apples on a school desk. The final "apple" in the row was a brightly colored, perfectly shaped orange. The message and subsequent agenda that the poster conveyed was of a new approach to education. Once again, we would be laboring at the task of rethinking teacher education by trying to bring together in a meaningful way, schools, society, teaching, and learning.

This rethinking of education eventually speculates on what it may mean to reform or change both education policy and practice. Does it mean to improve, or to adapt? Does it mean to reconfigure, or to attempt some form of significant change? If rethinking means change, what will be the nature of this change? Will it be radical, conservative, political and/or pedagogical?

To this end, this chapter attempts to rethink what it means to reform teacher education. I seek to understand the relationship between teacher education and inner-city activism by focusing on an alternative inner-city teacher education program: The Winnipeg Education Center (WEC). I examine inner-city teacher activism and issues of personal and institutional change not as a grand, one-dimensional activity prone to becoming swiftly ineffectual, but change that takes the form of sustained activism. This form of activism tends not to be loud, but lengthy, in duration; long enough to be meaningful and sustainable for the children and families in the inner city as well as for the schools that affect the well-being of these children and families. This form of activism is deeply powerful, as it affects changes that matter in direct ways through its involvement with ordinary people leading extraordinary lives.

With consideration of the kind of teacher education embedded within the context of inner-city education, this chapter begins to look at how a teacher education program such as the WEC might prepare students teachers to recognize, confront, and deal with the savage and complex realities of an inner-city school. Further, it highlights some of the ways in which preparation for the inner-city school context contributes to student efficacy and self-actualization—a self-actualization that, in some cases, may contribute to the formation of activist identities. This chapter looks at the development of the extraordinary everyday reality of inner-city education and the activism that may develop from involvement in such education programs—with specific reference to selected portions of the life story of one of the WEC graduates.

To this end, the thoughts of Jean McLeod, an inner-city teacher activist who graduated from the WEC in the 1980s, are considered. These thoughts—parts of Jean's life story—are a social construction taking the form of an interpretive biography.

## THE INNER-CITY CONTEXT

There are many myths associated with the inner city, a place frequently celebrated by the media or academy. Too often it is stereotyped as a violent, ugly area with an unstable and transient population. One common myth describes working in an inner-city school as similar to that of teaching in any school, except for the additional behavioral problems. Another registers the view that inner-city schools do not always attract the brightest and the best teachers. At best, this space is thought to be in constant need of "fixing" by people whose job it is to monitor the resources that find their way to the inner city.

There is little credence given to the stable populations that live in the area and choose to have their children attend neighborhood schools, plant gardens, or risk a small business venture, seemingly with no great difficulty or plans to leave. Although some people do leave the inner city for varied reasons, those who choose to remain do so cognizant of the problems and imperfections that often accompany such contexts, because it is their home, their community.

Teachers and administrators involved in inner-city education often experience the constant, active, and/or inadvertent dilemma of meeting the needs of the children in their care, while tackling systems that do not advocate for equity and social justice. These educators reflect a distinguished and organized group of teachers who carry a banner, which announces that the traditional educational system is inappropriate for inner-city children.

Although their actions seem to be in accordance with change advocacy, bystanders often interpret their actions as antagonistic in significant ways. However, their actions raise issues that point to the system not being fair, nor being equitable. And this is noted across every facet of education including funding, issues of diversity, resource allocation, and equal opportunity. Another relevant issue is that of appropriately meeting the needs of the disadvantaged. It is noted that the intellectual, physical, spiritual, or economic needs of inner-city children are not being met. This is also true of the significant Aboriginal population in Winnipeg.

Another note of significance is that of the role of women in the inner-city context. Women, who form the greater percentage of the student population, have been for years involved in "grass-root" community activities such as building "safe houses." These places of safety are based on principles of social justice and have developed as storefront sites where democratically run, community-based activities are central to the lives of their inner-city children.

These safe houses create a space where the basic physical and emotional needs of families can be met. They serve as transition sites between home and school, for single mothers and parents who are able to "help themselves" to the skills and resources necessary to sustain family life. These houses also provide the opportunity for children of these individuals to attend the neighborhood school ready to learn. Some of these maintained homes include: Andrew Street Family Center, Ma Maw Wi Chi I Ta Ta Family Center, North End Women's Resource Center, and the Native Women's Transition Center.

## THE WINNIPEG EDUCATION CENTER

Women who are active in these centers are often in similar ways active in their neighborhoods and inner-city schools. Many of the women who work confidently and purposefully (and usually quietly) in these safe houses and schools are teacher graduates of the WEC. It is important to understand the effect a program such as the WEC may have had in supporting women graduate teachers in becoming activists who, by choice and with determination, return to their communities to put their schools and their political houses in order.

This activist phenomenon evolved at the Winnipeg Education Center Bachelor of Education Program without any overt reference to activism in the formal university curriculum, in neither course requirements nor the expectations of students' professional suitability. However, the Center and its teacher education program clearly provide a unique space within which to examine and challenge the status quo assumptions of our society regarding race, ethnicity, class, and gender. Individuals in the program do not necessarily enroll to become activists, but many who engage with the program do develop an activist stance in response to the pedagogical environment to which they have been exposed. The program itself is considered alternative due to the nature of its teacher candidates and its mandate to prepare residents of the inner city to become teachers.

Consequently, the critical, equity-based character of the program has developed organically as a way to sustain the alternative status of its candidates as well as incorporate their experiences of marginalization. This epistemic privileging of "marginalized and oppressed voices" (Dei & Calliste, 2000, p. 36) is a particularly empowering and powerfully unique facet of the program. The WEC is a place where teacher candidates can examine the personal, pedagogical, and curricular reproduction of racism, sexism, and classism, and in response, challenge this reproduction at both the personal and social levels.

**THE WINNIPEG EDUCATION CENTER: PEDAGOGY OF SPACE**

The WEC has a 5-year, government-funded Bachelor of Education "Access Program," initially designed to meet the perceived needs of inner-city communities. One primary need is equity; another is a sense of legitimacy, understood as the ability of inner-city residents to teach their own children in their own neighborhood schools with an approach that is contextual and appropriate. The WEC is positioned at the intersection of equity and legitimacy and offers a program whose mandate works in response to both.

Since the time of its inception, the WEC has developed a unique recruitment and selection process. Related to this, its program development and political character have been built on principles of affirmative action, known in the province of Manitoba as the "Access Model." The original mandate was derived from an agreement with the Government of Manitoba, which stated that the WEC would equitably serve the minority populations residing in the core area of Winnipeg. Based on the demographics of the inner city in 1973 (the date of the Center's founding), the mandate was interpreted to mean that 50% of the yearly quota of students would be Aboriginal, 25% recent immigrants, and 25% would represent what was known as the "working poor." Selection criteria also specified that the applicant must be 21 years of age (proviso for mature student status at the University of Manitoba), and live, work, or have knowledge of the inner-city or a similar environment.

Most of the WEC's candidates are from the inner city, where they share and live the everyday reality of poverty and alienation from mainstream society. The difficult realities of their experiences were regarded as sites of knowledge and strength that could be used to inform their understanding of both the curriculum and their practice. Furthermore, their social position provided an important element of their acceptance into the program.

To enter the program, applicants also must demonstrate academic, financial, and social need. Academic need was considered to be the absence of the traditional university entrance requirements or an interrupted student history. Grade 12 was not mandatory but a minimum requirement of Grade 10 was a benchmark below which applicants' chances for academic success were considered problematic. Applicants' financial need was carefully considered and aid was allocated to welfare recipients, those with low family income, or those with some means to handle student loans or similar financial exigencies. Generally, as stated by Statistics Canada, a financial need describes one who is at or below the poverty line.

The social need of the applicants was the most subjective area to clarify, but was considered for those who would benefit from the supports the program offered to single mothers, survivors of abuse, neglect and/or family violence. These factors would have normally posed significant barriers to the applicants' ability to access regular, postsecondary education. However, consideration of these characteristics awarded the WEC an "alternative education program" status.

The applicants to the program were single parents, visible minorities, and recent immigrants. Many were raising families below the poverty line and had histories of abuse and family violence. They came from the inner city, First Nations reserve communities, or in the case of the immigrant students, regions such as the politically and poverty-stricken Santiago, Chile, and San Salvador. These unique categories were perceived as strengths not to be fixed or ignored but recognized and built upon. The applicants who were most in need of the program and who reflected the mandate of the school were selected.

The characteristics and categories already noted are indicative of the financial and social inequity that spawns the issues in which inner-city teachers find themselves immersed. The graduates who originate from this context may have been more predisposed to want to stop the reproduction of injustice and inequality, or they may have wanted to use the opportunity of their education to leave the inner city entirely.

Most significantly, it is the character of the candidates themselves that affect the WEC most profoundly. All of the students are from the inner city of

Winnipeg or what is identified as a similar environment. A number of the students came to the program with a knowledge and experience of living, studying, working, or receiving welfare, and of being parents of school-age children. At the same time, the support of a smaller setting with its academic supports, the immediacy of its counseling supports, its supportive and innovative timetables, and the opportunity for small class sizes offered by the WEC was designed to respond to the needs of candidates with a view of ensuring their success.

## TEACHER EDUCATION: WHAT IS ITS PURPOSE?

Trends in teacher education have evolved, matured, and receded for several decades, one central tendency often eclipsing another. These tendencies usually mark a "solution set" to the question "What is the main purpose for teacher education?" There appears to be two and possibly three, major ideological positions: The first is characterized as overtly and inescapably political, as reflected in the works of Zeichner (1993, 1996). In much of his work, Zeichner has developed an agenda for teacher education that supports strong, democratic, pedagogical environments responsive to issues of social justice in schools, the community, and professional organizations. Similarly Dei calls for "an educational agenda for social change" (Dei & Calliste, 2000, p. 35).

The second ideological camp is often presented as a bipolar argument of morality versus politicization, with the corollaries of education or training, professionalism, or vocation presented as the main goal of teacher education. The third ideological camp that I have added is derived from the work of Noddings (1992), *The Challenge to Care in Schools*. Here she has issued a challenge for teacher educators to contemplate a disparate purpose for teacher education; to establish simultaneously an all-encompassing understanding and method for enabling teachers to "care" for children, teaching, and schools. Another related view is seen in the work of Cochran-Smith (2004). In *Walking the Road: Race, Diversity, and Social Justice in Teacher Education*, she conceptualizes teacher education as the integration of a teaching problem and a learning problem aimed at social justice.

In the simplest sense, the purpose for teacher education that has developed at the WEC integrates all of these ideologies. There was no need to "take on society," which in part is represented by those opposed to politicized teacher education, as the "taking on of society" already existed implicitly within many candidates at the WEC. The teachers and administrators in the program recognized that candidates not only brought their experiences of society with them, but also their exposure to poverty, welfare, unemployment, uneven distribution of power, racism in the schools and community, gender insensitivity, family violence and marginalization, drug and alcohol abuse, effects of political and social alienation, inadequate education, and the indifference and betrayal of adults when they were children, inaccessibility to education and training as adults, and their experience with being single parents. The "society" that candidates brought immediately came into the arena of becoming a conscious teacher, which often meant being of the genre of teachers who promote and provide effective and equitable education for inner-city children. As a result, teacher education at WEC was not a dress rehearsal for life as a teacher but was a living examination of how one's life experiences must be integrated realistically with becoming an informed teacher.

Effective education for inner-city minority students meant coming to terms with child welfare and the caring for and about children and families of the inner-city community. It also meant engaging in a process of politicization that brought about a way to get things done. During this process, the first step was to address one's own individual socialization, the level of victimization that had resulted, the damage that this had inflicted, and the understanding of how important it was to know ones identity as a person before embarking on a teaching career. This process of identification was more and sometimes less of a success for each of the candidates that worked through the program. At this juncture, I examine the course of this process of identification as experienced by Jean McLeod.

## JEAN—A CASE STUDY OF TRANSFORMATION

This part of the chapter focuses on the perceptions of one graduate from the WEC and examines the impact that the Center had on the construction of her identity as an activist. Here we engaged in a consensual collaborative dialogue about the shared and embedded context of the WEC over an extended period of time. During this time, a dialogue developed that placed Jean in the position of student and myself as education professor. This social construction of her life story may be conceptualized as an ethical sensibility that first and foremost did not betray the trust that was freely given.

Working with Jean in developing her biography engendered a way of addressing practical realities rather than comparing people from a sense of prescriptive ideals or a posture of "high ground" morality. Her story found its place in a genre of ordinary people living extraordinary lives. The interpretation of Jean's biography unfolding as a "storied life" contributed to a method that does not need to judge people in order to appreciate and understand them. This methodology has been crucial in forming the ethical sensibility brought to her life story and its interpretation.

This method supported the construction of the meaning of inner-city activism as it grew within the exploration of the realistic contexts and contingencies of her life experiences. This is an attempt at searching into oneself, insights that at times tend to be overlooked in policy or reform research efforts. Social constructivism, the philosophical approach that informed this research process, did alert both Jean and me to the fact that not all activists are responsive in the same way to preconceived common interests such as caring, feminism, or commitment to culture.

Jean was a single mother for some time, living in the inner city and raising two young children. Later she remarried and now has two more children as part of a blended family. Her parents were both deaf and she grew up in a "deaf culture," where she acted an interpreter for her parents and learned "never to challenge the hearing authority." She also referred to herself as "the hearing child of parents of European lower class backgrounds."

Jean chose to begin her life story not with the usual "I was born and raised" but by emphatically outlining the significance that the WEC had on her life. "I think that WEC had a huge impact on my life. WEC gave me confidence. WEC gave me the opportunity to try on different roles that I never had the opportunity to try before."

For the first time, Jean felt she was not being kicked out of life, but instead invited in as an active participant. This created for her an ethos of possibility at the Center of respect, reciprocity, and reconceptualization. This ethos also provided a secure opportunity where the possibility of transformation could be realized. The ethos at the Center contributed to a form of transformative activity as Jean developed an understanding of what constituted real rather than illusionary choices. She was the student president one year where she saw "her ideas taking form and her ability being tested." The success that Jean experienced was transformational and encouraged the development of her activism:

> When we had problems I helped—we all helped. The WEC was a safe place to try and work these things out. I had experienced sexism all my life but this was the first time I learned and understood what it had done to me. Until then I always thought it was my fault.

In addition to teacher trainee, there were many challenging roles for women students to contend with: mother, wife, welfare mother, single mother, school dropout, abused wife, dutiful daughter, student, mature student, teacher aide, unemployed. A significant aspect of the success Jean experienced in becoming a teacher and later an inner-city community activist was her resilience. This resilience enabled her to transcend many of the perceived negative aspects of her life story. For Jean, the experience at the WEC was the first time the negative aspects of the roles ascribed to her or that she acknowledged were not considered as deficits, but instead as positive attributes that could contribute to the development of self-efficacy. It was her ability to question these ascribed roles and recognize them openly that enabled her to surpass anger and resentment, and furthermore to deliberately and thoughtfully use the physical and psychological safety net of the WEC to explore alternatives. Eventually, Jean was able to authentically examine her identity from within, as "my own skin that I don't keep in a drawer." These alternatives helped to relinquish the negative aspects of her many roles and responsibilities.

During our conversations, Jean often alluded to the notion of a "level playing field":

> We were all on a level playing field. We didn't compete with one another but were able to use our energy to help one another in our cohort group, to look past ourselves.... The mandate of the WEC afforded the student body the opportunity to avoid the initial forms of competition that often occur at other and more traditional learning institutions.

This sense of camaraderie and support contributed profoundly to building a space for informed social action. As a result of the WEC's unique environment, Jean was able to focus her time and energy addressing issues such as racism and gender bias, and to seek solutions to class privilege through the development of the principles of social justice.

WEC students like Jean were especially adept at understanding these issues. There was no need for textbook examples of the poor and oppressed or code words for racism, sexism, or class bias. Recognizing and naming these "isms" was a significant aspect of Jean's story and formed for her the confluence of activism and teacher education. It was, in fact, only after a summer of collaborating that she became comfortable with the use of the term *activist* when referring to herself.

Jean was comfortable with concepts such as *racism, sexism,* and *class bias,* albeit not always named directly and only when they referred to her work with children and families related to her own life experiences. The precipitation of her politicization and evolving activism occurred when she began to link the issues of her own experiences to that of the children and families in the inner-city community. Essentially, Jean came through the Center coupling her own identity formation along with the identities of inner-city children and their families. This process formed an indelible impression on her, evidenced in the following comment:

"I am an inner city teacher. I live in the inner city by choice. I struggle to be an inner city teacher and to understand what this could mean." The Center also provided her with a haven of legitimization."You people recognized me for who I was. I was let in and my life experiences were valued. I was allowed, even encouraged, to talk and even disagree about things."

The WEC was also a place where she was able for the first time to come to terms with her own negative school socialization, a socialization that had significantly hindered and immobilized her development as a person. She likens her negative Junior High experience as being similar to First Nation's people who had been placed in residential schools. Jean's ability to relate, learn from, and fully comprehend these experiences contributed substantially to her life as an activist. The major theme throughout Jean's life story has been her perceived need "to be real, to be who I am, and to know who I am." The Center provided a secure space for her to find her authentic self. The people at the "WEC automatically assumed I had something to say.... In the short 3 years that I was there, it was like this accelerated the making of me."

Jean has told us emphatically, as part of her life story, about the interplay between the roles that society ascribed to her and how WEC helped her to clarify them. Her teacher education program was one place and time period where these roles were intensified and ordered around learning to become an inner-city teacher. The sensitizing concepts that developed are those of *self-efficacy*, an *understanding of self* and *subjectivity*, *resistance*, and *resiliency*. Jean's life story can be traced through the historical antecedents that parallel the life of WEC. The timeline extends the pendulum that swings from reform to change, from an emphasis on practice such as mastery of learning to the development of a critical pedagogy, paralleled with the restoration of conservatism and the threat of globalization.

The naming of activism for Jean was a process that took time. When the grammar of Jean's language began to change from "but" to "and," she began to accept the possibility that she was becoming an activist. As she constructed her life stories, the use of "but" was a tropism for why things had happened to her. When she began to use "and," she began to construct ways of making sense of what had happened to her and how this contributed to her work and its influence on the lives of the children, families, and the community of the inner city. It was this use of "and" where activism began to be understood.

In constructing her life story to determine how she became an activist, the interwoven pieces of her life were connected and experiences named and then assembled as an emphatic recognition of "knowing who I am." What became clear as our work became more intense was the resistance that Jean demonstrated at being named when she did not understand what the naming meant or if she disagreed with its implications or if there was no connection to the children in the inner city. She did not use the term *feminist* because she did not understand nor accept what it meant, yet she held strong convictions of what it meant for her to be a woman. Not until she defined and understood what it might mean to be an activist would she call herself a feminist. The phrase "to be empowered" was never used by Jean; she was much more likely to use phrases such as "being real," "knowing who you are," and/or "getting connected." The resistance to being named before securing an understanding of the meaning of the name enabled Jean to be "real," "connected," and "whole." It meant that her activity as an activist would be purposeful, reciprocal, and highly productive. She became more and more confident.

I have come to understand that the premature naming of Jean in any sense as an activist could have become a repressive or romantic myth-making exercise. More to the point, I would not have learned anything of significance about her or how she came to know who she was. The resistance was justified; the spirit of difference and diversity Jean conveyed may have slipped away or become lost if she was named prematurely through a misguided attempt to empower her.

Most of us who worked at the WEC during Jean's candidacy had learned that one could not empower another; each individual can only do that for his or herself. What is possible is for each person to work toward their own liberation as part of the empowerment of others. This we learned from Freire (1968) and others, and was reinforced daily throughout the life and world of the WEC.

For all its complexity, the teacher education program at WEC was successful for Jean because it created a place where the human quality of generosity was able to flourish. This sense of generosity began with a spirited politicization, nurtured with caring and evolving around one's struggle to act ethically, expressed at the WEC as discovering the "real." This activity was not always pleasant or comfortable; nor was it always successful. Many students were unable to transcend the "I won't learn from you" phenomenon perpetuated as a protective power dynamic where learners willfully do not learn if they believe their identity is threatened, negated, and/or misunderstood.

The intimacy of the WEC community created an environment where ignoring or avoiding life experiences became virtually impossible. This "impossibility" was an integral part of the ethos of life at the Center. As a result, some people left the WEC program unchanged, and continued to feel angry, victimized, or indifferent. People were not always in agreement, and out of necessity began to develop and use a model of consensus. There was open confrontation at times. However, cohort members at the WEC were mostly a supportive learning experience.

The very nature of the WEC and the schools and community it serves has created a natural site of resistance to the status quo. In Jean's case, although she did not say that the WEC overtly taught her how to resist the social and political inequities that surrounded her, she did express awareness that somehow she was involved in something "progressive and innovative."

## WEARING HER OWN SKIN

My own pedagogical approach to both the curriculum and foundation courses is to explore with students where to look without telling them what to see. We work from the understanding that curriculum is not like life, but that curriculum is life. The manner in which Jean's experiences unfolded at the WEC reflects this conceptualization of *curriculum*. Jean did not name her activism until she was prepared to define it for herself. The process of this naming occurred within the activity of behaving like an activist while simultaneously discovering new personal confidence and insight about herself and her relationship to her community as a developing activist teacher. Jean did not rely on or remain behind a code that would dictate or camouflage the motivation and character of her activism. It was certainly an important moment when she said to me that her activism was "removing barriers for kids and families in the inner city." Although there is no "activism" course in the curriculum at the WEC, there was an environment that provided both the opportunity and encouragement to bring an activist initiative into her practice. In working toward her definition, Jean was also coming to terms with her own form of oppression. This insight I believe makes her a more resilient and affective activist.

Jean views the time she spent as a teacher education student at the WEC as one where she came into a better understanding of herself and her relationship with others. Specifically, part of her identity is significantly related to the children of the inner city. She spoke frequently of how the WEC provided the place for her to "wear her own skin," as a place that gave her the confidence to not "keep her skin in a drawer." Delpit (2003) writes:

> Just as our skin provides us with a means to negotiate our interactions with the world—both how we perceive our surroundings and in how those around perceive us—our language plays an equally pivotal role in determining who we are: it is the skin that we speak. (p. xvii). It is the inner-city activist Jean has become.

## POSTSCRIPT

Jean has worked in the inner city of Winnipeg as a teacher activist since graduation. She has worked both in schools and in the safe houses she has helped to establish. Jean is now pursuing graduate work and is interested in developing her expertise in Urban Education.

## REFERENCES

Cochran-Smith, M. (2004). *Walking the road: Race, diversity, and social justice in teacher education*. New York: Teachers College Press.

Dei, G. J. S., & Calliste, A. (Eds.). (2000). *Power, knowledge and anti-racism education*. Halifax: Fernwood.

Delpit, L. (2003). *The skin that we speak*. New York: The New Press.

Freire, P. (1968). *Pedagogy of the oppressed*. New York: Seabury Press.

Noddings, N. (1992). *The challenge to care in schools: An alternative approach to education*. New York: Teachers College Press.

Zeichner, K. (1993). Connecting genuine teacher development to the struggle for social justice. *Journal of Education for Teaching*, *19*(1), 5–20.

Zeichner, K. (1996). *Currents of reform in pre-service teacher education*. New York: Teachers College Press.

# About the Contributors

**Andrew Allen** is a former elementary school teacher and is currently an assistant professor in the Faculty of Education at the University of Windsor. His recent article (co-authored with Patrick Solomon), "The Struggle for Equity Diversity and Social Justice in Teacher Education," addresses some of the issues facing teacher education for social justice. His scholarly interests include beginning teachers' emerging identities and factors contributing to and affecting the process of learning to teach, particularly in marginalized communities.

**Wanda Brooks** is an assistant professor of elementary education at Temple University. She teaches graduate and undergraduate courses related to literacy acquisition, instruction, and assessment. Her research interests include examining the literacy development of African American students, multicultural children's literature, and middle-school students' reading processes. She has published in *The New Advocate*, *Journal of Children's Literature*, *English Journal*, and *The Journal of Negro Education*. Prior to becoming a university professor, Dr. Brooks taught elementary and middle school.

**Arlene Campbell** is a PhD candidate in the Faculty of Education, York University, Canada. Her areas of research interest include antiracist education, Black feminist thought, life writing, teacher education, and critical pedagogy. She is an African Canadian educator with over 15 years of teaching experience within the public school system. Her teaching experience includes elementary and middle-school teaching, as well as teacher in-service and pre-service instruction and school administration.

**Beverly-Jean Daniel** currently works as an instructor in the Faculty of Education, York University in Toronto, Canada. She also provides consulting services to various community agencies, hospitals, and boards of education. She has worked in the field of teacher education, sociology and gender studies, and currently teaches courses related to those areas. Dr. Daniel's interests include urban education, adjustment patterns of immigrant adolescent females, and African-centered feminist epistemology.

**Hyacinth Evans** is Professor of Teacher Education in the Institute of Education, University of the West Indies, Mona, Jamaica. She teaches graduate courses in teacher education and in qualitative research methods, and has conducted research on teaching and teacher education. Her research interests are in teacher learning and school reform. She has published widely on various aspects of teaching and teacher education. Her most recent book is *Inside Hillview High School: An Ethnography of an Urban Jamaican High School.*

**Carol Hordatt Gentles** is Lecturer in Education with the Institute of Education at the University of the West Indies, Mona, Jamaica. She works as an external examiner with teachers colleges in Jamaica, providing support in developing and implementing curricula for education courses. Her academic interests are critical pedagogy, the education and professional development of teachers, and qualitative research methodology. She is committed through her teaching and research to facilitating critical pedagogy in teacher education.

**Sonia James-Wilson** is an assistant professor at the University of Rochester in the United States, where she holds a joint appointment in the Departments of Teaching and Curriculum and Educational Leadership. She has worked in the field as a classroom teacher, educational researcher, consultant, and teacher educator in both Canada and the United States. Her research interests include urban and inclusive (antiracist) education, teacher leadership, educational reform, and integrated arts. Her writing is focused on ways in which social, cultural, and physical differences among people contribute to injustice and inequality in education.

**Randa Khattar Manoukian,** formerly an ESL teacher, is currently working toward her doctorate in education at York University. Her research focuses primarily on the philosophical dimensions of nonreductive pedagogies within a context of complexity, diversity, and social justice. She has co-authored, with R. P. Solomon and J. Clarke, "From an Ethic of Altruism to Possibilities of Transformation in Teacher Candidates' Community Involvement," in L. Pease Alvarez and S. R. Schecter's book, *Learning, Teaching and Community: Contributions of Situated and Participatory Approaches to Educational Innovation* (2005).

**Rupertia Minott-Bent** received her PhD at the University of Toronto and has taught at York University in the teacher education program. Her areas of specialization are computer-facilitated learning and urban education, where she has developed professional development programs for pre-service and certified teachers. Dr. Bent is currently a vice principal with the Peel District Board of Education, where she continues to mentor certified and pre-service teachers in computer-facilitated learning.

**Peter Murrell, Jr.** is Associate Professor of Urban Education at Northeastern University in Boston, Massachusetts, where he also is the Director of the Center for Innovation in Urban Education. Dr. Murrell's research focuses on the areas of the cultural psychology of learning, cognition, achievement and development, situated identity, and the formation of academic identity and scholastic agency among African American students in urban school contexts. His current professional work also focuses on developing schools of achievement through community, school, and university partnerships.

**Charlotte Reid** received her PhD from the University of Manitoba and has been involved for many years with the Winnipeg Education Center and the Bachelor of Education Program, teaching in the areas of Curriculum and Instruction and Educational Foundations. Her work focuses on social justice and inner-city teaching practices and providing access to teacher education for First Nation's and other "minoritized" peoples. In 2003, she was the recipient of the University of Manitoba's Social Justice Research award.

**Dia Sekayi** is currently the Faculty Chair of Research for the PhD programs in Education at Walden University. She has nearly a decade of experience an as academician (at Cleveland State University and Howard University) and spent several years teaching mathematics and science to elementary level students in Buffalo, New York. Dr. Sekayi earned her PhD in the Social Foundations of Education from the State University of New York at Buffalo. Her work has been published and presented nationally and internationally.

**Harry Smaller** is an associate professor in the Faculty of Education, York University, Toronto. His research interests include the history of state schooling systems, teachers' work, and teachers' unions. His teaching interests include history of education and educational foundations. Prior to working at York, he taught in the inner city in Toronto for many years, in elementary, secondary, and alternative schools.

**R. Patrick Solomon** is professor and coordinator of the Urban Diversity Teacher Education Initiative in the Faculty of Education, York University. He previously served as a school–community liaison with the Toronto public school district, providing better access to schooling for new and minoritized immigrant groups. His publications include: *Black Resistance in High School* (1992), *The Erosion of Democracy in Education* (2001; with John Portelli), and *Teaching for Equity and Diversity* (2003; with Cynthia Levine-Rasky). His current research includes a longitudinal study of graduate teachers, their strategies, and challenges of implementing diversity and social justice pedagogy in urban schools and communities.

**Lois Weiner** coordinates a graduate program for experienced urban teachers at New Jersey City University. Her first book, *Preparing Teachers for Urban Schools* (Teachers College Press, 1993), was honored by the American Educational Research Association for its contribution to research on teacher education. Her practical guide to teaching in urban schools, *Urban Teaching: The Essentials* (Teachers College Press), is used throughout the United States. Her research focus has shifted to how teachers are resisting (internationally) reforms associated with capitalism's global restructuring of education. She is editing a book on the subject.

**Patricia A. Young** is an assistant professor of literacy education at the University of Maryland, Baltimore County. Her research examines the history of African American instructional design and technology; race, ethnicity, and culture in instructional design and technology; and race and ethnicity in urban teacher education.

# Author Index

# Subject Index